HTML

for Web Developers

by

John Avila

Scott Jones Publishers

HTML for Web Developers
John Avila

099 XYZ
ISBN: 1-57676-028-6

Text Design and Composition: Bob Jones Graphics; chapter openers by Winona Avila
Cover Design: Heather Bennett
Book Manufacturing: Malloy Lithographing
Copyediting: Rebecca Wilhite
Sponsoring Editor/Publisher: Richard Jones

A Word About Trademarks

Additional Titles of Interest from Scott/Jones

Client-Side Programming for WWW Developers
Server-Side Programming for WWW Developers
by John Avila
Introduction to Programming Using Visual Basic 2nd Edition
by Gary Bronson
C by Discovery, 3rd Edition
by L. S. Foster
Starting Out With C++, 2nd Edition
by Tony Gaddis
Computing with Java: Programs, Objects, Graphics
by Arthur Gittleman
QuickStart to Internet Explorer 4!
by Leslie Hardin and Deborah Tice
Advanced Visual Basic, 2nd Edition
by Kip Irvine
Assembly Language for the IBM PC, 2nd Edition
by William B. Jones
Word for Office 97: Economy Pack
by Paula Ladd and Ralph Ruby
The Visual Basic 6 Coursebook
QuickStart in DOS for Windows 9x
QuickStart to JavaScript
A Short Course in HTML
ActiveX and the Internet
by Forest Lin
The Complete Computer Repair Textbook, 2nd Edition
by Cheryl Schmidt
Applications Programming with Visual Basic 5, 2nd Edition
by Mark Simkin
The Access Guidebook for Office 97
by Maggie Trigg and Phyllis Dobson
The Windows 98 Textbook
A Short Course in Windows NT for Beginners
by Stewart Venit

Table of Contents

Preface .... **v**

Chapter 1. Introduction **1**
1.1 A Brief History of the Web 2
1.2 What is a Web Site? 5
1.3 What is a Web Developer? 6
1.4 Hardware Resources 8
1.5 Software Resources 9
1.6 The Journey 10
1.7 Conventions 11

Chapter 2. HTML Basics **15**
2.1 The Basic HTML Document 16
2.2 Format Tags 29
2.3 Adding Graphical Elements 39
2.4 External Elements 51

Chapter 3. Hypertext Documents **61**
3.1 Implicitly Anchored Hyperlinks 62
3.2 E-mail with the A Tag 74
3.3 Explicitly Anchored Hyperlinks 76
3.4 Clickable Images 83

Chapter 4. Data Gathering and Layout Features: Forms andTables **101**
4.1 Forms Preview 102
4.2 Simple Forms 104
4.3 More Complex Forms 112
4.4 Tables 119

Chapter 5. Dynamic Content and Extensions: Applets and Frames **135**
5.1 Applets 136
5.2 Frames 145

Chapter 6. Cascading Style Sheets **157**
6.1 What are Cascading Style Sheets? 158
6.2 Defining a Style for a Single Document 160
6.3 More Rules and Properties 167
6.4 Defining Styles for Groups of Documents 188
6.5 Positioning Text for Interesting Effects 197

Appendix A. HTML Syntax **211**

Appendix B. Frames Syntax **245**

Index **247**

To Winona, Elaine, and Barbara

Preface

Who is this book intended for?

This book was written for people who want to be technically proficient in HTML. These will usually be persons who want to be "Web masters"—developing Web sites for themselves or others. These persons may need to know HTML at a level that would allow them to write software that could generate HTML documents automatically (such as the personalized response to a form filled out in a Web page).

This book is also written for persons who are not satisfied with the tools that generate HTML documents by "drag and drop" techniques. You can't always get exactly what you want with these tools. Finally, this is for persons who just want to take control over the process of developing Web pages themselves.

What is covered?

By today's standards of bloated books related to Internet technology, this is a small book. My philosophy as a teacher has been that the role of teaching is to teach you what you need to know so that you can teach yourself the rest. Once you see what the underlying ideas are in HTML and how things like tags work, the rest is just looking up the right tags and a little experimentation. This book will give you an understanding of how HTML is written and how to pull together the various components that you need to build the documents you want to create.

The overall plan

Even though HTML has only been around since 1990, it has a history. In Chapter 1 we examine some of this fascinating fast-paced history. Starting with Chapter 2 we examine HTML from the basics to advanced features. The focus is always on things someone who was involved with putting together web sites for others would want to know. The exercises and examples tend to be related to Web sites designed with a commercial flavor. In particular, we assume a fictitious customer called "Island Quest Travel" that is in the business of providing fantasy excursions to exotic islands. (Perhaps if enough copies of this book are sold, I can even try out one or two of these islands.) We make up various "problems" related to this customer and show how to put together the Web documents to meet the customer's needs. I have always found it easiest to learn something if it had a certain air of reality about it.

Classroom experience

The material in this book has been used as part of a class I have taught since 1997 entitled Web Programming. It's actually the first part of the class that goes on later to teach students how to program in Java to support a Web site. The class has been taught in workshop style.

Students get a little lecture and a lot of "hands-on" opportunity to try out what they're learning. The material on the enclosed CD-ROM is always available to the students on-line so that they can quickly start from existing examples to produce the documents they want. There is a reference to the Web-Archipelago site where students can obtain additional information or download copies of files that they can then use for their work. The contents of this site is essentially what is on the CD-ROM although the site will be more up to date.

This material can also be used in a more conventional classroom lecture model provided students are getting plenty of hands-on experience working with the examples on the CD-ROM. I would recommend that as students read the book, that they be close to a computer where they can be experimenting with the examples. Pushing an example to see "what happens if..." is a terrific way to quickly learn the material.

Each section is followed by a series of questions designed to get the student to think about the material just covered. These questions tend to be true-false questions or multiple-choice questions or simply questions with a short answer.

At the end of each chapter there are two sets of exercises. The first are ones that allow the student to modify and "play" with some of the examples in the text or generate relatively simple documents that utilize the material from the chapter. The second set are exercises that typically require a little more time and effort. These may involve putting together groups of HTML documents or simply exploring in more significant detail some aspects of the material in the chapter.

Conventions

In keeping with the theme of the Island Quest Travel customer, each chapter begins with a "treasure map" showing the route through the chapter. Each island corresponds to one of the sections. Sidebars are shown as sandbars. Some islands are more critical than others and the route shown may bypass some of the islands. These correspond to sections that are not critical on the first pass. Students may want to skip these and come back later as their need or desire dictates.

In addition to the map presented at the beginning of each chapter, we have adopted certain conventions that will help orient the reader as she or he progresses through the book.

Programs in their text file form and other text files are displayed in the form of a shadowed box with the name of the file appearing in a shaded line at the top of the box. For example, here is a sample HTML document.

File: `simple.html`

```
<HTML>
<HEAD>
   <TITLE>A Simple Document</TITLE>
</HEAD>
<BODY>
   Hello, WWW World.
</BODY>
</HTML>
```

Occasionally, we will explicitly display the syntax for HTML or Java. These will be denoted by a double-lined shadowed box. The following is an example.

Syntax rule

Unless the browser is explicitly commanded to do otherwise, all white space that is not a blank (such as tabs, end-of-line characters, etc.) is treated as a single blank. Multiple white space is collapsed to a single blank.

Sidebars which contain additional information that the reader may want to know and is usually an extension of the material covered in the regular portion of the text are also displayed using the double-lined shadowed boxes.

Finally, we have two appendices containing a list of the HTML tags (HTML 3.2) and the syntax for frameset documents.

Follow-on

This book is the first of a planned trilogy centered around the theme of the Web developer. The second book will cover "Server-side Web Programming" showing how to use Java (and a little Perl) to do the tasks that Web developers have to do such as processing those forms that appear on HTML documents. The third book will cover "Client-side Web Programming" showing how Java (and a little Javascript) is used on the client side to provide dynamic content to those Web documents.

Acknowledgments

I want to thank Richard Jones for suggesting this book and his patience waiting for me to finish it. I also thank Darin Okuyama for early discussions and ideas. I want also to thank the various reviewers whose comments have helped me focus and improve the content. These include (in alphabetical order) George Atkins from Southwestern Oklahoma State

University, Dwight Barnette from Virgina Tech, Paul Bladek from Spokane Falls Community College, Chakib Chraibi from Miami University, Paul Chase from Becker College, Ken Collier from Northern Arizona University, Anthony Klejna from Buffalo State College/ Niagra Community College, Jerzy Letkowski from Western Massachusetts College, and Jack Van Luik from Mt. Hood Community College.

I wish to thank Paul Chase and Mabel Chow for putting together the answers to some of the exercises. Ms. Chow's organization and web-based presentation of this important aspect of the book is particularly noteworthy.

Finally, I apologize to my spouse Winona for taking so much time away from her for this book. I can only hope that the skills that readers will acquire will compensate on some larger balance sheet.

John Avila
August, 1998

1. Introduction

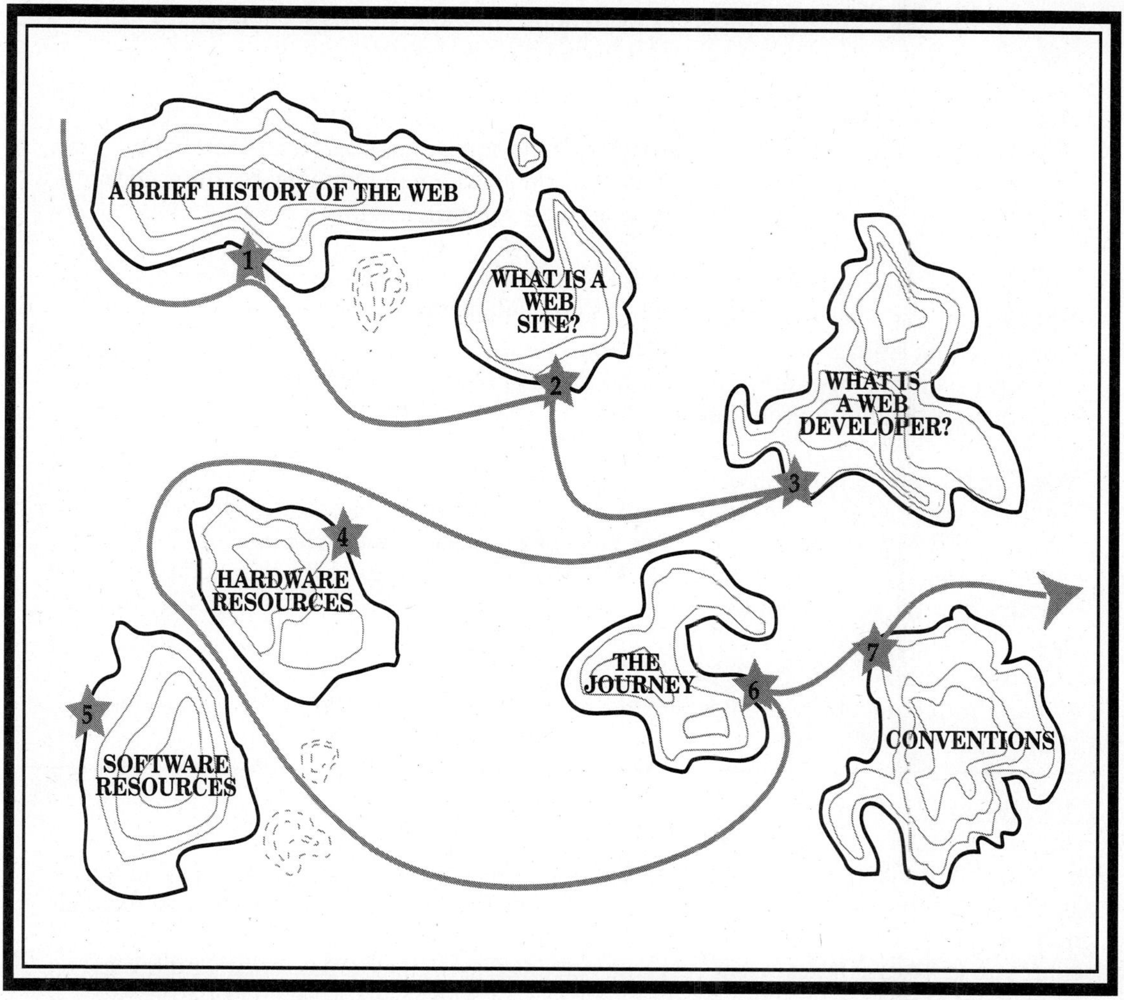

Chapter Preview

1.1 A Brief History of the Web
HTML and the ability to share documents in a universal way over the Internet dates back only to 1990. We list some of the persons involved in the early development and their contributions. We follow the development of browsers and Java to the present.

1.2 What is a Web Site?
Since this book is concerned with the development and maintenance of a Web site, it's important that we have a shared concept of what a Web site is.

1.3 What is a Web Developer?
We also use the term *Web developer* throughout this book. In this section we try to establish what Web developers are and what they are expected to do.

1.4 Hardware Resources
The Web developer must be concerned with the computers that deliver the Web documents as well as those used by users viewing these documents. In this section we identify some of the features that each of these computer platforms must have.

1.5 Software Resources
In addition to the hardware resources, the Web developer must be concerned with the software that resides on these platforms. In this section we look at some of the requirements of the operating system and some of the tools currently available for both the server-side and the client-side platforms.

1.6 The Journey
In this section we provide an overview of the book. We list briefly the topics we will cover and how they fit into the larger view of providing those who would like to become Web developers with the tools they need. We also describe the metaphor that we use throughout the book.

1.7 Conventions
Finally, in this section we describe some of the conventions used in the remainder of the book.

1.1 A Brief History of the Web

The World Wide Web (or just the Web) is all the information that you can access on this planet through the network known as the Internet. This information is accessible through small and large computers. Sometimes it's organized, often it is not. It's a place where people can interact. There are sounds and videos, text, images, animations, and three-dimensional worlds. This is the description given by Tim Berners-Lee in "WWW: Past, Present, and Future," *IEEE Computer*, October 1996.

From HTML at CERN to the browser wars

Berners-Lee was working as a physicist in 1990 at the European particle physics laboratory (CERN) when he developed the basic ideas behind the Web. From the beginning, the Web was designed to make it possible for persons with access to the Internet to easily exchange information. In particular, it should not matter if a person is using a PC or Macintosh or a Unix workstation. Each should have equally easy access.

One of the fundamental pieces making this possible was the development of HTML (for HyperText Markup Language). Berners-Lee defined this language as a means creating documents that could be shared between persons with access to the Internet. The brilliant aspect of this was the ability to provide imbedded links within these documents that would automatically fetch information from other locations on the Internet.

Actually, the idea of these "hyperlinks" was first proposed back in 1945 (!) by Vannevar Bush. Vannevar Bush was the "science Czar" during World War II, the person who decided which projects got funded by the US government. After the war he decided to write about some of his ideas on organizing information and in an article in the Atlantic Monthly in 1945, he proposed this fabulous idea.

It was not until the HTML language combined with the technology of the Internet that the idea could actually be implemented. Despite the goal of creating documents that were universally accessible, the first program (known as a browser) for viewing these "hypertext" documents was restricted to a specific platform (NeXT computers).

The earliest portable browser that allowed retrieval of Web documents from any platform was written by Nicola Pellow in 1991. This program, however, only allowed the viewing of text documents without graphics. In 1993, Marc Andreessen developed a more capable browser while he was at the National Center for Supercomputer Applications (NCSA). His program allowed persons to view graphical elements as well as text and could run on any computer that supported X Windows (originally a Unix-based windowing environment). This browser was known as Mosaic and was freely available to anyone who wished to download a copy from the Internet.

The incredible growth in the use of the Web can be measured in the number of requests by browsers from different machines to the computer at CERN that was serving Web documents. Between July of 1991 and July of 1994, this number increased by a factor of 10 each year. Starting at a level of requests from about 100 different computers per day in July 1991, the number had grown to almost 100,000 per day by July 1994.

In 1994, Andreessen went on to start up Netscape Corporation around an enhanced version of the Mosaic browser. He is the chief technical officer at Netscape today.

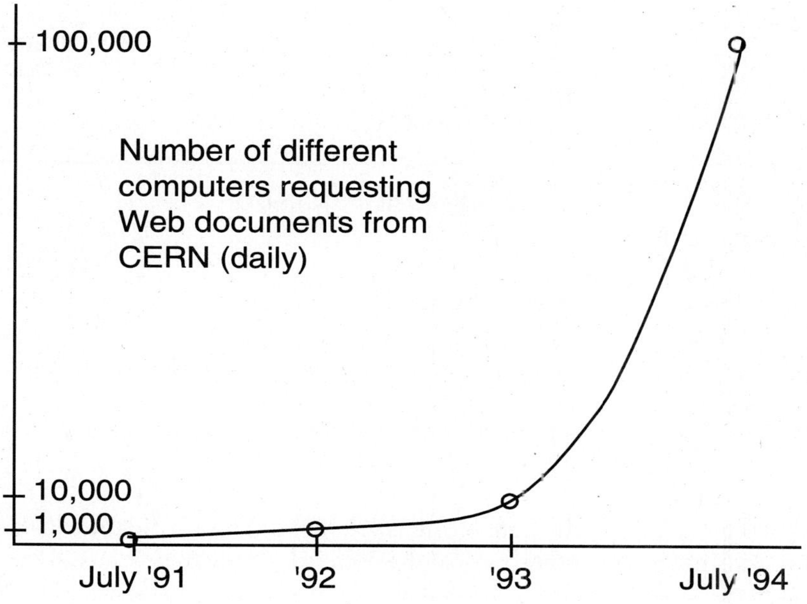

It was also in 1994 that the Java language found a home on the Web. People at Sun Microsystems began to use it for small applications (called applets) that could be downloaded at the time a user was viewing a Web site, execute on the user's machine and display output as part of a Web document. By the Summer of 1996, Netscape had introduced another language called JavaScript (which is unrelated to Java) for carrying out tasks associated with Web documents. Like Java, this language also executed on the viewer's computer.

Also in the Summer of 1996, Microsoft entered the Web browser business with its Internet Explorer. Since then, Microsoft and Netscape have been competing for marketshare by introducing new features and refining existing ones. The "browser wars" have been staged on a large scale and have recently involved even the U.S. Justice Department in a suit against Microsoft related to its inclusion of Internet Explorer as part of the Windows 95 operating system.

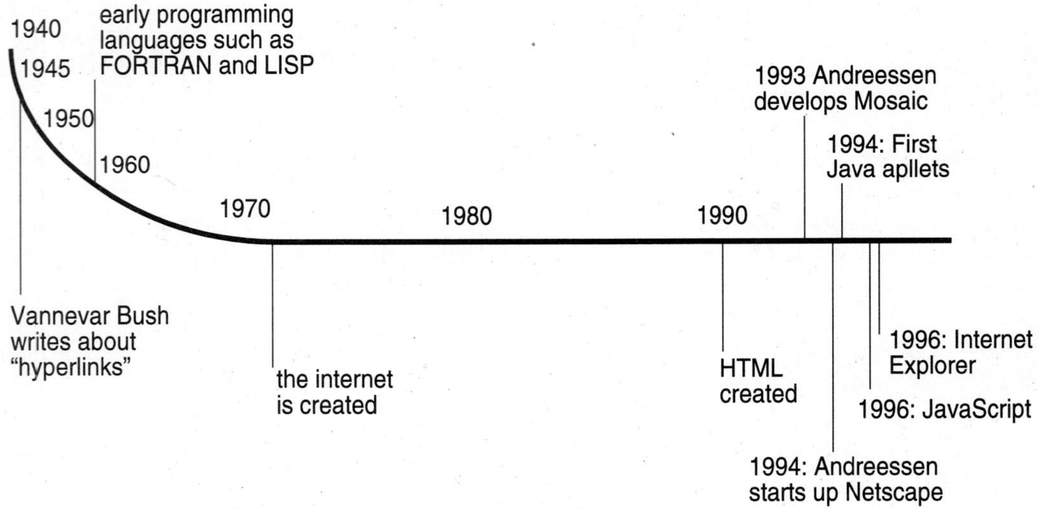

A brief history of the Web

Section review questions

True or false

1. Javascript was a precursor to the Java programming language.
2. Netscape is a browser that originated with the earlier Mosaic browser.
3. Applets are small Java programs that execute on the machine used to view a related Web document.
4. From the beginning, the goal of the Web was to provide documents to anyone with Internet access, regardless of the computer type they are using.

Multiple choice

5. Tim Berners-Lee
   (a) developed the HTML language.
   (b) was the one who first came up with the idea of linking documents together on the Internet.
   (c) developed the first browser.
   (d) all of the above.

6. Mark Andreessen
   (a) developed the first browser for viewing HTML documents.
   (b) was the first to develop a browser that could view graphics.
   (c) developed a browser that was capable of running on PCs, Macintosh, and Unix computers.
   (d) none of the above.

7. Between 1991 and 1994,
   (a) the number of requests for Web documents to the computers at CERN went up by a factor of 10 each year.
   (b) the number of different Web documents requested from the computers at CERN went up by a factor of 10 each year.
   (c) the number of requests for Web documents from different computers to the computers at CERN went up by a factor of 10 each year.
   (d) all of the above.

1.2 What is a Web Site?

This book is concerned with the development and maintenance of Web sites. What is a Web site? Anyone can put together a "home page" and have a Web presence. Here we mean something more specific.

Generally, a Web site will consist of a collection of Web documents. The term *documents* is used broadly to include text files, graphical images, sounds, Java applets, or other similar items. This collection of documents is usually associated with a company, whether it be a bank or a microbrewery.

The documents should provide a coherent image to the viewer. That is, these documents should be similar in appearance and have a "theme" that carries from document to document. We will explore this idea later in the book.

The Web site should also provide a service to the viewer, who is often a potential customer. The service may be just to convey information to the viewer about the company. It may be to allow the customer to ask for information about products that the company produces or even to purchase these products. It may even allow several customers to chat or share information with each other.

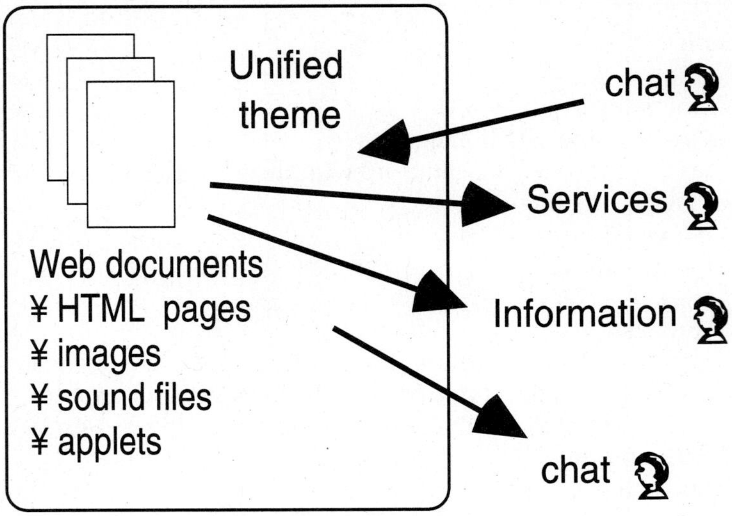

A Web Site

Section review questions

True or false

1. A Web site must be business related.
2. Web documents can be files containing data that can be played as sounds.
3. A Web site should have the appearance that each "page" is separate and stands on its own.
4. Chat "rooms" are inappropriate for a Web site.
5. A Web site should provide a service to the user.
6. A Web site devoted to a rock group would not fall into what is considered here to be a Web site.

1.3 What is a Web Developer?

Web developers put together and maintain Web sites. They may do it alone (taking direction from the appropriate representative of a company for whom the site is being developed), or as a member of a team. Some of these people may be technically oriented, others may have other skills.

Here we focus on the person who must provide the technical expertise to make a Web site functional. A Web developer will, in general, be a programmer. In addition to developing HTML documents, she or he may have to write programs that process data submitted by users viewing HTML documents and filling in forms. There are numerous other programming tasks that may be required to maintain and support a Web site.

Web developers must also be artists. Even if they are not directly responsible for the graphical content in a document, there are other issues relating to fonts and placement of visual information on the Web page that require an aesthetic sensibility. In fact, a master programmer is an artist even in the way his/her program is written and displayed in a text file.

In this book we will explore how to create HTML documents directly using a text editor to assemble them and a browser to view the results. There are many WYSIWYG (What You See Is What You Get) HTML editors on the market that allow you to assemble Web pages using "drag-and-drop" techniques, enter text right where you want it, and place images carefully on the page. Microsoft even includes software within their product that will automatically convert Microsoft Word documents into HTML documents.

So why should Web developers need to learn the basic HTML commands? There are two good reasons: (1) they may have to be able modify or "tweak" documents created by WYSIWYG software; and (2), they will have to be able to write software that will create these documents "on-the-fly." The former will sometimes be required when the software available doesn't quite produce what you wanted. The latter occurs (as an example) when a user enters data into a form and the program that processes such data is required to produce a response as a Web document returned to the viewer. Such programs must be able to generate the text file that makes up the HTML document. This means that the program's author must have mastered the HTML language.

Section review questions

True or false

1. A Web developer is one who puts together and maintains the Web documents associated with one or more Web sites.

2. A Web developer needs to let the designers determine the "look and feel" of a Web site.

3. Web developers are often part of a team of persons responsible for a Web site.

4. The Web developer will be concerned with artistic matters even in the way his or her text documents are arranged.

5. HTML documents can only be put together with text editors.

6. WYSIWYG editors can only be used for generating simple HTML documents.

7. Web developers will not use WYSIWYG editors for generating HTML documents.

8. HTML documents can be generated by programs instead of having to be written by a Web developer.

1.4 Hardware Resources

The Web developer will be concerned with two hardware platforms. Foremost will be the server. This is the computer that must deliver the Web documents to the viewer or process information supplied by a customer. It is also (in all likelihood) the computer used to maintain the Web site. The server must be powerful enough to support many requests for documents. The server must also have sufficient attached disk space to allow the storage of many Web documents for multiple Web sites.

The other platform that the Web developer must be aware of is the client platform. This is the computer used by the viewer of the Web documents. It might be an Intel-based PC or a Macintosh or a Unix workstation. Web developers may not have any control over the client platform but they must be aware of the variety. In general, HTML was developed with this variety in mind so that if one uses the right software, the hardware won't be a problem. In particular, HTML is an evolving language, but there is a standards body called the World Wide Web Consortium (W3C—www.w3.org) that determines the rules for HTML. Web documents that adhere to these rules will be viewable by anyone with any of the most widely used browsers regardless of the computer they are using.

Section review questions

True or false

1. The Web developer need only be concerned with the server hardware.

2. The Web server hardware platform should have enough disk space to support multiple Web sites.

3. The client platform refers to the computer that receives requests for Web documents and delivers them to requesting browsers.

4. If one uses HTML as defined by the standards body then essentially all browsers will be able to properly display the resulting Web documents.

1.5 Software Resources

A Web developer has several operating systems (OS) to deal with. The first is the OS on the server. It might be Unix, it might be Windows NT, or possibly another OS. Since the server has the job of supplying Web documents and probably is the platform used by the Web developer to develop and maintain Web sites, the OS should be one that supports multitasking (several tasks running concurrently). Unix and Windows NT are the primary choices since they have been designed with multitasking in mind.

Other software resources that concern the Web developer are software tools These tools may range from those that can create Web documents to ones that create material that supports Web documents. As an example, the tools for generating multi-media content for Web sites are quite advanced at this point. There are many software vendors that provide programs for manipulating photographic data or generating photographic-quality images directly. Other programs allow the creation of film "clips" that can be made available on Web sites. Still other programs provide the ability to create sound files that can be used in Web sites.

Section review questions

True or false

1. The Web developer must be careful not to use the same computer that is being used to deliver Web documents to users.

2. A program that creates HTML documents using visual "drag and drop" methods would not be useful to a Web developer.

Multiple choice

3. Unix or Windows NT is a good candidate for the OS on a server because each
   (a) is inexpensive and commonly available.
   (b) supports the ability to deliver many Web documents.
   (c) has been developed with the ability to do more than one thing concurrently.
   (d) none of the above.

1.6 The Journey

This book is designed to help you acquire the knowledge of HTML required to be a technical Web developer.

An outline

We will begin with a look at the basic HTML commands for displaying text and graphical elements in a browser window. Even though there are tools, as we mentioned above, for creating HTML documents without having to know HTML, Web developers have to be able to write software that can generate Web documents "on the fly." This requires that they understand the *syntax* (rules that define HTML) for creating these documents as the output from special-purpose programs. In a subsequent book we will show how to write these programs. In this one, we will provide the knowledge to be able to develop sophisticated HTML documents directly.

Once we have learned the basic HTML commands for telling the browser how to display text and place graphical elements, we will look at how to embed hyperlinks in our documents. Hyperlinks allow the user to jump to another document by clicking on a piece of text or a button or a portion of a graphical image.

From there we will examine how to create those boxes and buttons used to send information back to the server. These *form* elements come in a wide variety of types and we will learn how to build them all.

Tables are an element of HTML used to display data in an orderly array of rows and columns. We will learn how to do this as well as how to use this HTML element to take more control over the layout of text and graphics when we want to build sophisticated Web pages.

Although this book is not about Java applets, they have become an important part of Web pages and we'll see how to embed applets in our Web documents, even if we didn't write them.

In Chapter 5, we look at frames. Frames are a mechanism for subdividing a browser window into subwindows so that each can be updated independently of the others.

Finally, in Chapter 6 we look at a relatively new aspect of Web pages known as Cascading Style Sheets. Although some of the features provided by Cascading Style Sheets are still somewhat "buggy" in their implementation, this will eventually be overcome. Moreover, the capabilities provided for Web developers is too great to ignore.

In Appendix A we have a detailed description of each HTML "tag." This is meant as a reference offering more detail than we may have covered in the chapter where that tag appears. You will probably want to place a bookmark on that appendix since you will be referring to it frequently.

In Appendix B we have additional information regarding the use of "frameset documents."

The metaphor

We have used a metaphor of a sea journey throughout the book and in a supporting Web site. Each chapter begins with a treasure map showing the piece of the journey associated with that chapter. Each island is a section of the chapter. There are sandbars that represent various interesting topics providing additional material. The route shown in the map leads to the essential islands. Islands shown on the map but not on the route can be viewed as optional. The reader in a hurry can skip them, perhaps to return later. The reader who wants to acquire deeper skills will want to visit every island.

1.7 Conventions

In addition to the map presented at the beginning of each chapter, we have adopted certain conventions to orient the reader as she or he progresses through the book.

Text files and programs in their text file form are displayed in the form of a shadowed box with the name of the file appearing in a shaded line at the top of the box. For example, here is a sample HTML document.

File: `simple.html`

```
<HTML>
<HEAD>
   <TITLE>A Simple Document</TITLE>
</HEAD>
<BODY>
   Hello, WWW World.
</BODY>
</HTML>
```

Occasionally, we will explicitly display the syntax for HTML or Java. These will be denoted by a double-lined shadowed box. The following is an example.

Syntax rule

Unless the browser is explicitly commanded to do otherwise, all white space that is not a blank (such as tabs, end-of-line characters, etc.) is treated as a single blank. Multiple white space characters are collapsed to a single blank.

Occasionally we provide additional information that the reader may want to know, usually as extensions of the material covered in the regular portion of the text. These extensions are also displayed using the double-lined shadowed boxes.

We often make references to the Web-Archipelago. This is a Web site (`http://web-archipelago.com`) where basic information on HTML and related items can be found. The material in the enclosed CD-ROM mirrors the content on the Web-Archipelago at the time the book went to press. Changes in the Web-Archipelago will be made as necessary and you might want to check in periodically to see if anything new has appeared.

Now that we have set the overall plan, we are ready to begin the journey.

Exercises

1. Locate a copy on the Web of the paper from 1945 by Vannevar Bush in which he conceptualized the notion of a link. What medium did Bush visualize for the storage of documents? Explore the technology of the 40s to answer why it might have been difficult to create linked documents.

2. Use the Web to learn more about the Xanadu project envisioned by Ted Nelson. Nelson was the person who first coined the term *hypertext*. What was this project? Do you think it could be implemented in the Web?

3. One of the characteristics of hypertext documents (ones with links to other documents) is that the documents to which the links originally pointed may no longer exist, have been renamed, or have moved. What do you think it would take to make links so that they remain correct even if documents are moved or renamed? Having a Web master continually checking these links "by hand" is not the right answer.

4. Gopher was a means of sharing documents over the Internet that pre-dated the use of HTML and browsers. Locate information about gopher and describe how it was used. What limitations did it have? There is a primitive concept of links in gopher. How did a user navigate the Web? How is the gopher concept different from the Web?

5. Find examples on the Web of Web sites that do not provide a coherent image to the viewer. What is it about the sites you found that gives them a lack of coherency? Can you think of a way the problems might have been corrected?

6. Provide a list of items of information that a commercial Web site might want to collect from its viewers. It might be easier to answer this question if you envision a particular Web site (real or imaginary) and ask the question about that Web site.

7. Web sites can also be public service organizations (the local library or city offices). What do you think the significant differences would be for a Web developer who was putting together a Web site for such an organization?

8. What do you think it means to say that master programmers are artists in the way their programs are written and displayed in a text file? Give some examples of artistic and non-artistic programs.

9. How do you imagine a program would check to verify that the links in a Web document were still "live"? What would be the input to this program, and how would that input be used to determine if links were live?

10. Use the Web to check out several of the major server hardware platforms: Sun Microsystems, Digital, IBM, Intel. What features do they advertise to distinguish themselves from their competition?

11. Use the Web to check out the major server software vendors such as Apache and Windows NT (name at least three others). What does each offer to distinguish itself from its competitors? What hardware platforms is each product capable of running on? See if you can find information on the percentage of Web servers using each software product.

12. Locate Web sites for companies that market products for generating HTML documents using visual techniques (e.g. drag and drop). One such company is Adobe with their PageMill product. Name several others. What features distinguish the various products? On which platforms can each run? What system requirements do they have?

2. HTML Basics

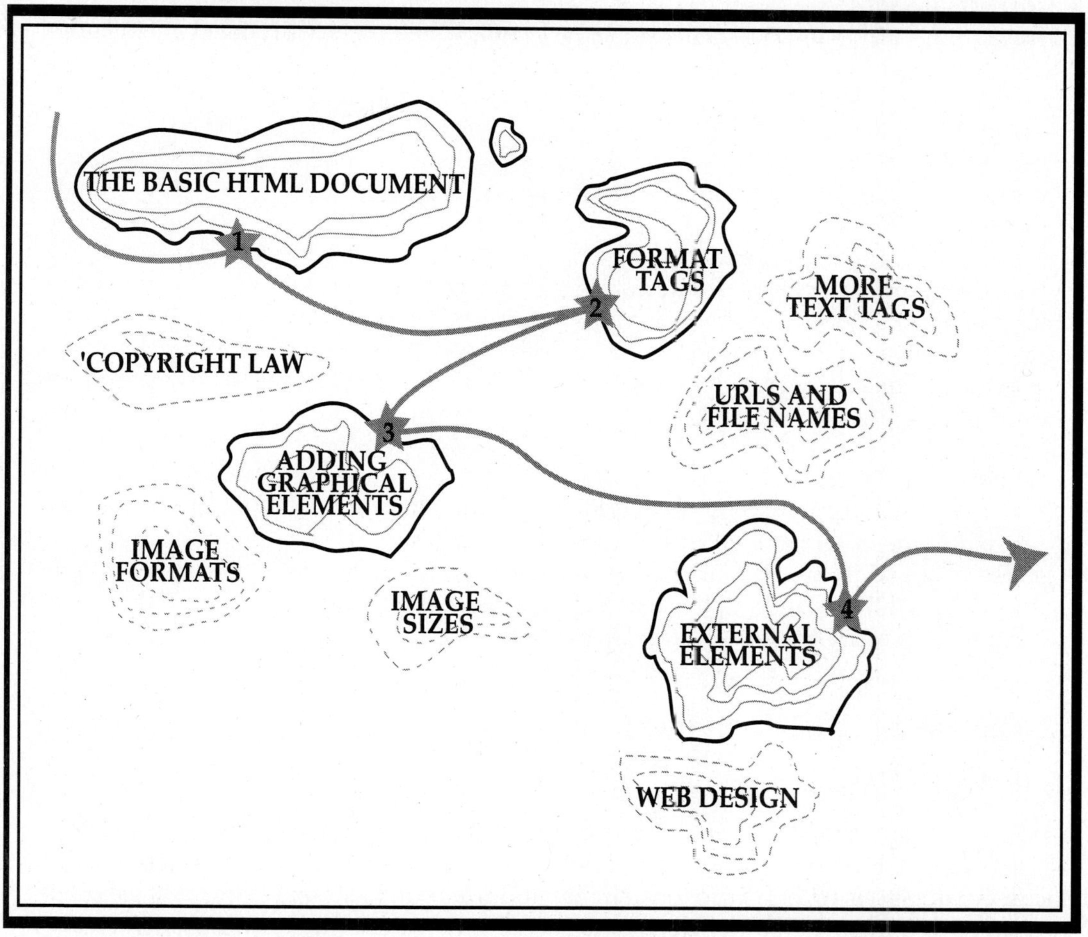

Chapter Preview

2.1 The Basic HTML Document
We start with a simple example showing the underlying structure of every HTML document. From there, we start building a Web site that will be a theme throughout the textbook. We set out a simple and practical strategy for developing HTML pages. We examine how the first HTML "tags" to represent line breaks, new paragraphs and horizontal lines are used to organize a document visually.

2.2 Format Tags
Formatting in HTML documents is partly accomplished by identifying elements of a document and letting the browser decide how to display them and partly by explicitly commanding the browser to display certain elements in specific ways. We look at both types of formatting tags in this section. Along the way we examine how to display characters that would normally have special meaning to the browser. Finally, we look at the HTML mechanisms for displaying lists.

2.3 Adding Graphical Elements
Web documents are pretty uninteresting without graphics. In this section we examine how to place graphical elements in our documents. We will also examine how to provide background color and texture to Web pages. We examine the issue of large graphical elements in Web documents, particularly the time it takes to download such documents.

2.4 External Elements
Good Web management dictates that HTML documents contain within them information about the document, its author, the date it was last revised, and other similar elements. In addition, HTML provides a tag that allows developers to place within the document information used by search engines to convey information about that document to users on the Web. We look at these items in this section.

2.1 The Basic HTML Document

Hello, WWW World

A Web document is made up of text and graphics. Behind the representation that you see using your Web browser is a simple text document containing the text portion of the Web document, together with instructions on how to format that text and how to incorporate the graphics elements. That text document incorporates formatting commands in a language called HyperText Markup Language (HTML). In this section we will examine a simple example of an HTML document.

Every HTML document has the following form:

The basic HTML document

```
<HTML>
<HEAD>
   <TITLE>The title of the document</TITLE>
</HEAD>
<BODY>
   text, graphics and other elements
</BODY>
</HTML>
```

Figure 2.1

For example, to create an HTML document displaying the string "Hello, WWW World." we would modify the form shown in Figure 2.1 to produce the `simple.html` file shown in Figure 2.2.

File: `simple.html`

```
<HTML>
<HEAD>
   <TITLE>A Simple Document</TITLE>
</HEAD>
<BODY>
   Hello, WWW World.
</BODY>
</HTML>
```

Figure 2.2

You may obtain this file (as well as virtually all other files in this textbook) from the enclosed CD ROM or the Web-Archipelago site (`http://Web-Archipelago.com/`). Alternatively, you can simply type it and save it on your local hard disk. Once you have created or located this file, you can view it with your Web browser. Depending on which browser you are using, you will have to select the *Open File* or *Open Location* item from the File menu and then direct the browser to the location of the file. The result should look like Figure 2.3.

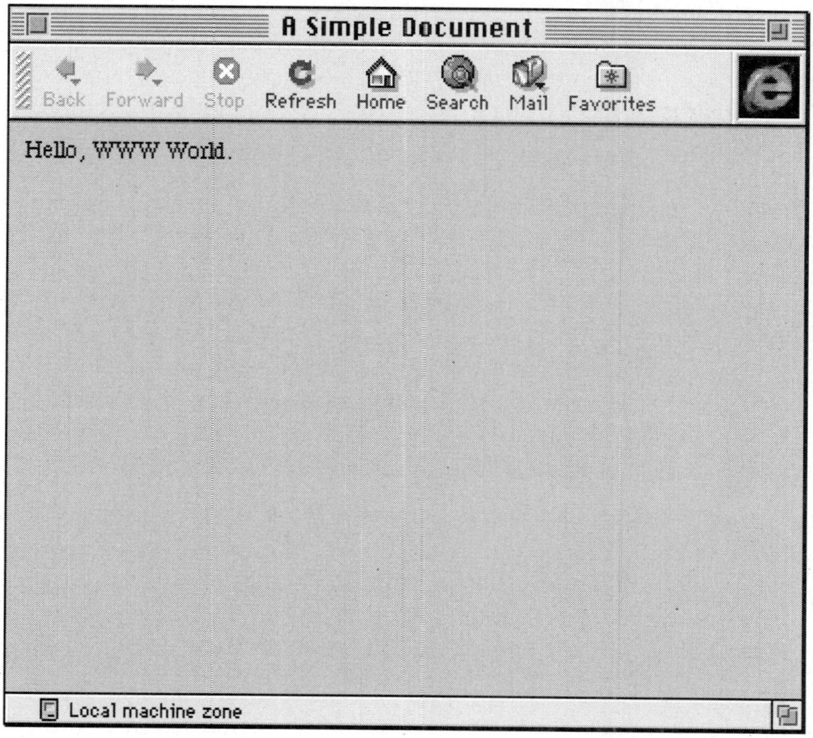

Figure 2.3

The first thing you should notice is that very little of the `simple.html` file actually was displayed by the browser.

Let's examine the `simple.html` file in detail. Notice that most of the document is made up of items of the form `<tag-type>` or `</tag-type>` where tag-type is one of several choices you see in the document. In fact, items that begin with the < character and end with the > character identify a *tag* in HTML. These tags are instructions to the browser. Most (but not all) tags come in pairs. The opening tag (such as `<HTML>`) is matched by a closing tag (`</HTML>` in this case). The tag identifies the material that is to be handled by the browser when it processes this tag. We will usually refer to the material between the opening and closing tag as the *contents* of the tag. The browser doesn't care if the tags are in uppercase letters or lowercase. We, however, will adopt the convention of using all uppercase letters. This makes the tags easier to locate visually when we are looking at a text file.

The `HTML` tag identifies the start of an HTML document and the `/HTML` tag identifies the end of a document. Every HTML document is made up of two major subsections: the head and the body. Notice how in our document we have a section beginning with the `HEAD` tag and ending with the `/HEAD` tag and a section beginning with the `BODY` and ending with the `/BODY` tag.

The head portion of the HTML document will contain (among other things) the title of the page displayed by the browser. In fact, if you examine the title bar in the browser window displaying the `simple.html` document (Figure 2.3) you will see the string of characters we have enclosed by the `TITLE` and `/TITLE` tags.

Finally, the body portion of the HTML document contains the short phrase, which is the only text displayed in the browser window. Most HTML documents will have the major portion of their content in the body section.

We mentioned earlier that tags need not be in uppercase letters although we will use that convention. Similarly, tags need not be placed at the beginning of a line as we have done. Good programming practices, however, dictate that we should attempt to prevent simple errors such as forgetting the closing tag to match the opening tag. As a result, unless the opening and closing tag and the enclosed material fits on one line (as it does in the TITLE example in Figure 2.1), we will line up the opening and closing tags vertically. Occasionally, we will also use indentation and align matching tags by indenting them the same amount.

Web document development

Since you will be building Web documents and experimenting with them, we recommend that the way to do this is to have your browser display its output in one window while your text editor displays its output in a separate window. The development cycle is shown in Figure 2.4. We will edit the text file, view the resulting document using the browser, go back and change the text file, and cycle through the process until you have the result you want.

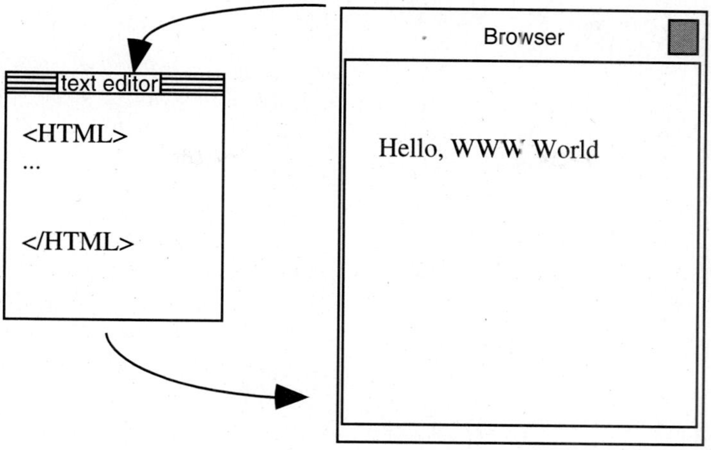

Figure 2.4

HTML documents must be simple text files. To develop these files you can use either a simple text editor or a more sophisticated word processor. If you use a word processor, however, be sure that when you save the file you save it in text format.

When you make a change to the HTML document in the text editor and wish to see its effect, first save the document in the text editor window. Then, in the browser window (assuming you are viewing the HTML document you are working on) be sure to *re-load* the document. Usually this can be done by just clicking on a re-load or refresh button.

The HTML document development cycle must take into account if the document is currently accessible to the world. If it is, then you must be aware that a browser somewhere on the net may request your document while you are working on it. The saved copy will probably be in a transitional state and not ready for display. Instead, work on a version of your document that is not available for public viewing. Once you have developed it to the point where it is ready, replace the public one with the one you have modified.

WYSIWYG ("What You See Is What You Get") tools for creating HTML documents generally hide the HTML source from you. As a Web developer, you will need to see the HTML source because you may want to write applications that produce HTML documents. Later, as you develop proficiency in HTML, you may want to start with one of these HTML document development tools and, if necessary, modify the resulting text documents.

© Copyright Law

The Internet has made it possible for anyone to publish material for others to view. This raises issues about copyright protection. How does copyright on the Web compare to that offered to other forms of publication such as books, music recordings, and pictures?

Article I of the Constitution of the United States states that Congress has the power to

promote the Progress of Science and useful Arts, by securing for limited Times to Authors and Inventors the exclusive Right to their respective Writings and Discoveries.

In 1909, the Congress passed a Copyright Act that indicated which things were eligible for protection:

Copyright protection subsists . . . in original works of authorship fixed in any tangible medium of expression, now known or later developed, from which they can be perceived, reproduced, or otherwise communicated, either directly or with the aid of a machine or device.

In 1976, Congress passed another copyright act and indicated in an accompanying report what it meant by these "tangible mediums of expression." In particular it stated

A work may be fixed in "words, numbers, notes, sounds, pictures, or any other graphic or symbolic indicia"; may be embodied in a physical object in "written, printed, photographic, sculptural, punched, magnetic, or any other stable form."

Generally, the courts have ruled that things like floppy disks, CD-ROMs, and other digital storage devices are all stable forms.

What this means is that Web documents are copyrightable. Moreover, the law doesn't specifically require that the "copyright" notice be present in the document for it to be copyrighted.

Copyrighted information may not be reproduced without the consent of the author (or someone to whom the author has given the right—like a publisher). But what does it mean to reproduce a Web document? In fact, each time the document is viewed by a browser it is being reproduced from its original form on the disk drive attached to the server.

There are provisions in the Copyright Act for "fair use" which means that you can use copyrighted work for purposes such as teaching, journalism, or research. Beyond that, determining fair use depends on things like whether or not someone is profiting from the copy and whether or not the copies affect the market value of the copyrighted work.

In general, it appears that viewing a Web document on a browser is fair use. Copying the material from a Web document and embedding it in another Web document or other published form without the permission of the original owner is not fair use.

Our first customer

Our first customer wants us to develop a Web site for them. They have some initial text they want incorporated into their *home page* . By now, you should have guessed that a home page is just an HTML document that is to be viewed by a Web browser. The home page is just the first document in a hierarchy of documents you may view when you go check out a particular location.

In order to be able to put together the home page for our customer, we need to learn about who they are and what they do. Island Quest Travel is a travel agency specializing in expeditions to exotic places. The agency wants to let its customers know the kinds of things they do and wants to encourage those that view their home page to browse and get interested in buying their services. Assume Figure 2.5 is what we have received from our client.

The text received from our client

Island Quest Travel can take you to exotic locations where you can walk in the footsteps of buccaneers and adventurers from the past. We can take you to places that are just dots on the map. We'll fly you there and back and even provide guides for special treks into jungles. Or if you prefer the sailing adventure, we will gather a crew and a ship and let you cruise mysterious islands.

Here are some of our services:

- **Planning**
We have dozens of locations that offer adventure and excitement and we can help you pick out just the right place.

- **Flight reservations**
Just leave it to us. We'll get you there and back. We will handle reservations with the major airlines as well as the local pilots for those special places not seen by most of the rest of the world.

- **Sailing accommodations**
For the buccaneer, we can charter sailboats and crews who will fix your meals and take you to those hidden island coves, where perhaps treasure is hiding in a nearby cave.

- **Guide services**
Islands often have jungles and we have the guides to take you to some of the temples from forgotten civilizations. These guides will provide everything you need in the way of meals and accommodations.

Figure 2.5

Of course we'll add graphics and all sorts of neat stuff later but let's start with getting this text in an HTML document and viewing it in our Web browser. We start by "pouring" the customer text into an empty document in our favorite text editor. We replaced the • character with the * character since the bullet is a special character not directly recognized by the browser. Next we add HTML tags for the HTML document components using Figure 2.1 as our guide and add some comment tags. Comment tags are identified by the four characters: `<!--` at the beginning, followed by the commented text and terminated by the three characters `-->`. They can be placed anywhere in your document. The browser will ignore comments and they will not be displayed on the Web page. They will, however, be useful to us as Web developers. The result is the document you see in Figure 2.6.

A note about the comments at the beginning of the file. It is always a good idea to identify the name of the file and the project you are working on. We will also adopt the standard of supplying the name of the programmer, the date of the last modification, and copyright information. This last item means the contents of the document belongs to the named parties. In particular no unauthorized use of your work can be made except to view it in the usual way on the Web.

File: `IQTravel_2a.html`

```
<HTML>
<!--File: IQTravel_2a.html-->
<!--Project: Island Quest Travel Site-->
<!--Programmer: J. Avila-->
<!--Last modified: 5/20/1998-->
<!--Copyright J. H. Avila, 1998. All rights reserved.-->
<HEAD>
   <TITLE>Island Quest Travel</TITLE>
</HEAD>
<BODY>
  Island Quest Travel can take you to exotic locations where
  you can walk in the footsteps of buccaneers and adventurers
  from the past. We can take you to places that are just dots
  on the map.  We'll fly you there and back and even provide
  guides for special treks into jungles. Or if you prefer the
  sailing adventure, we will gather a crew and a ship and let
  you cruise mysterious islands.

  Here are some of our services:

  * Planning
  We have dozens of locations that offer adventure and excite-
  ment and we can help you pick out just the right place.

* Flight reservations
Just leave it to us. We'll get you there and back. We will
```

```
    handle reservations with the major airlines as well as the
    local pilots for those special places not seen by most of the
    rest of the world.

    * Sailing accommodations
    For the buccaneer, we can charter sailboats and crews who
    will fix your meals and take you to those hidden island coves
    where perhaps treasure is hiding in a nearby cave.

    * Guide services
    Islands often have jungles and we have the guides to take you
    to some of the temples from forgotten civilizations. These
    guides will provide everything you need in the way of meals
    and accommodations.
</BODY>
</HTML>
```

Figure 2.6

We open this file from the browser and what we see is what's shown in Figure 2.7! What happened?

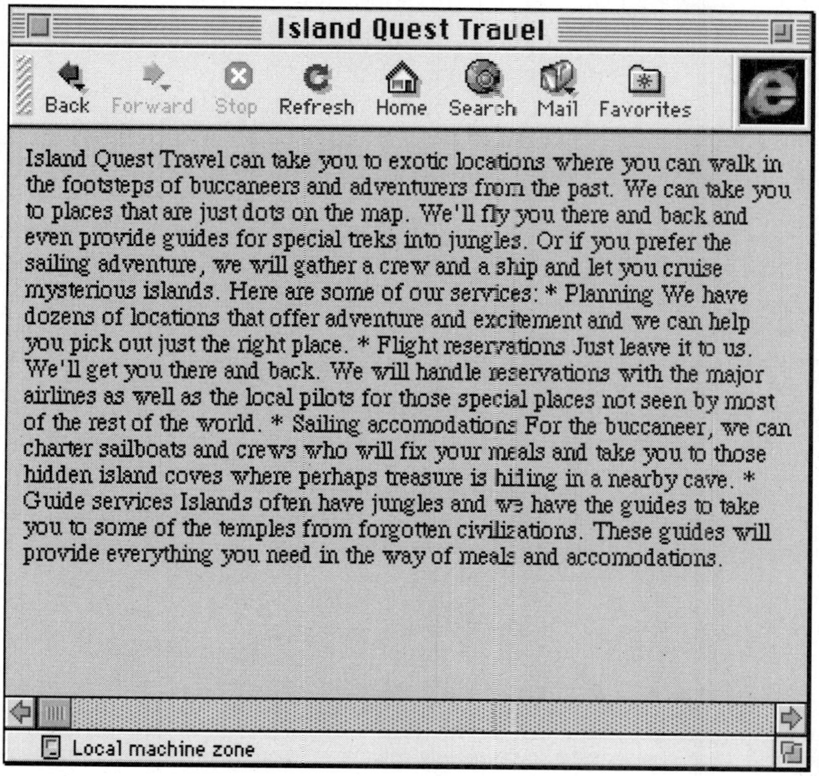

Figure 2.7

What happened is that the browser has its own rules for how to display text. In particular, it has to account for the fact that the browser window can be re-sized by the user and the browser tries to fill out the available space. All those return characters that we embedded in the text file are not taken literally by the browser. "White space" is the generic name given to characters that don't print. The return character, tabs, and blank spaces are all examples of white space. The rule that governs how white space is rendered by the browser is given in the following box.

Syntax rule

Unless the browser is explicitly commanded to do otherwise, all white space characters such as the blank (created with the space bar), tabs, end-of-line characters, etc. are treated as a single blank. Multiple white space characters are collapsed to a single blank.

The `P`, `BR`, and `HR` tags

As we see in Figure 2.7, there is essentially no formatting information preserved from our original document. HTML is a document formatting language and if you want things formatted, you must put in the instructions to make it happen! This includes information about when to start a new paragraph or where to break a line and start a new line.

The `P` tag identifies a paragraph. The trailing `/P` tag is optional in HTML. The browser can determine the end of the paragraph from other tags. It will cause the browser to skip a line and to start the subsequent text on a new line. Closely related is the `BR` tag (for BReak), which will simply cause the browser to place subsequent text (or other items) starting on a new line. The `BR` tag does not have a matching closing tag.

Finally, there is an `HR` tag (with no matching closing tag) which will cause a simple horizontal rule (line) to be placed in the document by the browser. This line will extend the full width of the browser window.

Let's use these new tools to improve the appearance of our document. The result is shown in Figure 2.8. In Figure 2.9 we see how the browser renders this document. It's an improvement over the original but we can do more. In the next section we will continue to improve this document.

File: `IQTravel_2b.html`

```
<HTML>
<!--File: IQTravel_2b.html-->
<!--Project: Island Quest Travel Site-->
<!--Programmer: J. Avila-->
<!--Last modified: 5/20/1998-->
```

```
<!--Copyright J. H. Avila, 1998. All rights reserved.-->
<HEAD>
   <TITLE>Island Quest Travel</TITLE>
</HEAD>
<BODY>
<P>
  Island Quest Travel can take you to exotic locations where
  you can walk in the footsteps of buccaneers and adventurers
  from the past. We can take you to places that are just dots
  on the map.  We'll fly you there and back and even provide
  guides for special treks into jungles. Or if you prefer the
  sailing adventure, we will gather a crew and a ship and let
  you cruise mysterious islands.
<P>
<HR>
<P>
   Here are some of our services:
<P>
   * Planning
<BR>
  We have dozens of locations that offer adventure and excite-
  ment and we can help you pick out just the right place.
<P>
   * Flight reservations
<BR>
  Just leave it to us. We'll get you there and back. We will
  handle reservations with the major airlines as well as the
  local pilots for those special places not seen by most of the
  rest of the world.
<P>
   * Sailing accommodations
<BR>
  For the buccaneer, we can charter sailboats and crews who
  will fix your meals and take you to those hidden island coves
  where perhaps  treasure is hiding in a nearby cave.
<P>
   * Guide services
<BR>
  Islands often have jungles and we have the guides to take you
  to some of the temples from forgotten civilizations. These
  guides will provide everything you need in the way of meals
  and accommodations.
</BODY>
</HTML>
```

Figure 2.8

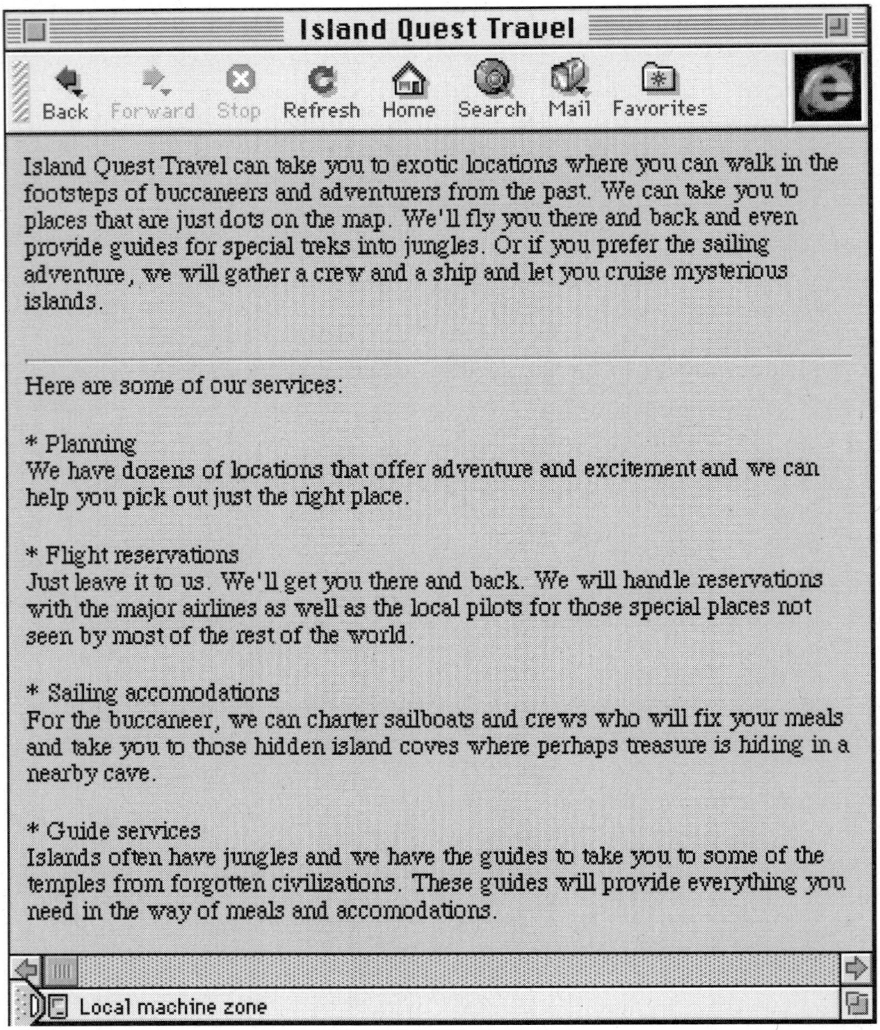

Figure 2.9

Some simple browser experiments

While you are viewing the document shown in Figure 2.9 with your browser, you should experiment with changing the size of the browser window. Usually this is accomplished by clicking and holding the lower right corner of the window and "pulling" the corner to make the window wider or narrower, taller or shorter. Pay careful attention to the way the text is displayed. In particular, notice that the browser will automatically wrap the text to accommodate the size of the window.

Browsers also allow you to change the font type and size. Find out how to do this by checking the options menu for your browser and try changing the font size or font type to see the effect of displaying the Island Quest Travel Web document.

Section review questions

True or false

1. HTML documents are plain text files that can be read by a simple text editor.

2. Every HTML document has two major subsections: a `HEAD` section and a `BODY` section.

3. Every HTML tag is identified by the < and > characters.

4. All HTML tags come in pairs such as `<BODY>` and `</BODY>`.

5. A home page is just the first document in a hierarchy of documents that make up a Web site.

6. The `P` tag is treated by the browser as if two `BR` tags were issued in succession.

7. A `P` tag will cause the browser to skip a line and indent to indicate the beginning of a new paragraph.

8. An `HR` tag visually divides the Web document into two sections.

9. Resizing the browser window will result in some text being cut off along one of the edges of the window.

Multiple choice

10. A Web document that displays using a browser consists of
    (a) a text file with the text portion and another file with HTML commands that tell how to format the text and place graphical elements on the screen.
    (b) a text file with embedded HTML commands that tell how to format the text and place graphical elements on the screen.
    (c) a file containing text and graphics that can only be read by the browser.

11. The HEAD portion of an HTML document contains only
    (a) graphical elements but no text.
    (b) the title of the document.
    (c) HTML instructions on how to display the contents of the Web document.
    (d) none of the above.

12. The contents of a tag is
    (a) the material between the opening tag and the matching closing tag.
    (b) the material between the < character and the matching > character.
    (c) the name of the tag.

13. The use of uppercase letters for tags is
    (a) required by the HTML language specifications.
    (b) optional but a good idea so that the Web programmer is able to identify these tags.
    (c) only necessary for the major tags such as HTML, HEAD, and BODY.

14. Vertical alignment of opening and closing tags is
    (a) used only when the tags and the contents cannot be contained on a single line.
    (b) required by the browser to correctly format the contents of the tag.
    (c) used to help Web programmers so that they do not forget the matching closing tag.
    (d) none of the above.

15. Assume you are viewing an HTML document using a browser. Changes that you make in the HTML text file using an editor will
    (a) only immediately affect the text file and not the display in the browser window.
    (b) be visible immediately upon saving the changes in the text file.
    (c) only be visible in the browser window once you re-load the document.
    (d) (a) and (c).

16. WYSIWYG editors for creating Web documents
    (a) should never be used by a Web developer.
    (b) should always be used by a Web developer.
    (c) eliminate the need to know HTML commands for a Web developer.
    (d) should be used to develop documents directly but cannot be used if the HTML document is the output of a program.

17. Comments in an HTML text file
    (a) can be placed anywhere in the file.
    (b) are denoted by the <!-- characters prior to the comment and the characters --> following the comment.
    (c) will not be displayed by the browser.
    (d) all of the above.

18. White space is
    (a) ignored by the browser.
    (b) used by the browser as a guide in displaying the text file.
    (c) only used by the browser if it consists of a tab or an end-of-line character.
    (d) none of the above.

2.2 Format Tags

Header tags

HTML provides the ability to format titles to sections of your document. You can mark a section title by using the `Hn` opening tag before the title and the `/Hn` closing tag following the title. Here `n` denotes a number from 1 to 6. The most important sections have the smaller numbers, the less important sections have the larger numbers. The browser generally will place all section titles in boldface type and will make the more important sections a larger type size.

The Island Quest Travel Web page that we have been working on is particularly bland at this point. Let's display the title of the Web page in the body of the document as the first line of the document. We will do this by using the `H2` Header tag. (You should experiment with an alternate choice of `H1` or `H3`.) The resulting change will be reflected in the first few lines of the body section of the document:

```
...
<BODY>
<P>
<H2>Island Quest Travel</H2>
...
```

In addition, let's use the header tags to set off the list of services provided by Island Quest Travel. The result is the following modification for the first of the service items:

```
...
Here are some of our services:
<P>
<H4>Planning</H4>
  We have dozens of locations that offer adventure and excitement
  and we can help you pick out just the right place.
...
```

We have used a higher number in the header tag to indicate that the list of services is less important than title of the document itself. The choice of `H4` instead of `H3` was dictated by the size of the font used by the browser to render headers and you may find that you would prefer something else.

Logical and physical tags

The name, Island Quest Travel, appears in the first paragraph. We would like to accentuate that in some way. In HTML there are tags known as "character tags" that allow us to identify sections of text as having a particular property. For example, we can use the `EM` tag to ask the browser to *emphasize* a section of text or we can use the `CITE` tag to treat a section of text as a *citation* (a quoted section from some other source). The browser is programmed to respond to these tags by making appropriate changes to the text between the opening and matching closing tags. These tag types are known as *logical* tags because you are identifying the nature of the element you are marking and not telling the browser how to display it. In one browser you may get text appearing in boldface when you ask for emphasis. In another you may get italic type.

In addition to these logical tags there are *physical* tags that allow you to specify the way in which the text is displayed. Many HTML authors will choose the physical tags just because it gives them a little more control over the look of the document displayed by the browser. In the Web page for Island Quest Travel we want to see the name of the company appear in italics. As a result, we modify the first paragraph of the HTML document so that the name Island Quest Travel is bracketed by the I and the /I tags as follows:

```
...
<I>Island Quest Travel</I> can take you to exotic locations where
you can walk in the footsteps of buccaneers and adventurers from
the past. We can ...
```

You will learn about other tag types. We will explore some of these issues in the exercises.

Metacharacters

As one approach to setting off the list of services, let us try bracketing the name of each service by the characters << and >>. For example, assume we want to see

```
<<Planning>>
```

as the appropriate heading.

We have a problem. The < and the > characters have special significance to the browser because they are used to identify tags. They are known as *metacharacters*. For this reason we cannot simply place these characters in the text of the document without confusing the browser. HTML handles this problem by having an alternate way of representing these characters. In this case, the < character is represented by < (including the semi-colon) and the > character is represented by > . There are other metacharacters and these have their own similar representations. Check out the Web-Archipelego site for pointers to sites that will give you these details.

Now we can put these pieces together to obtain the latest version of the Island Quest Travel Web page. The HTML is shown in Figure 2.10 and the document as rendered by a browser is shown in Figure 2.11.

File: `IQTravel_2c.html`

```
<HTML>
<!--File: IQTravel_2c.html-->
<!--Project: Island Quest Travel Site-->
<!--Programmer: J. Avila-->
<!--Last modified: 5/24/1998-->
<!--Copyright J. H. Avila, 1998. All rights reserved.-->
<HEAD>
   <TITLE>Island Quest Travel</TITLE>
</HEAD>
<BODY>
<P>
<H2>Island Quest Travel</H2>
  <I>Island Quest Travel</I> can take you to exotic locations
  where you can walk in the footsteps of buccaneers and adven-
  turers from the
  past. We can take you to places that are just dots on the
  map.  We'll fly you there and back and even provide guides
  for special treks into jungles. Or if you prefer the sailing
  adventure, we will gather a crew and a ship and let you
  cruise mysterious islands.
<P>
<HR>
<P>
   Here are some of our services:
<P>
<H4>&lt;&lt;Planning&gt;&gt;</H4>
  We have dozens of locations that offer adventure and excite-
  ment and we can help you pick out just the right place.
<P>
<H4>&lt;&lt;Flight reservations&gt;&gt;</H4>
  Just leave it to us. We'll get you there and back. We will
  handle reservations with the major airlines as well as the
  local pilots for those special places not seen by most of the
  rest of the world.
<P>
<H4>&lt;&lt;Sailing accommodations&gt;&gt;</H4>
   For the buccaneer, we can charter sailboats and crews who
will fix your meals and take you to those hidden island coves
where perhaps   treasure is hiding in a nearby cave.
<P>
<H4>&lt;&lt;Guide services&gt;&gt;</H4>
   Island often have jungles and we have the guides to take you
to some of the temples from forgotten civilizations. These
guides will provide everything you need in the way of meals and
accommodations.
</BODY>
</HTML>
```

Figure 2.10

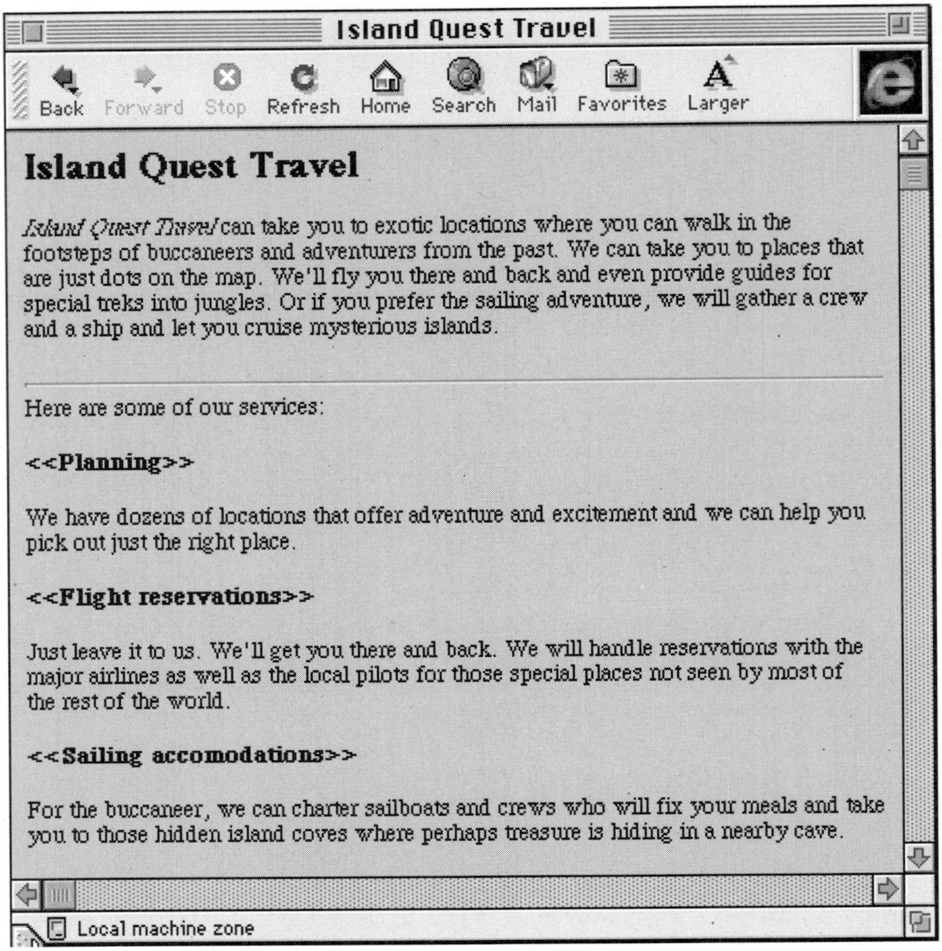

Figure 2.11

More Text Tags

Physical tags

The `FONT` tag

HTML provides for a number of other text formatting tags that have not been mentioned. Some tags are logical tags in which we tell the browser **what** the enclosed text is (e.g. a definition or a quote) and let it determine **how** to display that text. The other tags are physical tags in which we tell the browser directly how to display the enclosed text.

Here we will mention a few of these text formatting tags. All of the tags associated with HTML 3.2 are found in Appendix A.

The FONT tag is a physical tag that allows us to direct the browser to use a specific size and even allows us to manipulate the color of the text enclosed between the opening and closing tags.

Look at the following example:

```
<FONT SIZE="+1">This text is shown slightly bigger</FONT>
```

Here the text shown between the opening and closing tags will be displayed as one size larger than whatever the size of the font before and after the FONT tag. Notice that we have an additional component within the opening tag. The SIZE item is called an *attribute*. Attributes provide additional direction to the browser. They are parameters associated with the particular tag. Most tags have attributes. They always appear with the opening tag. If there are multiple attributes for a tag, their order is unimportant. The SIZE attribute can also specify an absolute font size (the choices are 1 (smallest) to 7 (largest). It is always safer to have the value of the attribute quoted, although not all values need be quoted.

Syntax rule

Attributes may be followed by an equals sign and some *value*. Some attributes do not define values. Others assume a default value if none is specified. White space is allowed around the equals sign. Although there are some value names that don't have to be surrounded by double quotes, it is always acceptable to use them.

If there is more than one attribute for a particular tag, the order in which they are listed is not important. Multiple attributes are separated from each other by a blank space.

There is an additional attribute for the FONT tag. You can specify the color of the text between the opening and closing tags by using the COLOR attribute. Color is an attribute that appears in other tags and the value assigned to this attribute can be specified in two different ways. For some colors, the name of the color will be sufficient. For others, a code is used to indicate the color. This code is of the form #RRGGBB where RR, GG, or BB is a two-digit hex number between 00 and FF. Here is a list of the colors known to the browser by their name.

Black	#000000	Gray	#808080	Maroon	#800000	Purple	#800080
Green	#008000	Olive	#808000	Navy	#000080	Teal	#008080
Silver	#C0C0C0	White	#FFFFFF	Red	#FF0000	Fuchsia	#FF00FF
Lime	#00FF00	Yellow	#FFFF00	Blue	#0000FF	Aqua	#00FFFF

In an attribute, the value of the color can always be one of these names (e.g. `COLOR="Silver"`). Other colors not named here can be obtained by using the hex representation. This may require some experimentation. In many cases, HTML file generation software will allow you to select a color from a color wheel and the appropriate hex tag will be generated for you.

The `PRE` tag

In some instances the layout of certain sections of text is critical and you do not want to let the browser make any modifications. For example, if you wanted to display a computer program it would be important to preserve indentation. The `PRE` tag (for `PRE`-formatted) will let you do this. The enclosed text will be placed in the document so as to preserve the layout you have provided. In particular, the browser will use a mono-spaced font where all the characters are equally wide to preserve your layout. One issue is that you may not use embedded metacharacters such as < or & and must use their replacement form. In addition, the `PRE` tag has an attribute named `WIDTH` whose value is the maximum number of characters in any line of the pre-formatted text. By specifying a value for this attribute, the browser can pick the font size that will best allow the text to fit in the browser window.

Logical tags

The `EM` and `STRONG` tags

These are two logical tags. The first indicates to the browser that the enclosed text is to be emphasized. Usually this means rendering it in an italic typeface.

The second tells the browser to strongly emphasize the enclosed text. Usually this means to render it in boldface type.

The `SUB` and `SUP` tags

In some examples, we need to use subscripts or superscripts. These tags will render the enclosed text so that it appears either slightly below or above the surrounding text (as appropriate).

Each of the text formatting tags behave in a similar way. You should experiment with new ones to see how they work so that you can add them to your list of tools for creating Web pages that will deliver what your customer wants. See Appendix A for a comprehensive list of these tags.

Lists

One of the things we haven't completely resolved with our customer's original text (Figure 2.5) is the way in which we displayed the list of services. We were able to make the Web document look similar to the original print document using the header tags. There is a better way.

Lists are common in documents and HTML has tags for producing them. There are two kinds of lists: ones whose items are not numbered and ones whose items are numbered. For numbered lists we use the `OL` tag (ordered list). For unnumbered lists use the `UL` tag.

For either case, the content of the list (between the opening and closing tags) contains the list items. Each item is preceded by an `LI` tag but there is no matching closing tag. For example, in the Island Quest Travel Web document we handle the list of services as seen in part in Figure 2.12. The indentation is not required by the browser but clearly useful to the human reader. As part of our HTML page design conventions we shall indent list items by three spaces (don't use tabs because that will be too dependent on the text editor).

from File: `IQTravel_2d.html`

```
...
<UL>
   <LI><B>Planning</B>
      <BR>
      We have dozens of locations that offer adventure and
      excitement and we can help you pick out just the right
      place.
   <LI><B>Flight reservations</B>
      <BR>
      Just leave it to us. We'll get you there and back. We
      will handle reservations with the major airlines as well
      as the local pilots for those special places not seen by
      most of the rest of the world.
   <LI><B>Sailing accommodations</B>
      <BR>
      For the buccaneer, we can charter sailboats and crews who
      will fix your meals and take you to those hidden island
      coves where perhaps treasure is hiding in a nearby cave.
   <LI><B>Guide services</B>
      <BR>
      Islands often have jungles and we have the guides to take
      you to some of the temples from forgotten civilizations.
      These guides will provide everything you need in the way
      of meals and accommodations.
</UL>
...
```

Figure 2.12

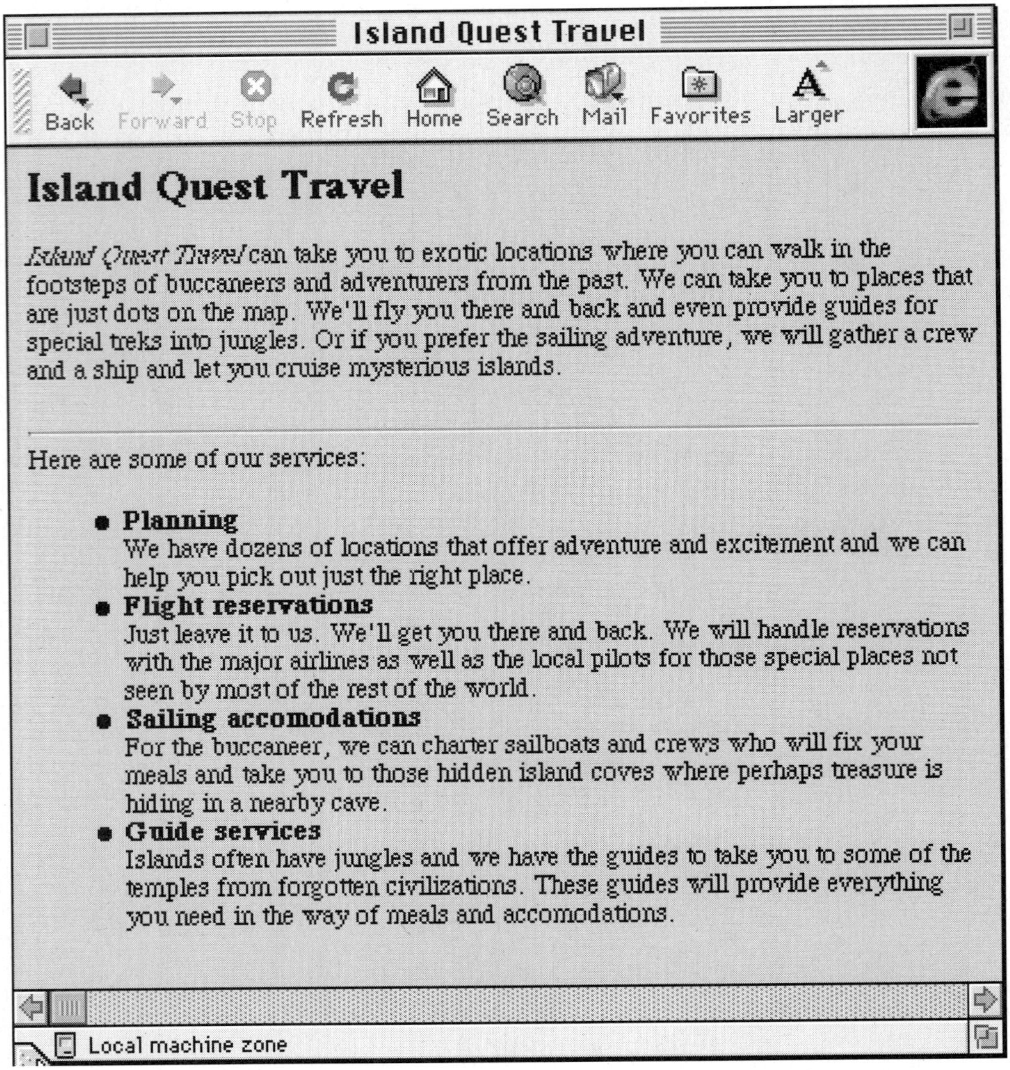

Figure 2.13

In Figure 2.13 we see how the new file is rendered by a browser. The browser handles unnumbered lists by placing a • or bullet character at the start of each list item. There is an attribute for the `UL` tag that allows you to change the character that will be displayed before each list item. The `TYPE` attribute lets you select "disk" (a filled-in circle), "square," or "circle" (an open circle) as the character of choice. The disk is the default.

List items can, in fact, be other lists. In this way, you can create sublists within lists. This can be particularly useful if you have a complex outline such as a multi-level table of contents. In such cases the major list may be a list of chapters. Within each chapter may follow a list of sections. We'll explore this in the exercises at the end of this chapter.

Section review questions

True or false

1. The `H6` tag will result in a smaller sized font than the `H1` tag.
2. The `Hn` tags are usually used to denote the title of a chapter or section of a document.
3. A physical tag tells the browser how to display some element.
4. A logical tag tells the browser about the element but does not directly tell it how to display a particular element.
5. The `Hn` tags are physical tags.
6. The `CITE` tag is used for short quotes from other sources.
7. The `I` tag is a physical tag.
8. An attribute is a parameter that may be part of a tag to give the browser additional direction.
9. It is never incorrect to enclose the value of an attribute within double quotes.
10. If a tag takes more than one attribute, then all attributes must be present and given values.
11. Text marked with the `STRONG` or `EM` tags must always be displayed identically by the browser.
12. The following HTML text: `A<sub>n</sub>` will be rendered by the browser as: A_n.
13. List items can contain inner sublists provided they are of the same type as the outer list.
14. If you modify an ordered list to insert new list items, the browser will automatically take care of the numbering.

Multiple choice

15. Metacharacters are
    (a) characters that are not usually part of the character set available on the computer.
    (b) not characters at all but small icons.
    (c) characters that usually don't display in the browser window.
    (d) characters that have a special meaning to the browser.

16. Using the `FONT` tag allows one to
    (a) change the size of the font for the text within its contents.
    (b) set the color of the text within its contents.
    (c) make the text within its contents either smaller or larger than the surrounding type.
    (d) all of the above.

17. The `PRE` tag will
    (a) result in preserving the alignment of text.
    (b) align text provided there is no white space within the content of the tag.
    (c) allow embedded metacharacters without having to represent them by their alternate form.
    (d) all of the above.

18. In order to produce the following list:
    - Maui
    - Molokai
    - Kauai

    one should use the following HTML code:

(a)
```
<OL>
   <LI>Maui
   <LI>Molokai
   <LI>Kauai
</OL>
```
(b)
```
<UL>
   <LI>Maui
   <LI>Molokai
   <LI>Kauai
</UL>
```
(c)
```
<OL>
   <LI>Maui</LI>
   <LI>Molokai</LI>
   <LI>Kauai</LI>
</OL>
```
(d)
```
<UL>
   <LI>Maui<BR>
   <LI>Molokai<BR>
   <LI>Kauai<BR>
</UL>
```

2.3 Adding Graphical Elements

The Web is really about images. Documents that are text-only are not going to attract the attention of the viewer in the way that documents with graphical elements will. These elements can be in the form of pictures or fancy computer-generated graphics but they can also be in the form of simple little buttons and banners. We'll start with these smaller elements and then explore the fancier ones.

There are many sites which allow you to freely copy simple graphical elements in the form of horizontal lines and colorful balls that will let you add "punch" to your pages. (You may locate these items through the Web-Archipelago site). A little later in this section (under the heading Download it!) we'll tell you how to obtain these graphical items for your own pages.

Now we'll revisit our work so far on the Island Quest Travel Web document. First, instead of using the rather plain horizontal line produced by the `HR` tag, we are going to use a colored dividing line. This line is contained in an image file named `blue_rule.gif`. To insert this line in our document, we replace the `HR` tag with the following:

```
<IMG SRC="graphics/blue_rule.gif">
```

The `IMG` tag (for image) is used to insert a graphical element in the document at the point where the tag appears. The `SRC` attribute (for source) is required and tells the browser where to locate the desired graphics file. The name that appears here brings up the issue of how Web servers locate HTML documents or graphical image files.

URLs and File Names

The Web server is responsible for delivering Web documents on request from client browsers. The server software usually does not have access to the entire file system. A branch of the file system is allocated to the Web server as the place to look for documents that match incoming requests. The root directory in this branch is called the *document root*. The browser doesn't have to know the location of this document root directory in the larger file system. It only needs to know the location of a document relative to this root directory.

When identifying a Web document, we are by now accustomed, as a result of browsing the Web, to a name such as

```
http://Web-Archipelago.com/textBook/ch02/IQTravel.html
```

This name is known as a URL (Universal Resource Locator). The first portion (`http:/`) tells the Web server software that the communication between the server and the client will involve a particular set of rules or a protocol known as the hypertext transfer protocol. The next portion of the URL (`Web-Archipelago.com`) identifies a particular Web server on the Internet. This is the so-called *domain name* of the Web server. The domain name identifies where in the Internet this particular Web server is found. In this case, the com part indicates this server belongs to the commercial portion of the Web. The `Web-Archipelago` part of the domain name identifies a particular computer.

The last portion of the URL (in this case `textBook/ch02/IQTravel.html`) identifies the name of a file relative to the root directory.

Sometimes the Web server can locate a file without having to specify the full URL. For example, in the name of the image we are using above to replace the `HR` tag (`graphics/blue_rule.gif`), we have what is called a *relative path name*. Since the domain name is not given, the Web server will assume that it will be identical to that of the document in which the reference appears. Thus, in this case, the file `blue_rule.gif` is located in a subdirectory named `graphics` within the same directory containing the HTML document in which the `IMG` tag appears.

It's a good idea to place your graphics files in a separate directory from the HTML document to avoid confusion. We have done that here. The `blue_rule.gif` file is contained in the `graphics` subdirectory.

We also want to add the colorful balls mentioned above. We'll use these instead of the • character at the beginning of the list items. Now, however, we won't be able to use the `UL` tag because there is no way to omit the • character and the presence of both the colored ball and this bullet character would appear very awkward. Fortunately there is a variant of the unnumbered list known as a definition list which we can invoke with the `DL` tag. The definition list is meant to allow for a list of terms, each of which is defined by a short piece of text. Instead of the `LI` tag, we must use the `DT` tag to identify the term and the `DD` tag to define it. The closing tags are optional since the browser can easily tell the end of the term or definition from the other tags.

Rewriting the section of the text corresponding to the list we had before in Figure 2.12 and including the new graphical horizontal line, we obtain the document shown in Figure 2.14. Viewing the file with a browser gives us Figure 2.15.

from: `IQTravel_2e.html`

```
...
<P>
<IMG SRC="graphics/blue_rule.gif">
<P>
Here are some of our services:
<P>
<DL>
   <DT><IMG SRC="graphics/smallWhiteBall.gif"><B>Planning</B>
   <DD>
      We have dozens of locations that offer adventure and
      excitement and we can help you pick out just the right
      place.
  <DT><IMG SRC="graphics/smallRedBall.gif"><B>Flight reserva-
  tions</B>
  <DD>
      Just leave it to us. We'll get you there and back. We
      will handle reservations with the major airlines as well
      as the local pilots for those special places not seen by
      most of the rest of the world.
  <DT><IMG SRC="graphics/smallBlueBall.gif">
      <B>Sailing accommodations</B>
  <DD>
      For the buccaneer, we can charter sailboats and crews who
      will fix your meals and take you to those hidden island
      coves where
      perhaps treasure is hiding in a nearby cave.
  <DT><IMG SRC="graphics/smallGreenBall.gif"><B>Guide ser-
  vices</B>
  <DD>
      Islands often have jungles and we have the guides to take
      you to some of the temples from forgotten civilizations.
      These guides will provide everything you need in the way
      of meals and accommodations.
</DL>
...
```

Figure 2.14

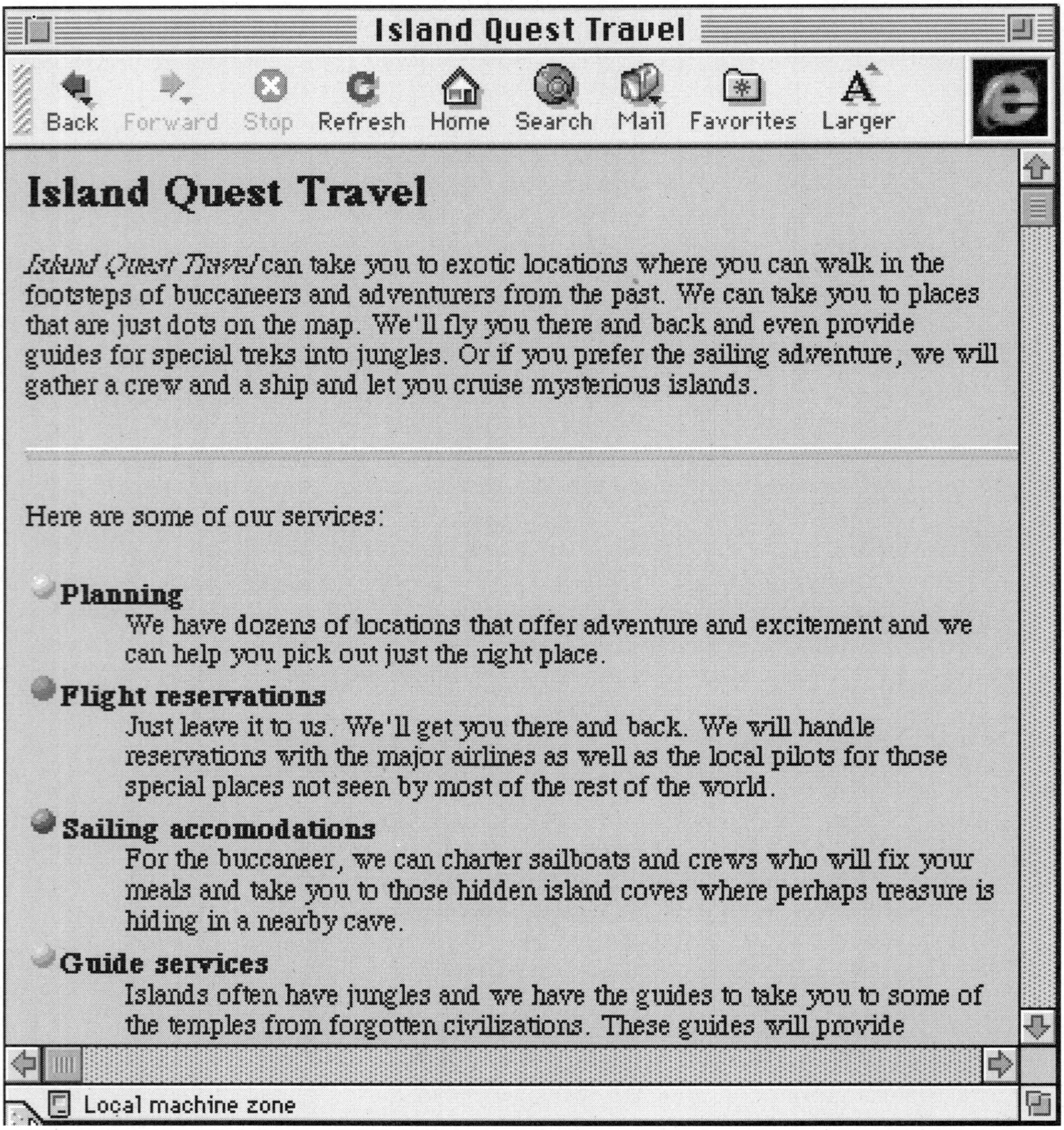

Figure 2.15

Download it!

Many people on the Web have made many images, such as the ones we have been using, available without charge. This is one of the wonderful characteristics of the Web—people helping people. You might consider making some of your tools available as well when you have some wonderful items to share with others. We have collected a number of sites where you can download these images and placed links to them on the Web-Archipelago site.

Most of these sites have instructions on how to make a copy of any images you may wish to download. In the absence of instructions, you can usually hold the right mouse button down (the one mouse button for Macs) on the desired image until a menu appears letting you choose to save the image on your hard disk. However, please observe copyright laws. If you have not been given permission to make a copy of someone's images, don't do it. Respect the work of your Webmates.

Background color

One of the easiest ways to add color to your Web documents is to use some of the attributes of the `BODY` tag. In particular, the `BGCOLOR` attribute allows you to change the background color from the blue-grey default value. For example, let us modify the Web page for Island Quest Travel so that the background color is more in keeping with an island or aquatic theme. We can use any of the color values described earlier in the box entitled **More text tags**. In particular let us pick "aqua" as the background color. To do this we need only change the `BODY` tag to the following:

```
<BODY BGCOLOR="aqua">
```

There are other attributes to the `BODY` tag. For example we can change the color of the text by using the `TEXT` attribute. We will explore this in the exercises. One problem that you as a Web page designer must be aware of is the fact that text may be difficult to read if the color of the background and the color of the text are too much alike. There are other problems as well with PCs that don't have the ability to display more than 256 colors. When this happens, the browser will often attempt to fake the color by picking a nearby color and then making the color of every *n*th pixel a mixing color that will hopefully fool the eye into thinking the background color is the desired one. Unfortunately, the result is usually a pattern of dots that makes the text very difficult if not impossible to read. Be aware of your audience as you determine your colors. One way to do this is by trying to view your Web page using different browsers and different computers.

Image Formats

There are several graphics formats recognized by browsers. The most common is GIF (Graphics Interchange Format) developed by CompuServe. It allows up to 256 colors. It has been extended to a format named GIF89A which allows two important features if you have the software that can take advantage of them. The first is "transparent" backgrounds. By selecting one color from the graphic to be the same as the background color of the HTML document, you can achieve the effect of a graphic floating on a transparent layer, allowing the background to be visible through the image.

The second feature allows one graphics file to contain multiple images that are cyclically displayed to produce an animated graphical element. You have probably seen examples of this on many of the Web sites today that have advertising in the form of a banner at the top of the page that cycles between several different images.

You can create your own by using available software to generate the individual "stills" and then using other software to assemble them into an animated GIF file. See the Web-Archipelago site for pointers to sites where you can get more information on this feature.

The GIF format is a compression format, meaning that redundant information is removed from the file to provide a much smaller file that is faster to transmit over the Internet.

Another graphics file format is JPEG (from the Joint Photographic Experts Group). JPEG files can display 24-bit color images which makes them more popular for displaying photographic images. Like GIF, JPEG compresses images. Unlike GIF, the compression is "lossy" meaning that some information is lost when the image is compressed and the decompressed image generated by the browser will not be as good as the original. Still, the results are usually quite acceptable, especially given that the files can be dramatically reduced in size.

More recently, the World Wide Web Consortium has adopted a specification to replace the GIF format. This format is known as PNG (Portable Network Graphic). This format is lossless (there is no loss of information in the compression).

See the Web-Archipelago site for pointers to sites with much more information on graphics formats for Web documents.

Larger graphics

Most Web sites have a theme graphic that clearly identifies the site visually. In a separate graphics program we have created such a graphic for our Island Quest Travel customer. That file has been saved as `IQTravel.gif`. Let's add that to the IQ Travel Web page. We start with the `IQTravel_2e.html` file and place the graphic with the `IMG` tag. The `IMG` tag will place an image in the document at the point of the tag. One drawback of this is that even if we use the `P` tag to isolate the image, it will be left-justified. Fortunately there is another tag (`CENTER`) that will place the image in the center of the document.

Let's put some of these recent additions to the IQ Travel Web page into one document. These changes now reflect the choice of a background color of "aqua," the insertion of the graphic centered at the top of the page, the blue line to replace the horizontal rule, and the use of the small colored balls for the list of services. The resulting HTML document is shown in Figure 2.16 and the result of viewing it with the browser is shown in Figure 2.17.

File: `IQTravel_2f.html`

```
<HTML>
<!--File: IQTravel_2f.html-->
<!--Project: Island Quest Travel Site-->
<!--Programmer: J. Avila-->
<!--Last modified: 5/24/1998-->
<!--Copyright J. H. Avila, 1998. All rights reserved.-->
<HEAD>
   <TITLE>Island Quest Travel</TITLE>
</HEAD>
<BODY BGCOLOR="aqua">
<P>
<CENTER><IMG SRC="graphics/IQTravel.gif"></CENTER>
<P>
  <I>Island Quest Travel</I>can take you to exotic locations
  where you can walk in the footsteps of buccaneers and adven-
  turers from the past. We can take you to places that are just
  dots on the map.  We'll fly you there and back and even pro-
  vide guides for special treks into jungles. Or if you prefer
  the sailing adventure, we will gather a crew and a ship and
  let you cruise mysterious islands.
<P>
<IMG SRC="graphics/blue_rule.gif">
<P>
  Here are some of our services:
<P>
<DL>
  <DT><IMG SRC="graphics/smallWhiteBall.gif"><B>Planning</B>
  <DD>
      We have dozens of locations that offer adventure and
      excitement and we can help you pick out just the right
      place.
  <DT><IMG SRC="graphics/smallRedBall.gif"><B>Flight reserva-
  tions</B>
  <DD>
      Just leave it to us. We'll get you there and back. We
      will handle reservations with the major airlines as well
      as the local pilots for those special places not seen by
      most of the rest of the world.
  <DT><IMG SRC="graphics/smallBlueBall.gif">
      <B>Sailing accommodations</B>
  <DD>
      For the buccaneer, we can charter sailboats and crews who
      will fix your meals and take you to those hidden island
```

```
    coves where perhaps treasure is hiding in a nearby cave.
 <DT><IMG SRC="graphics/smallGreenBall.gif"><B>Guide services</B>
 <DD>
      Islands often have jungles and we have the guides to take
      you to some of the temples from forgotten civilizations.
      These guides will provide everything you need in the way
      of meals and accommodations.
</DL>
</BODY>
</HTML>
```

Figure 2.16

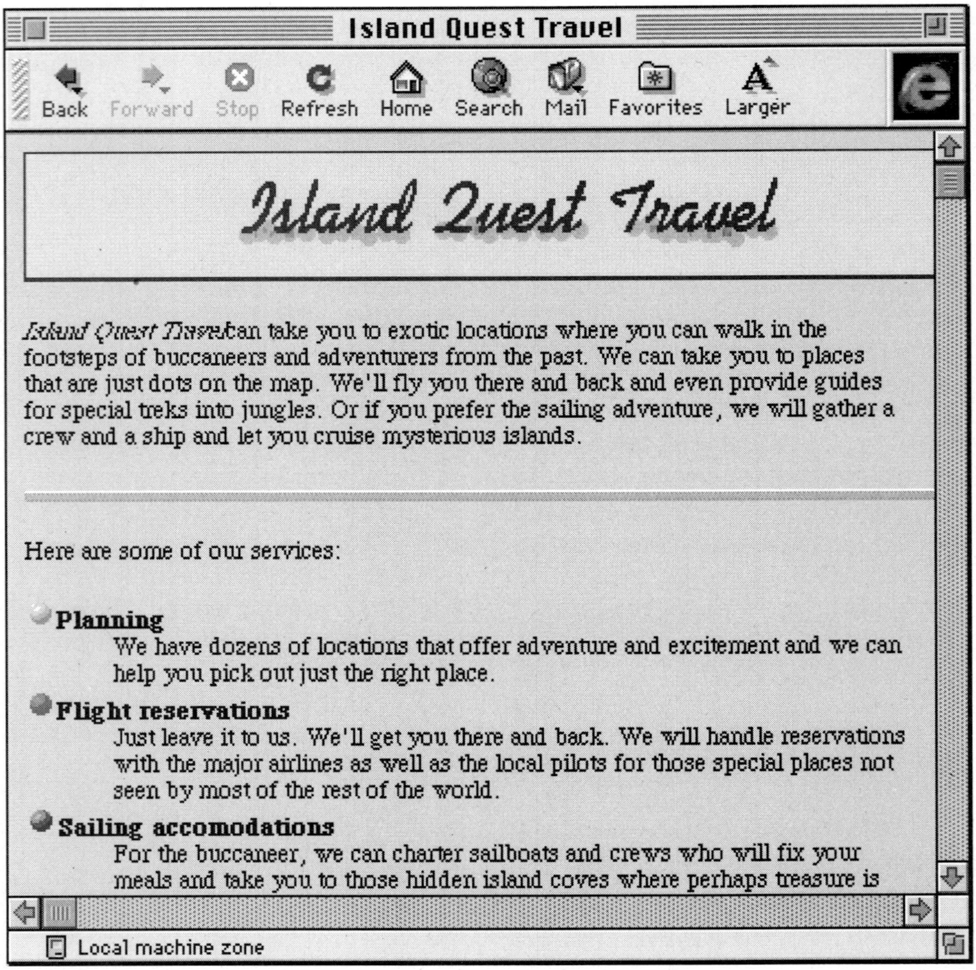

Figure 2.17

Background images

We've seen how to make the background of an HTML document a solid color. Using the BACKGROUND attribute of the BODY tag, we can display a graphical element as the background. To be precise, if we identify a graphics file in the value of the BACKGROUND attribute, then that file will appear as the background *behind* the text and other graphical elements in the document.

Starting with the document shown in Figure 2.16, modify the BODY tag so that it reads as follows:

```
<BODY BACKGROUND="graphics/watermark.gif">
```

The graphics file watermark.gif contains a white background with the text "Island Quest Travel" displayed faintly in aqua in a staircase fashion. The file itself would fill up a small portion of the entire Web page if only one copy were shown. With the BACKGROUND attribute, the browser will *tile* the background with the graphic contained in the named file. This means that the graphic is repeated horizontally and vertically until it completely covers the background. As a result, a well chosen graphics file can be used very effectively to produce a pleasing effect. One such effect is to produce *textures* that give the impression of a subtle patterned background. We explore this in the exercises.

You can view the Island Quest Travel page with the watermark.gif file for the background (IQTravel_2g.html) in Figure 2.18. As you can see the effect is almost that of a watermarked paper on which the other elements have been placed.

Figure 2.18

Image Sizes

It's important to take into consideration the ability of your audience to download the images you place on a Web page. The chart below shows sample times for downloading several moderately sized images using a 28.8K modem. Today, these modems are considered to be about the slowest still acceptable for viewing Web pages. Nevertheless, many are still in use.

The figure 28.8K refers to the number of bits per second that the modem is guaranteed not to exceed. Since there are 8 bits to a byte, such a modem is incapable of transmitting data any faster than 3600 bytes per second. Data transmission of an image using the modem contains information in addition to that image. There are other things that slow transmission, such as the number of other users sharing the server.

The chart below (Figure 2.19) shows an experiment in which a number of moderately sized files were downloaded over a 28.8K modem. The observed data suggests (at least for this case) a more realistic rate of 1070 bytes per second. The optimal rate is shown for comparison.

To give you a reference, a small picture (GIF format) measuring about 180 pixels wide by 200 pixels tall (about one-third of the width and one-half the height of your browser window) is about 24K bytes of data. For our Island Travel customer Web page, the size of the logo or the horizontal line each is about 2200 bytes and the size of the colored balls is only about 100 bytes.

By keeping your viewer in mind, you can provide a much more positive Web experience. The alternative may be to have a viewer quit in disgust after waiting minutes to download a few images that may not be central to the message.

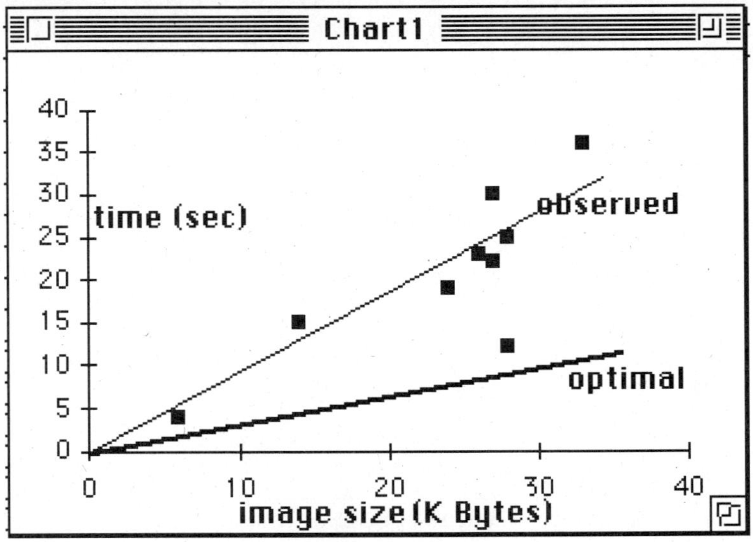

Figure 2.19

Section review questions

True or false

1. The `IMG` tag is used for placing images in your HTML documents.

2. The `SRC` attribute of the `IMG` tag must contain the full path name of the file.

3. The value of the `SRC` attribute in an `IMG` tag may not refer to a document on a different Web server.

4. The domain name identifies a particular Web server on the Internet.

5. The `GIF` graphics format is "lossy."

6. The `JPEG` graphics format is "lossy."

7. Both `GIF` and `JPEG` graphics formats support the same number of colors.

Multiple choice

8. If the `SRC` attribute in an `IMG` tag is `/graphics/green_ball.gif` then
   (a) we are asking for a file named `green_ball.gif` located in a subdirectory called `graphics` within the directory containing the HTML document with the relevant `IMG` tag.
   (b) we are asking for a file named `green_ball.gif` located in a subdirectory called `graphics` in the root directory for the file system on the server.
   (c) we are asking for a file named `green_ball.gif` located in a subdirectory called `graphics` in the document root directory for the Web server.
   (d) the given value of the `SRC` attribute is an error.

9. If the URL given as the value of the `SRC` attribute in an `IMG` tag is `http://Web-archipelago/pix/ch10.gif` then
   (a) `ch10.gif` is in a subdirectory named `pix` which, in turn, is a subdirectory of the document root directory associated with the Web server on the `Web-archipelago.com` site.
   (b) `ch10.gif` is in a subdirectory named `pix` which is a subdirectory of the root directory for the file system on the machine named `Web-archipelago.com`.
   (c) `ch10.gif` is in the subdirectory `pix` which is the document root directory for the Web server on `Web-archipelago.com`.
   (d) none of the above.

10. If the URL given as the value of the `SRC` attribute in an `IMG` tag is `pix/ch10.gif` then
    - (a) `ch10.gif` is in the directory named `pix` which contains the HTML document in which the `IMG` tag appears.
    - (b) `ch10.gif` is in the directory named `pix` which is a subdirectory of the one containing the HTML document in which the `IMG` tag appears.
    - (c) `ch10.gif` is in the directory named `pix` which is a subdirectory of the document root directory for the Web server containing the HTML document in which the `IMG` tag appears.
    - (d) none of the above.

11. If you want to use a definition list to produce the following:

    Fiji
      True South Pacific beauty and tranquility.
    Molokai
      The old Hawaii before the hotels.
    Pico
      Mid-Atlantic treasure still undiscovered.

Then the HTML should be

(a)

```
<DL>
   <LI>Fiji<BR>
       True South Pacific beauty and tranquillity.
   <LI>Molokai<BR>
       The old Hawaii before the hotels.
   <LI>Pico<BR>
       Mid-Atlantic treasure still undiscovered.
</DL>
```

(b)

```
<DL>
   <DT>Fiji<BR>
       True South Pacific beauty and tranquillity.
   <DT>Molokai<BR>
       The old Hawaii before the hotels.
   <DT>Pico<BR>
       Mid-Atlantic treasure still undiscovered.
</DL>
```

(c)

```
<DL>
   <DT>Fiji
   <DD>True South Pacific beauty and tranquillity.
   <DT>Molokai
   <DD>The old Hawaii before the hotels.
   <DT>Pico
   <DD>Mid-Atlantic treasure still undiscovered.
</DL>
```

(d) none of the above.

12. The BGCOLOR attribute of the BODY tag can
    (a) take the name of a color as its value.
    (b) take any of the hex values of the form #RRGGBB.
    (c) cause problems viewing text in an HTML document.
    (d) all of the above.

13. Graphical images chosen for a background
    (a) can be quite small because the browser repeats the image over and over horizontally and vertically until it fills up the entire window.
    (b) must be large enough to cover the entire browser window area.
    (c) must be wide enough to span the width of the window although the height is taken care of by repeating the image over and over vertically.
    (d) none of the above.

14. A 56K modem will transmit
    (a) at most 56K bits of data per second.
    (b) at most 7K bytes of data per second.
    (c) a 42K image in no less than 6 seconds.
    (d) all of the above.
    (e) none of the above.

2.4 External Elements

Development information

There are a number of things you will want to do to keep the information on your Web pages professionally organized. We've indicated the comments at the beginning of the HTML document that identify the name of the file (if you see a printed copy, you'll know which file to get if you want to make changes).

In addition, we recommend that the programmer be identified along with the date of the most recent modification. This last item is particularly important when you want to update many files. By modifying the date you will have a much better chance of knowing which files still haven't been modified and which are likely to have been modified. Because the modification date is important to the readers of your Web documents as well, we recommend that you make this information visible on the page.

The ADDRESS tag will allow you to make this information visible in a standard way on all your pages. From now on we will use this tag to provide the following information on every Web document:

programmer (e-mail address)
most recent modification date
copyright information

The Table 2.1 shows the information that should appear in every HTML document.

Information	Location in the HTML document
HTML document file name:	Comment at the beginning
Project:	Comment at the beginning
Programmer and e-mail address:	`ADDRESS` tag at the end
Last modification date:	`ADDRESS` tag at the end
Copyright:	`ADDRESS` tag at the end

Table 2.1

Here is how these modifications appear on the Island Quest Travel Web page.
At the top of the document we have

```
<HTML>
<!--File: IQTravel_2h.html-->
<!--Project: Island Quest Travel Site-->
<!--See the ADDRESS tag below for additional information-->
```

and at the bottom of the document we have

```
<ADDRESS>
<FONT SIZE="-1">
   Programmer: J. Avila<BR>
   <B>avila@web-archipelago.com</B><BR>
   Last modified: 5/24/1998<BR>
   &copy; J. H. Avila, 1998.
   All rights reserved.
</FONT>
</ADDRESS>
</BODY>
</HTML>
```

Notice the need for the `©` to represent the © character and the `&` to represent the & character. Also we have used the `FONT` tag to reduce the size of the font slightly so that it will not be intrusive on the Web page.

The browser generally renders the text enclosed within the `ADDRESS` tag in italics and slightly indented from the left margin.

In Figure 2.20 we have shown the end of the Web document contained in the file `IQTravel_2h.html`. Notice that the `ADDRESS` tag produces the small notice in the lower left corner of the window. The information is there if the user needs to know it, but it won't interfere with the rest of the document.

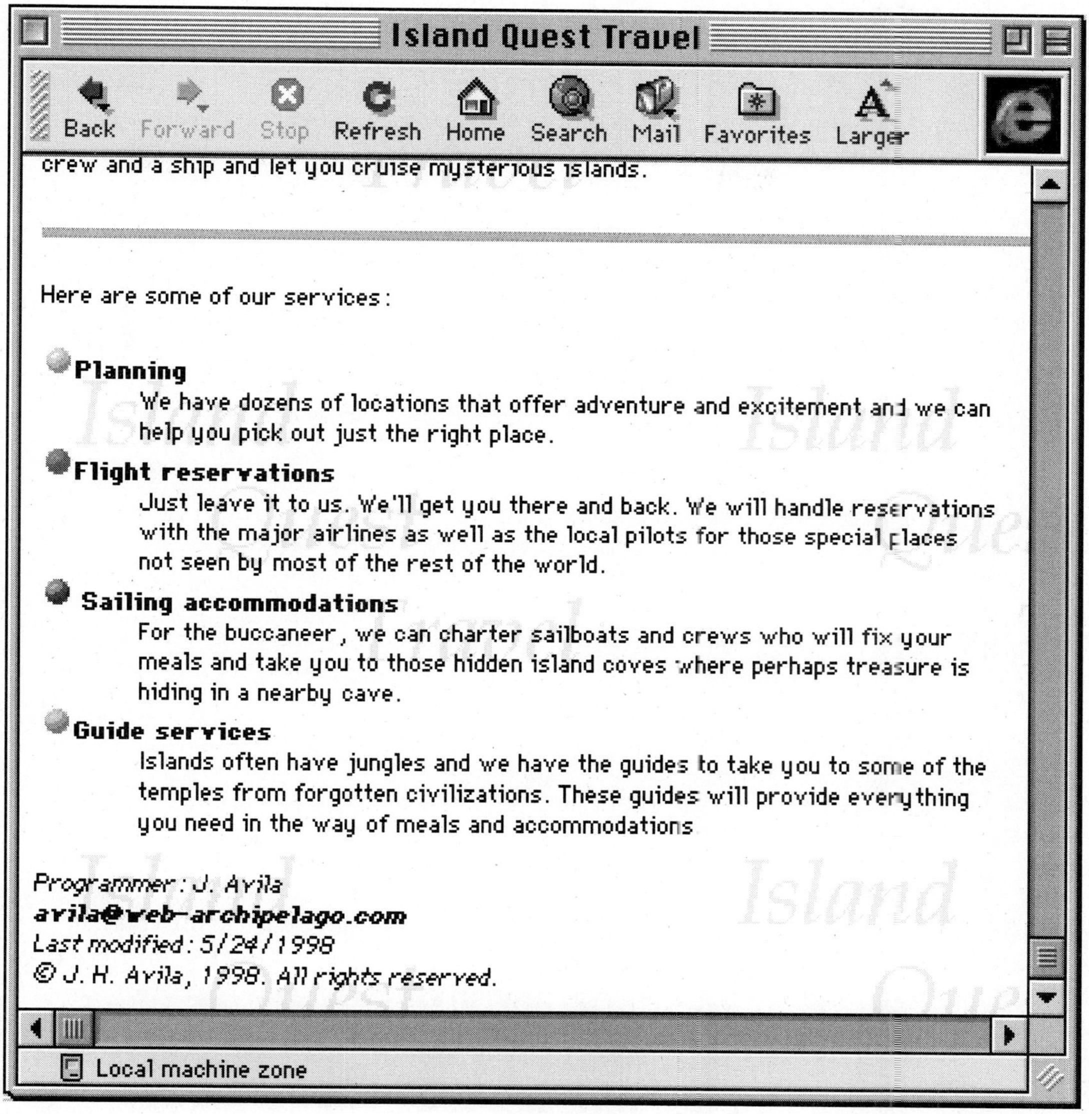

Figure 2.20

Meta information

HTML provides a `META` tag, which is used to convey information about the document to programs that access the document. As an example, search engines are widely used by persons looking for Web documents containing specific keywords. These search engines scan HTML documents and extract keywords directly from the document text. These keywords may or may not accurately reflect the information content of the document. As an author of an HTML document, you can supply your own keywords that will be read by search engines. Not all search engines use these author-supplied keywords, but many do. For example the following tag could be used in our Island Quest Travel customer Web pages:

```
<META NAME="keywords" CONTENT="island travel adventure">
```

Some search engines, when they select your HTML document to respond to a query from a user, will give the title of the document along with a few sentences about the document. If you do nothing, these sentences will be the opening text of the document. You can use the `META` tag, however, to supply your own short text description, as in

```
<META NAME="description" CONTENT="Travel to exotic island loca-
tions with our vacation packages">
```

The `META` tag is placed in the `HEAD` portion of the HTML document (instead of the `BODY`).

Web Design

It's one thing to put together Web pages that have text and graphics with colors and clickable stuff. It's another to make these pages useful and informative. As we learn how to build Web pages in the coming chapters, it's good to have some guidelines.

Roger Black has a terrific book on Web design entitled *Web Sites That Work* (Adobe Press, 1997). In there he has a number of rules on what you should and shouldn't do when you design Web pages. Here are five of the do's that he suggests.

1. *Put content on every page.* Each Web page must convey information. If you use images and icons, they must contribute to what you want to say. Having blinking things and scrolling banners isn't the secret to a great Web page.

2. *The first color is white, the second is black, the third is red.* Black and white provide the best contrast, whether it's black text on a white background or white text on a black background. Red is a powerful color that can be used with white or black. Humans are "pre-wired" to respond to red and good designers take advantage of this.

Here's a view of the site: `www.iab.com`. The images are compelling and part of the message. Notice the effective use of white (background) with black and red text.

3. *A cover should be a poster.* The "home page" or the first page that users see when they visit a site should immediately grab their attention. As Black says: "A single image of a human being—preferably Madonna—will sell more magazines than multiple images or all type."

Here is an example of several of Black's do's. The Web site is one of the many Madonna Web sites (`www.stanford.edu/~jwb/Madonna/`). Notice the heavy use of black and white and how much this "home page" looks like a poster for the pop artist.

4. *Make everything as big as possible.* Even if you can't say as much on a screen if you use larger type, what you say will have more impact. Notice how in the following example (`www.porsche-usa.com/home.html`) the large format of the text gets the message out loud and clear.

5. *Get lumpy!* This means to vary the rhythm. The Web is not a book: a section title, paragraph, paragraph, another section title, etc. This is boring. Have blocks of text but not all aligned. Have images but place them in "interesting" locations on the page relative to each other and to the text.

In the following example we have a definitely "lumpy" layout for the *USA Today* Web site (`www.usatoday.com`). The familiar logo, headlines, pictures, all work together to convey a sense of action and excitement that draws your attention all around the page. Definitely not boring.

Section review questions

True or false

1. We recommend that the date shown on a Web document be the date the document was originally created.

2. The modification date shown on a Web document will be automatically updated by the browser.

3. `META` tags contain information that may be used by search engines examining your HTML document.

4. `META` tags must appear in the `BODY` portion of the HTML document.

5. If the `META` tag is not present in your HTML file, no search engine will be able to display information about your document to others on the Web.

6. If you have a `META` tag to supply keywords, you must also have one to supply a description to search engines.

Multiple choice

7. The `ADDRESS` tag can be used to
   (a) let the user know the author of a document.
   (b) let the user know the date of the most recent modification to a document.
   (c) offer essentially any information the Web developer may wish to give to the viewer about the authorship or ownership of the Web document.
   (d) all of the above.

8. The home page of a Web site should
   (a) have a significantly different look from the other pages in a Web site.
   (b) introduce the Web site and contain a somewhat lengthy statement about the purpose and goals of the site.
   (c) should introduce the Web site and provide an opportunity for user feed-back.
   (d) introduce the Web site and provide a "road map" to guide the user to other parts of the site.

9. The choice of colors in a Web site should be
   (a) consistent from page to page and kept simple.
   (b) harmonious within each page but different pages should be viewed as standing on their own.
   (c) kept to lighter colors if possible.
   (d) (a) and (c)
   (e) (a) and (b)

Short excursion exercises

1. Start with the HTML document: `simple.html` and modify it so that the title is "My home page." Replace the "Hello, WWW World." string with an appropriate greeting for you.

2. Modify the `IQTravel_2b.html` file so that there are two horizontal lines just before the phrase "Here are some of our services:" and then a single horizontal line between each of the paragraphs that describe the services offered.

3. Change the header tags in the file `IQTravel_2c.html` so that the first header ("Island Quest Travel") is rendered using the `H1` tag and each of the services headers are rendered using the `H2` tag.

4. Modify the `IQTravel_2d.html` file so that each of the names of the services ("Planning", "Flight reservations", etc.) are displayed in a different color.

5. Modify the `IQTravel_2d.html` file using an ordered list instead of an unordered list for the list of services. Look up the `OL` tag in Appendix 1 and use uppercase roman numbering.

6. Modify `IQTravel_2d.html`. Instead of using the `Hn` tag, use the `FONT` tag and the `CENTER` tag to place the opening title ("Island Quest Travel") in the center at the top of the page. Make aqua the color of the title.

7. Find a Web site where graphical icons are available for free downloading. Locate an icon to represent the "under construction" sign you might see along the highway. Place it in the `simple.html` file so that it is centered at the top of the page.

8. In `IQTravel_2f.html`, the shade of aqua that is displayed may be too harsh. Since aqua is an "alias" for the hex representation #00FFFF, try using the hex representation and then modifying the value to get a softer aqua color. Since the hex digits are 0, 1, 2, 3, 4, 5, 6, 7, 8, 9, A, B, C, D, E, F, clearly the green and blue components are at maximum value. Try using smaller hex digits in the green and blue components.

9. Find a location on the Web that has small images that can be used for texture and replace the background image in `IQTravel_2g.html`. Try to find a texture appropriate to the theme of the Island Quest Travel customer.

10. If you are using a 28.8K modem, what is the fastest time (approximately) you can expect to download a 20K byte image? What is the more likely time it will take? (Consult Figure 2.19.)

11. Modify `IQTravel_2h.html` to add an appropriate `META` tag supplying keywords to a visiting search engine.

12. Modify `IQTravel_2h.html` to add an appropriate `META` tag supplying a description of the document to a visiting search engine.

Longer voyage exercises

13. Browsers are designed to ignore tags they don't understand and to try to make reasonable choices when you forget certain items. Start with the `simple.html` file and try the following:
    - leave off the `HTML` tag and its companion closing tag.
    - put the `HTML` tags back in and leave out the closing `/TITLE` tag.
    - put the `/TITLE` tag back in and leave out the opening and closing `BODY` tags.
    - put the opening `BODY` tag back in but leave out the `/BODY` tag.

    Report your findings.

14. Take the `IQTravel_2a.html` file and try placing the contents of the body of the document between opening and closing `PRE` tags. This takes care of preserving the format in the HTML document and might be useful if you need to make text documents available quickly in a situation where the visual content is not as important.

15. In the `IQTravel_2b.html` file, replace all occurrences of `<P>` by `<BR><BR>`. Is there any difference in the document viewed in the browser?

16. Start with `IQTravel_2d.html` and use the `FONT` tag so that each paragraph in the unnumbered list is rendered in a different color. For example, render the paragraph related to "Planning" in blue and then pick an assortment of colors for each of the other three paragraphs. What happens if you pick a color close to that of the background?

17. How would you modify the `IQTravel_2d.html` file to make each letter of the main title header a different color?

18. Look up the `OL` tag in Appendix A. In particular examine the available attributes. Then create an HTML document with the following table of contents:

    I Introduction and History
      i A history of the Web
      ii Why the World Wide Web is so important
      iii Professional results require professional skills
      iv New programming paradigms: smaller focused applications
      v The future of the WWW (in terms of programming)
    II Web site basics
      i Hardware resources (hardware diagram)
      ii Software resources (software diagram)
      iii Human resources

    What if you wanted to replace the second (inner) level with an unnumbered list instead of a numbered list?

19. Start with the `IQTravel_2f.html` file and modify it so that the text "Island Quest Travel" that appears in italics at the beginning of the document appears two font sizes larger and in red. Note the design flaw having the font in the logo different than the font in the text.

20. Start with the `IQTravel_2f.html` file and modify it to use the vertically aligned logo for the Island Quest Travel customer (in `IQTravel_vert.gif`). Look up information on the `IMG` tag and use the `ALIGN` attribute to place the logo image on the right of the Web document. Have the text above the horizontal blue bar wrap around the left of the image and then have the blue bar and the subsequent list displayed below the bottom level of the logo. You will have to examine the `BR` tag and use the `CLEAR` attribute to make this happen. Try the various values available for the `CLEAR` attribute to see their effect.

21. Change the background color of the `IQTravel_2f.html` file to "teal". How would you fix the document to make it readable?

22. Locate a picture on the Web that fills up about half the window when viewed in the browser. Note its URL. Create a simple Web document (start with `simple.html`) with no text and use the `IMG` tag (the value of the `SRC` attribute will be the URL of the picture file) to place this picture in the document. Open the HTML document from your browser and time how long the document takes to display. You might want to reload the file several times and measure the download delay each time. If you save the picture file locally, you can check to see how large the file is in bytes. From the speed of your modem and the size of the file, what percentage of the maximum speed were you able to attain?

23. If you have access to graphical tools, try to put together the home page for a small business Web site (fictitious or otherwise) in your city or town (a toy store would be a fun site). See if you can place all the information in about one screenful as viewed in the browser. In the next chapter we will see how to link documents so, for now, plan on leaving lower level details to other pages. See if you locate free graphical elements on the Web that you have permission to use and download them to your hard drive. Work with the placement of graphical elements and text to make it easy for viewers to locate the information they are looking for.

24. Put together a sampler test page. This HTML document will be useful for testing how various attributes will appear in different environments. Pick a background color and leave the text color as the default. Then generate multiple lines of text, each line a different color. Have lines with different sizes of fonts. Let the text tell you which color it's in. For example:

    This line uses text of color #8080FF.

    Try to create a page that will allow you to try different combinations. Then pick several background colors and try to view your document on as many different browsers and platforms as possible. Put together a report with your observations. A class project could be to collect these observations into a class sampler with results of these tests as a Web document.

3. Hypertext Documents

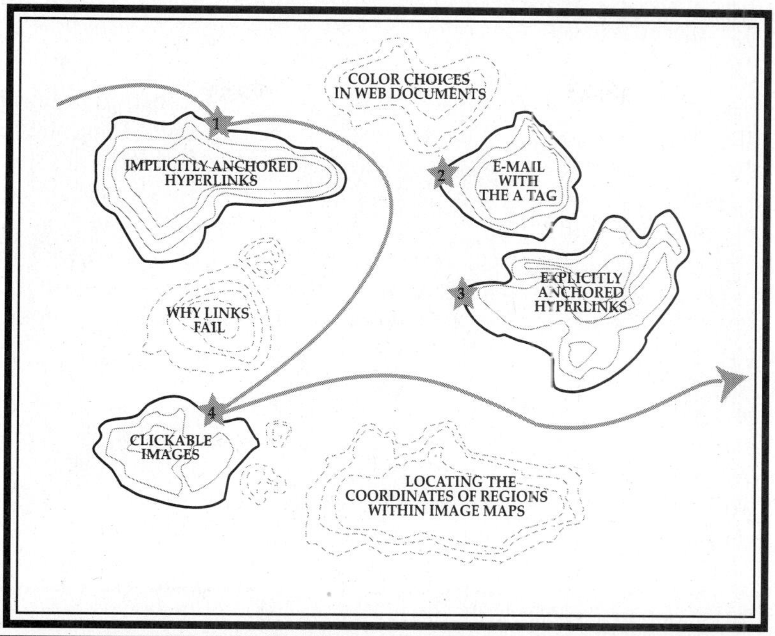

Chapter Preview

3.1 Implicitly Anchored Hyperlinks
The ability to link documents together is the most important feature of HTML. We revisit the Quest Travel Home Page and learn how to place links in this document that make other documents just a "click away." We learn how to turn text or small graphical elements into these links.

3.2 E-mail with the `A` Tag
HTML allows us to use the `A` tag to start up an e-mail message program by clicking on what appears to be a hyperlink. We take a quick look at this nice feature and show how it can be used with the `ADDRESS` tag to allow users to send feedback to the author of an HTML document.

3.3 Explicitly Anchored Hyperlinks
A link can take you to another document. We can refine the target of a link so that we travel to a particular point in a document, even the same document in which the link is located. We explore this in this section.

3.4 Clickable Images
It's possible to have an image that is sensitive to mouse clicks. In this section we learn how to identify those regions within images that we want to turn into hyperlinks. There are "server-side" and "client-side" versions of clickable images and we examine the differences and how to implement each type.

3.1 Implicitly Anchored Hyperlinks

Linking to other documents

The most important feature of the Web is the ability to click on a section of text or some other element on a Web page and have the browser display another document as a result. Because of this aspect, these documents are referred to as *hypertext*. This ability frees the viewer from having to read documents in a linear way such as we do with printed documents. Instead we have the ability to follow ideas and our interests as we view documents (provided there are links to take us where we want to go). In this section we learn how to create these non-linear documents by placing links in our HTML files. These links are usually referred to as *hyperlinks* although we will generally use links and hyperlinks interchangeably.

In order to create a hyperlink we need two things (see Figure 3.1):

- the element (text or graphics) on the Web page which will be sensitive to mouse clicks;
- the `URL` of the document to which the browser will "link" when a mouse click is detected in the sensitive area.

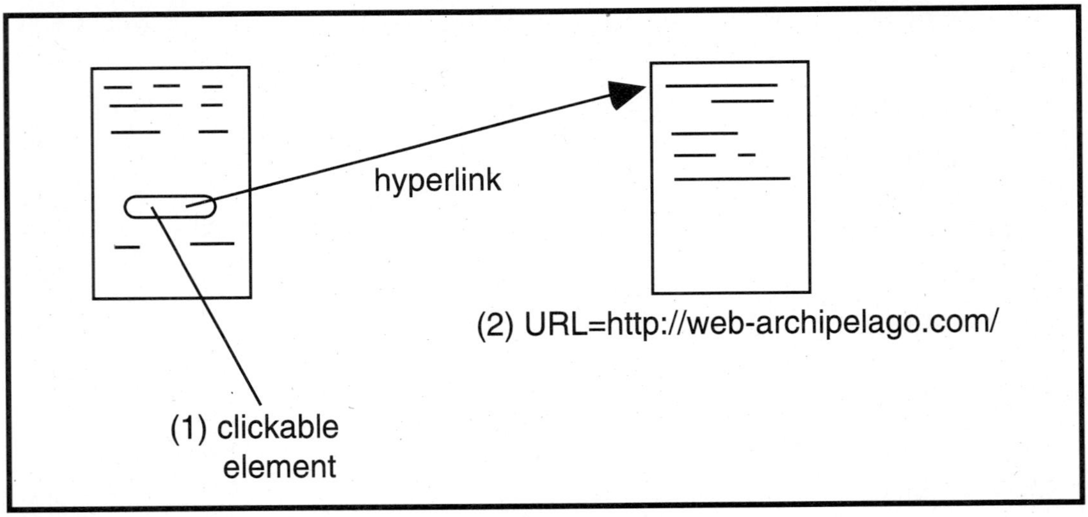

Figure 3.1

We use the term *implicitly anchored hyperlink* (there are explicitly anchored hyperlinks) to represent a hyperlink of this form. The term *anchor* refers to the position in the target document that the viewer will see as a result of clicking on the sensitive text. For the simplest case, this position is the start of the target document. We refer to this as an implicit anchor.

Suppose that we want to add a link from the Island Quest Travel home page to our Web-Archipelago site. Near the end of the Web document we want the following sentence: "Visit the Web-Archipelago site, one of the places where you can gain more information about other island adventures." The *hot text* or portion that will be sensitive to mouse clicks will be the expression "Web-Archipelago site". When the user clicks on this phrase we want the browser to display the home page for the Web-Archipelago site.

Once we have selected the hot text, we need to determine the location of the document to which we wish to link. The URL for the Web-Archipelago site is `http://web-archipelago.com/`

The `A` tag (for anchor) is the HTML mechanism to create hyperlinks. The implicitly anchored hyperlink has one required attribute, the `HREF` attribute (for HTML Reference). The syntax is as follows:

```
<A HREF="URL for the destination"> clickable element </A>
```

The tag is placed in the HTML document so that the clickable element appears in the appropriate place relative to the other elements in the document.

In our case this becomes

```
Visit the <A HREF="http://web-archipelago.com/">
Web-Archipelago site</A>, one of the places where you can gain
more information about other island adventures.
```

Figure 3.2 shows the Island Quest Travel Web page with this link added. The added material is shown in boldface type.

File: IQTravel_3a.html

```
<HTML>
<!--File: IQTravel_3a.html-->
<!--Project: Island Quest Travel Site-->
<!--See the ADDRESS tag below for additional information-->
<HEAD>
  <TITLE>Island Quest Travel</TITLE>
</HEAD>
<BODY BACKGROUND="graphics/watermark.gif">
<P>
  <CENTER><IMG SRC="graphics/IQTravel.gif"></CENTER>
<P>
  <I>Island Quest Travel</I>can take you to exotic locations
  where you can walk in the footsteps of buccaneers and adven-
  turers from the past. We can take you to places that are just
  dots on the map.  We'll fly you there and back and even pro-
  vide guides for special treks into jungles. Or if you prefer
  the sailing adventure, we will gather a crew and a ship and
  let you cruise mysterious islands.
<P>
```

```
    <IMG SRC="graphics/blue_rule.gif">
<P>
   Here are some of our services:
<P>
<DL>
  <DT><IMG SRC="graphics/smallWhiteBall.gif"> <B>Planning</B>
  <DD>
      We have dozens of locations that offer adventure and
      excitement and we can help you pick out just the right
      place.
  <DT><IMG SRC="graphics/smallRedBall.gif"> <B>Flight reserva-
  tions</B>
  <DD>
      Just leave it to us. We'll get you there and back. We
      will handle reservations with the major airlines as well
      as the local pilots for those special places not seen by
      most of the rest of the world.
  <DT><IMG SRC="graphics/smallBlueBall.gif">
      <B>Sailing accommodations</B>
  <DD>
      For the buccaneer, we can charter sailboats and crews who
      will fix your meals and take you to those hidden island
      coves where perhaps treasure is hiding in a nearby cave.
  <DT><IMG SRC="graphics/smallGreenBall.gif"> <B>Guide ser-
  vices</B>
  <DD>
      Islands often have jungles and we have the guides to take
      you to some of the temples from forgotten civilizations.
      These guides will provide everything you need in the way
      of meals and accommodations.
</DL>
  Visit the <A HREF="http://web-archipelago.com/"> Web-Archi-
  pelago site</A>, one of the places where you can gain more
  information about other island adventures.
<P>
<ADDRESS>
<FONT SIZE="-1">
  Programmer: J. Avila<BR>
  <B>avila@web-archipelago.com</B><BR>
  Last modified: 5/24/98<BR>
  &copy; J. H. Avila, 1998.<BR>
  All rights reserved.
</FONT>
</ADDRESS>
</BODY>
</HTML>
```

Figure 3.2

A portion of the document with the hyperlink is shown in Figure 3.3 as it appears in a browser window.

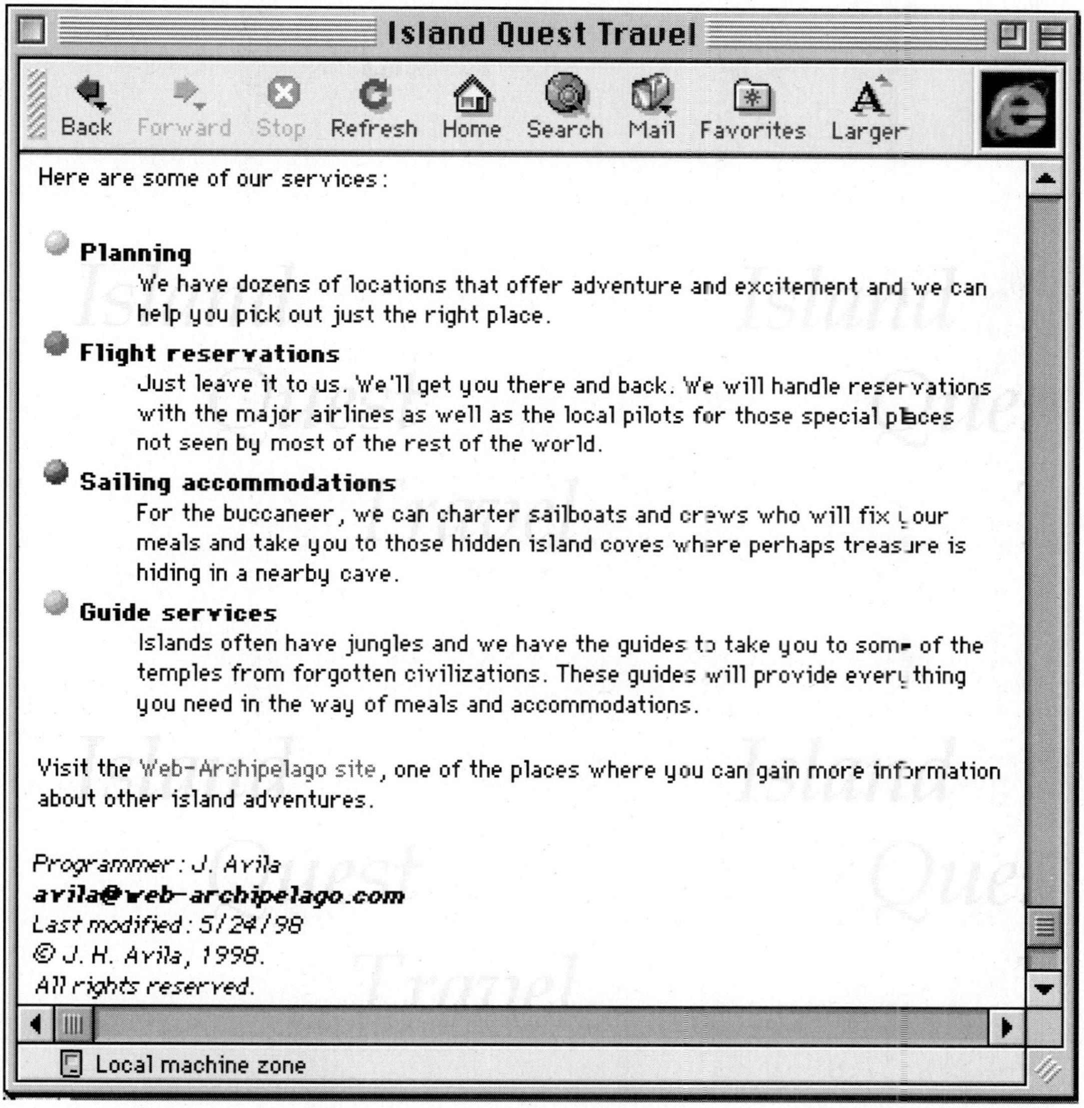

Figure 3.3

What if the document to which you want to link is local to your server? For example, suppose the document is in the same directory or a subdirectory of the one containing the link. Then the `URL` value of the `HREF` attribute can be simply the local file name relative to the directory in which the document with the link is located. For example, in the Island Quest Travel Web site, instead of placing all the information in one document, it is better to divide the information among several documents. Users only visit those they want to see and it takes less time to download one of the shorter documents. We also want to organize the directory structure in which these files are stored to match the hierarchical organization of the Web pages. We shall have a series of Web documents that will correspond to the services section of the first page. Consequently we create a subdirectory named *services* within the directory containing the Island Quest Travel home page document. Within that directory we have an HTML document named *planning.html* that has the specific information about planning trips. We wish to link the first of the service items named in the home page to this document. We show that section of Figure 3.2 in Figure 3.4. The portion in boldface type is the modification. When we identify a local document in this way we do **not** put in the `http://` portion of the full URL. Notice also how we can place the clickable text with its character formatting tag within the scope of the `A` tag.

Linking to a local document

```
Here are some of our services:
<P>
<DL>
  <DT><IMG SRC="graphics/smallWhiteBall.gif">
     <A HREF="services/planning.html"><B>Planning</B></A>
  <DD>
```

Figure 3.4

Setting the attributes for clickable text

In Figure 3.3, you will probably have noticed that the clickable text has a different color than the non-clickable text. Depending on the options you have picked within your browser, you may find that the text is underlined as well as a different color. For example, if the user selects the *Preferences* item in the Edit menu of the Internet Explorer browser, he or she will be given the possibility of selecting default colors for several items as shown in Figure 3.5. The color of the text , the color of the background, the color of clickable text that has already been viewed, and whether or not to display clickable text as underlined are all available choices. These are the default values in the browser.

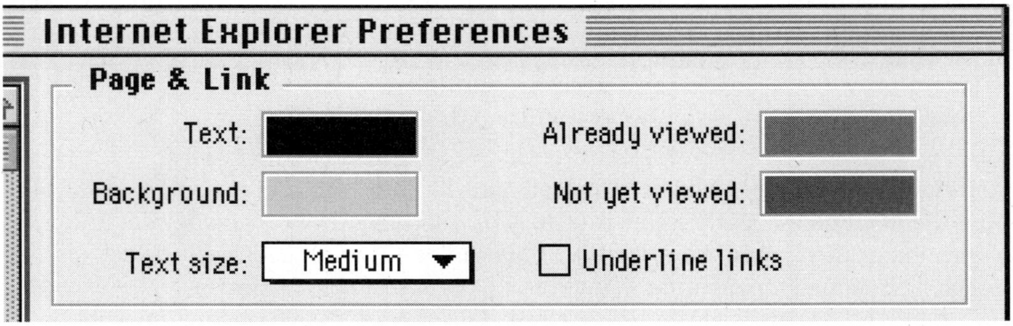

Figure 3.5

You can override these color choices through attributes associated with the `BODY` tag which we introduced in the previous chapter.

In particular there are four attributes that affect the color of the text in your document:

`TEXT`	for normal text in the HTML document
`LINK`	for hyperlinks
`VLINK`	for those hyperlinks that have been previously visited
`ALINK`	for active hyperlinks as you press the mouse button

Each takes a value that is a color. (See the section on the `FONT` tag in the previous chapter.)

The user does have the capability (also in the preferences menu item) to prevent the HTML document from imposing the color choices made in the `BODY` tag. Most users, however, will have set the options so that the HTML document can override the default choices. Please see the box below on the need to be careful with your choice of colors. We will assume here that the document will determine the text color according to the values of the attributes listed above.

The `TEXT` attribute value determines the color of ordinary text. Usually the default is black.

The `LINK` attribute value determines the color of links or clickable text. The default value is usually blue. Seeing text in this color alerts the user to the presence of a link.

Once a link has been previously clicked and the corresponding document viewed, the browser changes the color of the clickable text to the value of the `VLINK` attribute (for Viewed Link). Normally the `VLINK` is a contrasting value from that of `TEXT` or `LINK` to let users know that they have followed this path before. One especially useful feature is that during a single browsing session, previously visited links will be marked with this color even in new documents that are viewed as a result of following other links. The browser keeps track of those previously visited `URL`s and marks links to these documents appropriately. This is useful in avoiding looping back on previously visited documents unintentionally.

Finally, the `ALINK` (for Active Link) value is the color in which the clickable text is displayed while the mouse button is held down. If there were two pieces of clickable text next to each other then when you held the mouse button down over the clickable text, you would see that only a portion of the text would change color, telling you that there was another link there.

Color choices in Web documents

Unfortunately, the choice of colors for text and background can make your document difficult to view. With regard to the color of background and text, a rule of thumb is that if you set one of the BODY attributes (e.g. BGCOLOR, TEXT) then you should set them all.

If you do not set BGCOLOR, for example, then the default value will be used by the browser. If the default set by the user is the same as the value you chose for the LINK or VLINK attributes, it would appear to the user that the clickable text had disappeared!

It is also unwise to choose the value of the LINK attributes to be the same as that of VLINK. If this happens it is impossible to tell whether links have already been visited. As mentioned above, the browser keeps track of previously visited links so that they are marked even in newly-downloaded documents.

Since the color of visited links will persist once they have been selected, it is important to pick colors that are informative but not distracting. Always test your documents for their visual impact by viewing them—including testing the color of visited links.

As an example of the use of these attributes, the following BODY tag represents a modification of the IQTravel_2f.html file where the color attributes have all been set:

```
<BODY BGCOLOR="aqua" TEXT="blue" LINK="maroon" VLINK="white"
      ALINK="red">
```

As we saw in the previous chapter, colors can be represented by a six-digit hex number or, in some cases, by a name (such as we used here). The colors that are available to you on your Web pages are not all the possible colors that you could represent with 6 hex digits (that would be almost 17 million). The colors you can display depend on the monitor you use, the graphics card that is in your computer, and the software that you are using. There is not much in the way of agreement in the industry about which colors are universally available.

All machines that can display any color can represent 256 colors. What happens if you represent a color in an HTML document by its hex digit form and it is not one of the colors that your computer can display? There are various strategies that have been developed. One of these is called "dithering." Dithering tries to fake the color you wanted by using a blend of the available colors. A blend will be made by using one color and then replacing a pixel every so often with a pixel of another color so that the overall effect to the eye is the color you wanted. Unfortunately, the replaced pixels are usually very regularly spaced (e.g. every 4th pixel or every 3rd pixel) so that the result can sometimes be the appearance a background pattern that can make text almost impossible to read.

There is a set of 216 "safe" colors that have been adopted that will not trigger dithering if you are using Netscape on a Mac or PC. These also behave well using Internet Explorer. Recall that the six hex digits are just a triple of two-digit hex numbers corresponding to the amount of red, green, and blue present in the color. The safe colors use only the two-digit hex numbers: 00, 33, 66, 99, cc, ff.

We have put together an HTML document in the CD-ROM that will display the value of each of these 216 colors. This document (colorTable.html) uses a feature that is not standard HTML but it displays "correctly" both in Internet Explorer and Netscape. A portion of the color table is shown in this screen image.

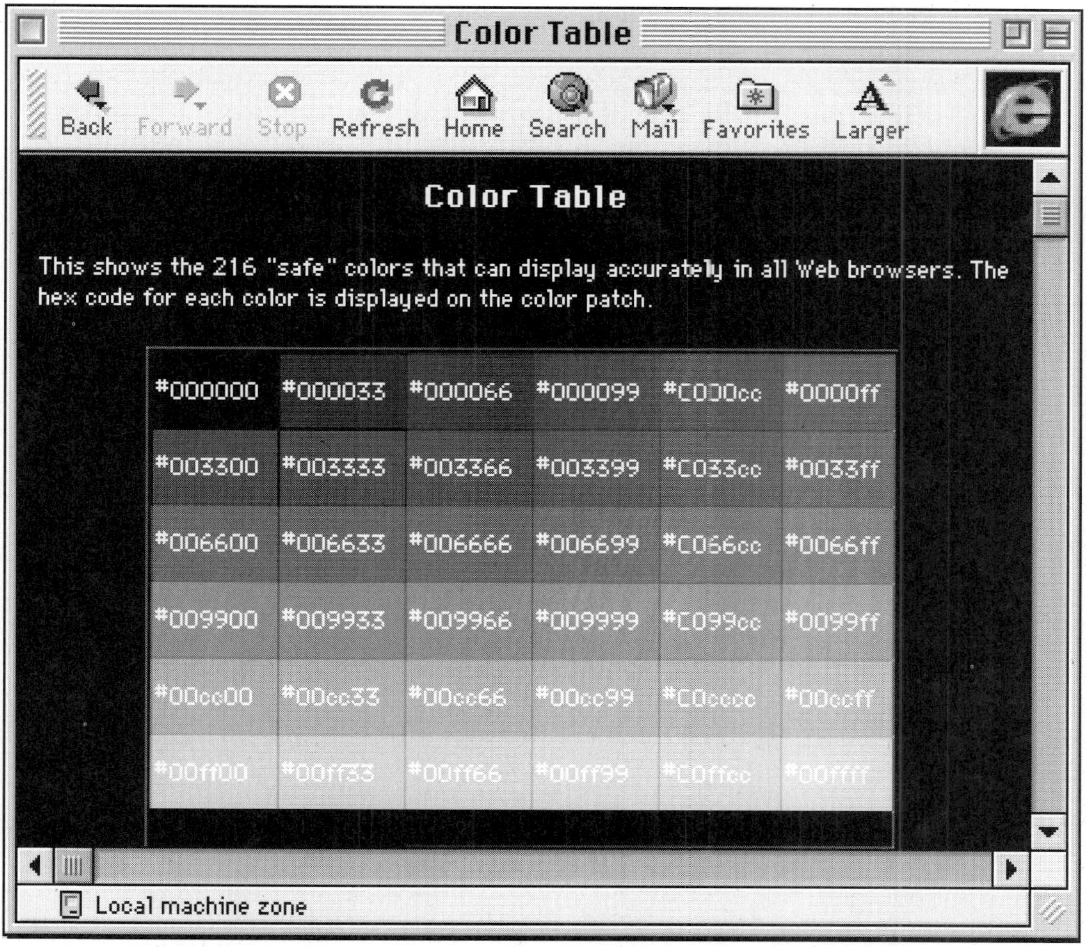

Creating button links

The link elements are not restricted to text. For example, it is sometimes more effective in a particular situation to have a graphical image be a clickable element. The `A` tag supports this. Just place the `IMG` tag for the clickable image between the opening and closing sections of the `A` tag.

As an example, recall the list of services from the Island Quest Travel home page. Earlier we created a link using the list item header text as the clickable element. It would be possible to make the small colored balls as the clickable element instead. Let's take the same example of linking to the file "`services/planning.html`" from the corresponding item in the list. Here is the modified list item (see Figure 3.2):

```
<DT><A HREF="services/planning.html">
   <IMG SRC="graphics/smallWhiteBall.gif"></A> <B>Planning</B>
```

In the file `IQTravel_3b.html` we have accumulated the changes described in this section starting with the earlier version of the home page without the watermark background. In Figure 3.6 you will see that the colored balls are now surrounded by a small maroon box. Maroon is the color assigned to links in the `LINK` attribute of the `BODY` tag and the colored box surrounding the graphical element is the manner in which the browser indicates the clickable element.

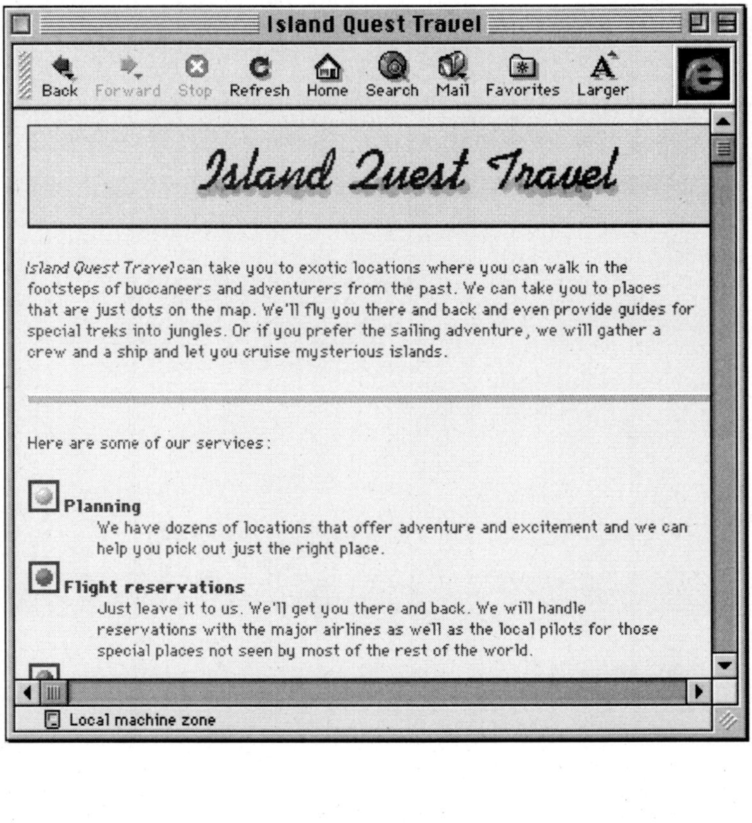

Figure 3.6

One problem with the use of the small graphical elements as links is that the user may not recognize the box as a clickable item. One alternative is to place both the small graphical element and the adjoining text between the opening and closing portions of the A tag:

```
<DT><A HREF="services/planning.html">
   <IMG SRC="graphics/smallWhiteBall.gif"> <B>Planning</B></A>
```

The result is that the user can click on either the text or the graphical element.

The presence of the borders around the clickable graphical elements is visually awkward. These borders can be eliminated using the BORDER attribute of the IMG tag and giving it a value of 0:

```
<DT>
   <A HREF="services/planning.html">
      <IMG SRC="graphics/smallWhiteBall.gif" BORDER="0">
      <B>Planning</B>
   </A>
```

The ball icon is still clickable, as is the text. The resulting document is IQTravel_3c.html and a portion of it showing the links is shown in Figure 3.7.

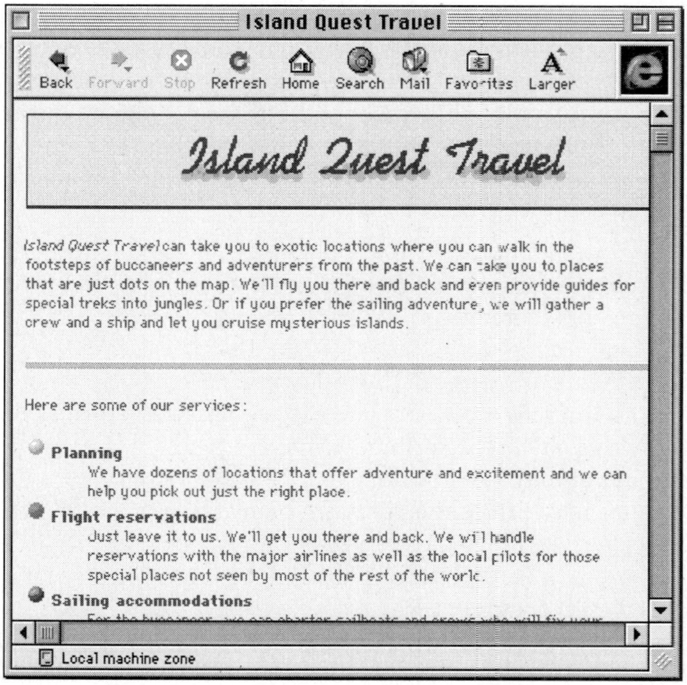

Figure 3.7

Why Links Fail

There are two major types of error messages that you may see when you click on a link and find that you do not obtain the desired Web document.

The first error message tells you that the file could not be found.

If this happens, then the `URL` which is the value of the `HREF` attribute no longer points to an existing file. There are several possible causes:

(1) the `URL` was incorrect in the HTML document;
(2) the owner of the file represented by the `URL` has moved the file to a different location—such as a different directory;
(3) the file has been deleted and no longer exists.

The second error message tells you that the URL does not have a DNS entry.

If this happens then the browser is indicating that it could not find the server whose name appears in the `URL`. To understand the cause for the error we have to understand how a document is fetched from another site on the internet. The name that appears in the `URL` that identifies the server (e.g. web-archipelago.com) must be translated into its IP (Internet Protocol) address. This IP address consists of four 2- or 3-digit numbers separated by a period (e.g. 130.65.86.41). Only the IP address locates a node on the internet. Certain machines on the internet are designated as *domain name servers (DNS)*. This means that they supply IP addresses corresponding to the name of a server.

When the browser attempts to request a document from the Web, it must first convert the name of the server (from the `URL`) to an IP address. It sends out a request to a name server to do this. One possibility is that the name servers on the internet have no IP address for the given name. Another possibility is that the name server doesn't respond within a pre-determined time (e.g. 30 seconds) which then leads the browser to issue the message.

If there really is no IP address for the given name then the `URL` value of the `HREF` attribute may simply be incorrect.

A time-out may be the result of one of the following:

(1) the network traffic is too heavy and the requested IP address did not arrive back within the pre-determined time;
(2) the `DNS` server may itself be busy;
(3) there may be network connectivity problems.

In the case of a time-out, it is worth trying the link again. Often a second click will result in the desired Web document.

Section review questions

True or false

1. The clickable portion of a hyperlink can only be a section of text.

2. The clickable region associated with a hyperlink is completely contained between the opening A tag and the closing /A tag.

3. The A tags used for hyperlinks should be grouped together at the beginning of the BODY portion of the HTML document.

4. The contents of an A tag can contain text-formatting HTML tags.

5. The value of the VLINK attribute should be the same as the value of the TEXT attribute.

6. Clickable text corresponding to a hyperlink will change color to the value of the VLINK attribute only for the time that the user is viewing the document containing the link.

Multiple choice

7. A hypertext document is
   (a) any HTML document on the Web.
   (b) an HTML document with a clickable region that triggers the display of another document.
   (c) an HTML document with animated images.
   (d) an HTML document that cannot be printed in a linear way.

8. The URL for a particular document is
   `http://web-archipelago.com/clientA/home.html`
   In that document is a hyperlink to a document named services.html in the same directory.
   (a) The HREF for this hyperlink must have the value
   `HREF="http://web-archipelago.com/clientA/services.html"`
   (b) The HREF for this hyperlink must have the value
   `HREF="services.html"`
   (c) Either of the two values in (a) or (b) will be correct.
   (d) Neither of the two values in (a) or (b) will be correct.

9. Given an image contained in a file named "`orderImage.gif`" which of the following will turn that image into a hyperlink?
   (a) `<A HREF="orderImage.gif">place an order today</A>`
   (b) `<A HREF="order.html"><IMG SRC="order.html"></A>`
   (c) `<A HREF="order.html"><IMG SRC="orderImage.gif"></A>`
   (d) `<IMG SRC="orderImage.gif"><A HREF="order.html">`

10. If a hyperlink fails,
    (a) the domain name server is "down."
    (b) the Web document which is the target of the hyperlink no longer exists.
    (c) the `URL` of the target document is incorrect.
    (d) Any of the above.
    (e) All of the above.

Short answers

11. What two items are necessary to have a hyperlink in a Web document?

12. What does the value of the `TEXT` attribute of the `BODY` tag determine?

13. What is the purpose of the `ALINK` attribute of the `BODY` tag?

14. Why are the following choices in combination not a good idea?
    `BGCOLOR="white" TEXT="blue" LINK="black" VLINK="white" ALINK="red"`

15. What is the purpose of the `BORDER` attribute of the `IMG` tag?

16. What is a domain name server?

17. What is the relationship between a domain name and an IP address?

3.2 E-mail with the `A` Tag

In addition to providing a mechanism for linking to other documents, the `A` tag is used for allowing a viewer to author an e-mail message. Usually, the recipient is the author of the Web document and the mechanism is a means of providing feed-back about the document itself.

We will adopt this use of the `A` tag as well within the `ADDRESS` tag element that we have been using to convey author information. The method is to use a special value for the `HREF` attribute. The value takes the following form:

```
HREF="mailto:recipient@location"
```

For example

```
HREF="mailto:avila@web-archipelago.com".
```

If we examine `IQTravel_3c.html` we see that the `ADDRESS` tag is now

```
<ADDRESS>
<FONT SIZE="-1">
   Programmer:
   <A HREF="mailto:avila@web-archipelago.com">
   J. Avila</A><BR>
   Last modified: 5/24/98<BR>
   Copyright &copy; J. H. Avila, 1998.<BR>
   All rights reserved.
</FONT>
</ADDRESS>
```

We have now made the programmer name the clickable text, which now, if the user clicks on it, will open a window such as we see in Figure 3.8. Notice that the recipient of the e-mail message already appears in the To: section. Now users can simply type a message and send it.

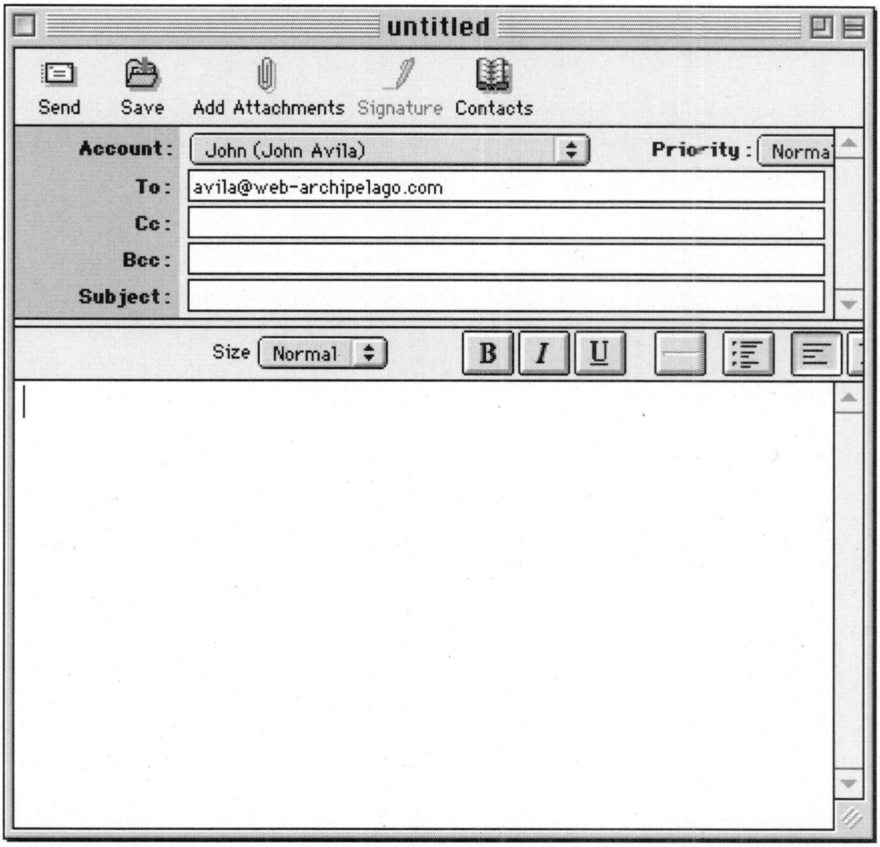

Figure 3.8

Section review questions

True or false

1. There is a special `EMAIL` attribute to allow users to send electronic mail using the `A` tag.
2. To send e-mail using the `A` tag, the contents of the `A` tag must contain the e-mail address of the recipient.
3. Although the `A` tag can be used to create a link to the e-mail program, users must still fill in the appropriate field to indicate who is to receive the message.

Short answer

4. What is the purpose of the mailto: form of a `URL` in the `HREF` attribute of the `A` tag?

3.3 Explicitly Anchored Hyperlinks

If you specify an HTML file as the target of a link, you will see the beginning of the document when it is presented by the browser. We referred to this type of hyperlink as an implicitly anchored hyperlink.

Often, however, you may wish to have the browser take you to some point within the document so that the top of the browser window corresponds to that point. This is particularly useful if the document is lengthy and has many sections. What we want is to place *explicit anchors* in a document so that hyperlinks can link to these places within the document. The `A` tag is used to identify these explicit anchors or places to which the browser can link.

For explicitly anchored hyperlinks, we use the NAME attribute instead of the HREF attribute. The value of the NAME attribute becomes a label that identifies a location to which a hyperlink can point. The value of the NAME attribute must be a string. The string should be simple (usually a single word), yet identify the label uniquely.

As an example of the use of explicitly anchored hyperlinks, assume that we have a long Web document containing many sections. At the beginning of this document we have a table of contents that appears something like Figure 3.9.

A table of contents document to which we want to add hyperlinks

Table of Contents

1. The early inhabitants of Guadalajara
2. Historical sites within the city
3. Places to visit within the state of Jalisco
4. How to get more information before your trip

Figure 3.9

Immediately following the table of contents, we have the text for each of the sections, one following the other. We want to be able to link directly from the table of contents to any of the sections without having to start at the beginning of the document and then scroll to the appropriate section. To do this we will establish each section header within the document as a location to which an explicitly anchored hyperlink can link. We display that portion of the body of the HTML document showing the target locations corresponding to each of the four sections in Figure 3.10.

Creating explicit anchors

```
<P>
<H3><A NAME="sec1">The early inhabitants of Guadalajara</A></
H3>
<P>
  The first peoples in this area in the mountains of central
  Mexico were ...
<P>
<H3><A NAME="sec2">Historical sites within the city</A></H3>
<P>
  A good place to start is the plaza and the area near the
  Cathedral...
<P>
<H3><A NAME="sec3">Places to visit within the state of
Jalisco</A></H3>
<P>
  Lake Chapala is a beautiful region within a few hours of
  Guadalajara...
<P>
<H3><A NAME="sec4">How to get more information before your
trip</A></H3>
<P>
  One of the first places to start is the Web site for tourist
  information...
<P>
```

Figure 3.10

Syntax rule

The A tag when used with the NAME attribute requires non-empty content (the items between the opening and closing portions of the tag).

The A tag may not contain an Hn tag (headers) but may be contained within Hn tags. In other words, if you want to use a header as a clickable item, you must place the A tag within the contents of the Hn tag. For example

```
<H2><A HREF="historical.html/">Historical sites</A></H2>
```

but **not**

```
<A HREF="historical.html/"><H2>Historical sites</H2></A>
```

As we see in Figure 3.10, we create the explicitly anchored hyperlinks by placing the header text (but not the header tags) within the A tag. We use the NAME attribute and assign a value that will uniquely identify this point in the document.

Once we have explicit anchors, how do we link to these points within documents? This involves using the HREF attribute with a modification. If *name* is the value of the NAME attribute for the explicit anchor within a document, then append #*name* to the URL of the file containing the HTML document. When the browser displays the appropriate document, the location of the explicit anchor appears at the beginning of the browser window.

For example, the file containing the HTML document fragment shown in Figure 3.10 is guadalajara.html. In another document if we want to link to the location corresponding to the third section we would see something like this

```
The Guadalajara Web site contains other
<A HREF="guadalajara.html#sec3">places to visit in Jalisco.</A>
```

Perhaps more commonly, the locations are referenced directly from within the document containing them. To continue with this example, let us place links to the appropriate sections directly into the table of contents list as follows:

```
<CENTER><H2>Table of Contents</H2></CENTER>
<P>
<OL>
    <LI><A HREF="#sec1"><B>The early inhabitants of Guadalajara
    </B></A>
    <LI><A HREF="#sec2"><B>Historical sites within the city</B>
    </A>
```

```
   <LI><A HREF="#sec3"><B>Places to visit within the state of
   Jalisco</B></A>
  <LI><A HREF="#sec4"><B>How to get more information before
  your trip</B></A>
</OL>
<P>
```

Notice that if the target of a hyperlink is within the same document, then only the appropriate `NAME` attribute value, together with the '#' character, needs to appear in the value of the `HREF` attribute.

The contents of the full `guadalajara.html` is shown in Figure 3.11.

File: guadalajara.html

```
<HTML>
<!--File: guadalajara.html-->
<!--Project: Guadalajara tourism-->
<!--See the ADDRESS tag below for additional information-->
<HEAD>
   <TITLE>Visit Guadalajara</TITLE>
</HEAD>
<BODY BGCOLOR="white" TEXT="green" LINK="maroon" VLINK="lime"
      ALINK="red">
<P>
<CENTER><H2>Table of Contents</H2></CENTER>
<P>
<OL>
  <LI><A HREF="#sec1"><B>The early inhabitants of Guadalajara
  </B></A>
  <LI><A HREF="#sec2"><B>Historical sites within the city</B>
  </A>
  <LI><A HREF="#sec3"><B>Places to visit within the state of
  Jalisco</B></A>
  <LI><A HREF="#sec4"><B>How to get more information before
  your trip</B></A>
</OL>
<P>
<HR>
<P>
<H3><A NAME="sec1">The early inhabitants of Guadalajara</A></
H3>
<P>
  The first peoples in this area in the mountains of central
  Mexico were ...
```

```
<P>
<H3><A NAME="sec2">Historical sites within the city</A></H3>
<P>
  A good place to start is the plaza and the area near the
  Cathedral...
<P>
<H3><A NAME="sec3">Places to visit within the state of
Jalisco</A></H3>
<P>
   Lake Chapala is a beautiful region within a few hours of
   Guadalajara...
<P>
<H3><A NAME="sec4">How to get more information before your
trip</A></H3>
<P>
   One of the first places to start is the Web site for tourist
   information...
<P>
<ADDRESS>
<FONT SIZE="-1">
   Programmer:
    <A HREF="mailto:avila@web-archipelago.com">J. Avila
    </A><BR>
   Last modified: 5/24/98<BR>
   Copyright &copy; J. H. Avila, 1998.<BR>
   All rights reserved.
</FONT>
</ADDRESS>
</BODY>
</HTML>
```

Figure 3.11

We can view how the browser represents this document in Figure 3.12. If the user clicks on the first item in the Table of Contents, he or she will see the document now with the first of the explicit anchors or labels appearing at the top of the window as in Figure 3.13.

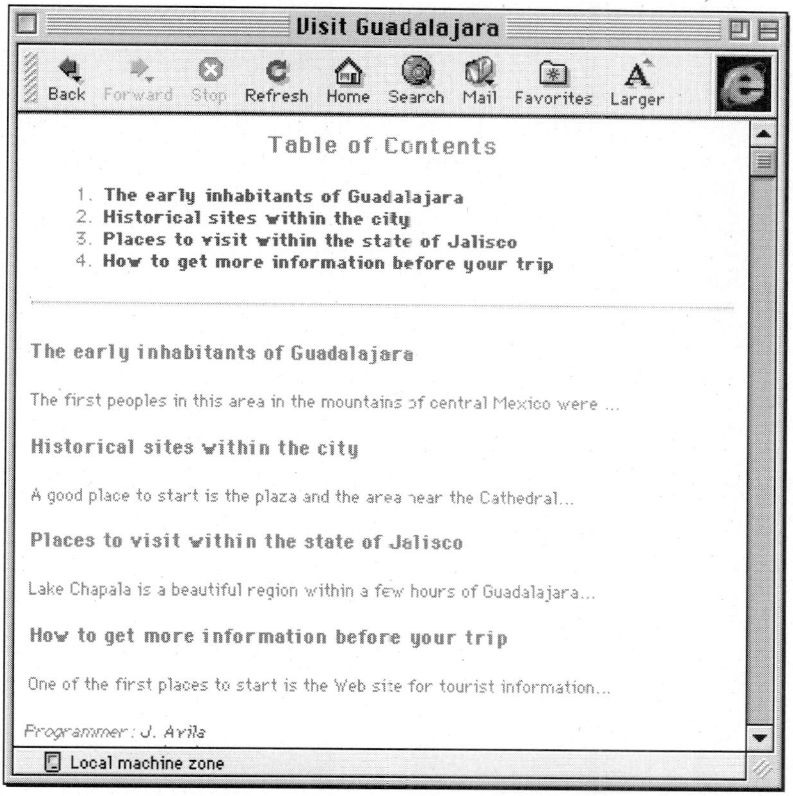

Figure 3.12

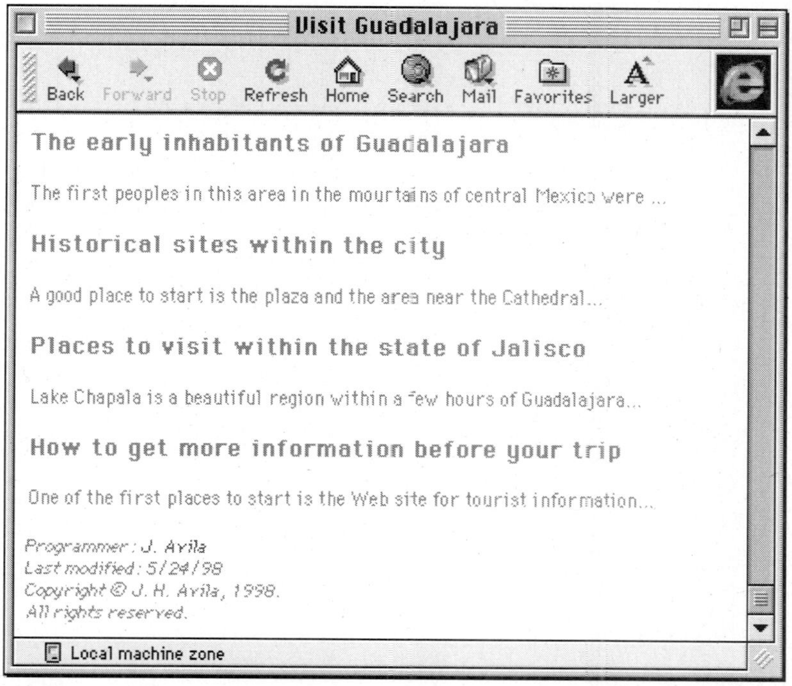

Figure 3.13

Section review questions

True or false

1. An explicit anchor refers to the target of a hyperlink.

2. An explicit anchor can be placed only at the beginning of an HTML document.

3. If the target location of a hyperlink is an explicit anchor, then the document containing the explicit anchor will be displayed starting at the point of the anchor.

4. The value of the NAME attribute used to identify an explicit anchor must match the value following the '#' character in the HREF attribute of the corresponding hyperlink.

5. The A tag, when used to establish an explicit anchor, must have text or a graphical element between the opening A tag and the closing /A tag.

6. Explicit anchors can only be used as target locations within the same document in which the hyperlink appears.

Multiple choice

7. If clicking on a hyperlink results in viewing the start of the target document, the hyperlink
   (a) must have been explicitly anchored.
   (b) must have been implicitly anchored.
   (c) could have been either implicitly anchored or explicitly anchored.
   (d) could not have been either implicitly anchored or explicitly anchored.

8. If the following tag appears in an HTML document:
   <A HREF="#history">How we got where we are</A>
   then you will expect to find which of the following somewhere else in the document?
   (a) <A NAME="history">History</A>
   (b) <A HREF="#historyAnchor">History</A>
   (c) <A NAME="#history">History</A>
   (d) <A HREF="history">History</A>

3.4 Clickable Images

Many Web sites have images with "hot-spots" that are clickable. A good example is the image shown in Figure 3.14. Suppose that this image represents a map of a town with a Web site for tourists who may be interested in visiting that community.

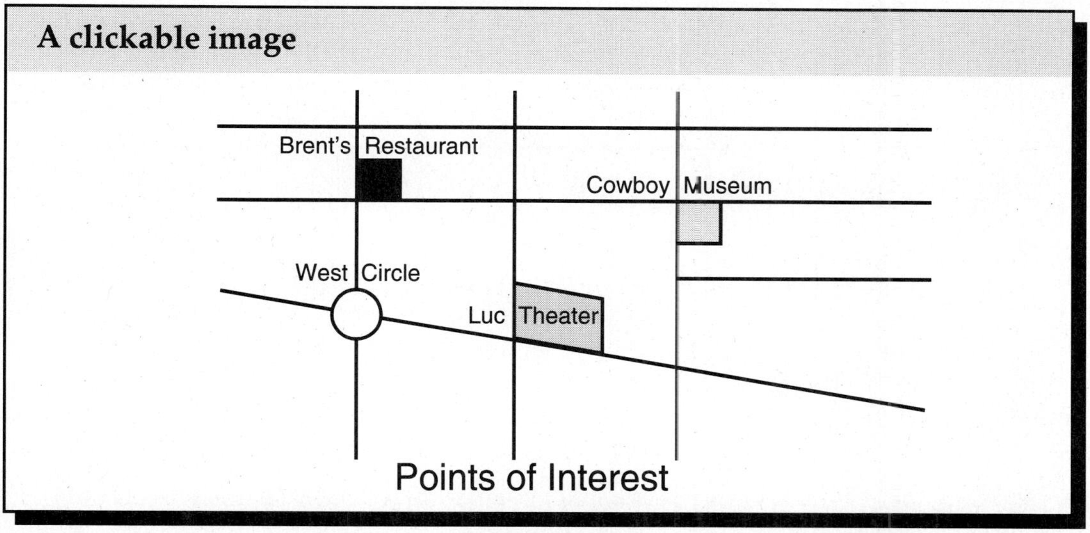

Figure 3.14

We would like to make it possible to have users click on any of the colored regions of the map and have a separate Web document appear for the corresponding point of interest. There are two ways of doing this. One involves "server-side" image maps, the other involves "client-side" image maps.

In the case of server-side image maps, a mouse-click is detected by the browser and its coordinates are transmitted to a server. The server has to determine if the coordinates fall within a region of the image that is a hyperlink. If so, the appropriate Web page is served to the client. With client-side image maps, the coordinate checking and linking to appropriate Web pages is all done on the client side without the help of a remote server.

Client-side image maps

Although server-side image maps came first, a drawback is the necessity to involve the server in processing the coordinates of the mouse click. A better solution is to use client-side image maps that allow this processing to be handled by the browser on the user end. This is far more efficient. In fact, with the advent of client-side image maps, it makes little sense to use the server-side approach except to support older web documents. We will, however, describe server-side image maps below.

The technique for client-side image maps is straightforward. In our example, we place the inline image of the map shown in Figure 3.14 using the `IMG` tag in our HTML document with the following:

```
<IMG SRC="graphics/townMap.gif" USEMAP="#townMap">
```

The USEMAP attribute takes a URL for a value or the name of a "label" which identifies a location within the present document. This location will be used by the browser to get map information. In this case the '#' character identifies the target as a label occurring within the current document (see the section on explicit anchors). In particular, townMap will be the value of a NAME attribute for a new tag type: the MAP tag. The MAP tag is used to identify the hot-spot regions within the image. The MAP tag for our example is shown in Figure 3.15.

Client-side image map

```
<MAP NAME="townMap">
<AREA SHAPE="rect" HREF="BrentsRestaurant.html"
      COORDS="109, 60, 136, 82">
<AREA SHAPE="rect" HREF="cowboyMuseum.html"
      COORDS="302, 82, 328, 108">
<AREA SHAPE="circle" HREF="cwestCircle.html"
      COORDS="109, 150, 16">
<AREA SHAPE="poly" HREF="LucTheater.html"
      COORDS="205, 133, 205, 166, 257, 173, 257, 146">
</MAP>
```

Figure 3.15

The value of the NAME attribute in the MAP tag must coincide with the value of the USEMAP attribute in the IMG tag for the related clickable image. In the content of the MAP tag we see another new tag, the AREA tag. We include as many of these tags as there are hot-spots in the image. In our case there are four. The three attributes for the AREA tag and the appropriate values are displayed in Table 3.1.

Attribute	value
SHAPE	the choices are rect (rectangle) circle poly (polygon) default
COORDS	integers separated by commas usually denoting x,y pairs
HREF	the URL of the document to be displayed

Table 3.1

The origin of the coordinate system is the upper left corner of the image and the x axis is positive to the right and the y axis is positive down (see Figure 3.16). All values are given in integer (whole number) values representing the number of pixels from the left edge of the image (x) or the top of the image (y).

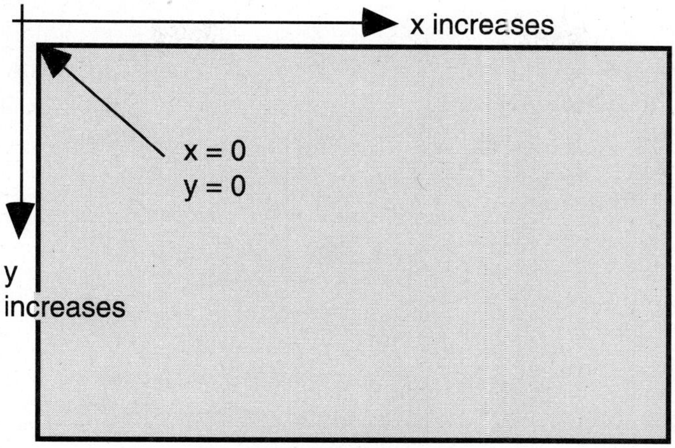

Figure 3.16

The shape identifies the shape of the hot-spot in the image. The extent of the hot-spot is determined by the COORD attribute. For a rectangle, the first pair of numbers represent the x, y coordinates of the upper left corner of the rectangle and the second pair represents the lower right corner. See Figure 3.17.

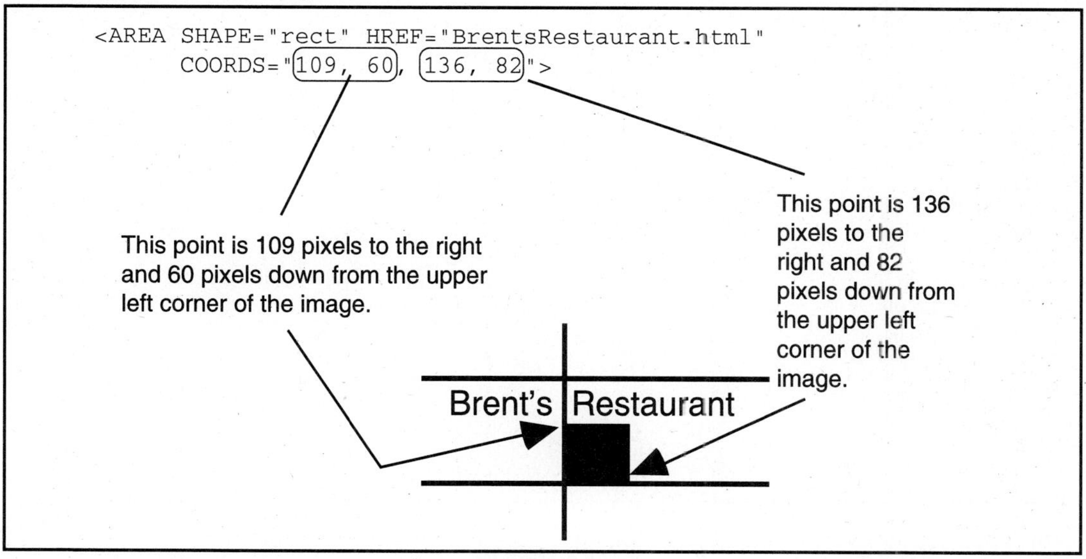

Figure 3.17

For a circle, the first pair of numbers in the `COORDS` attribute represents the center of the circle and the third number represents the radius. All numbers are integer values denoting pixels. See Figure 3.18.

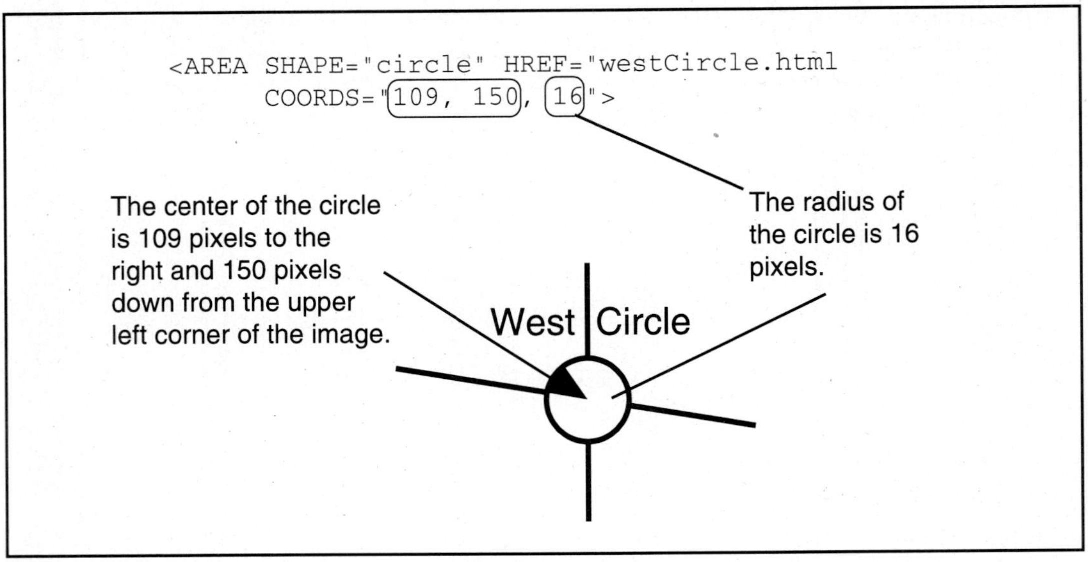

Figure 3.18

For a polygon, the value of `COORDS` represents x,y pairs corresponding to the vertices of the polygon. The sides of the polygon are formed by connecting the first pair to the second pair, etc. The last side is formed by connecting the last x,y pair to the first. See Figure 3.19.

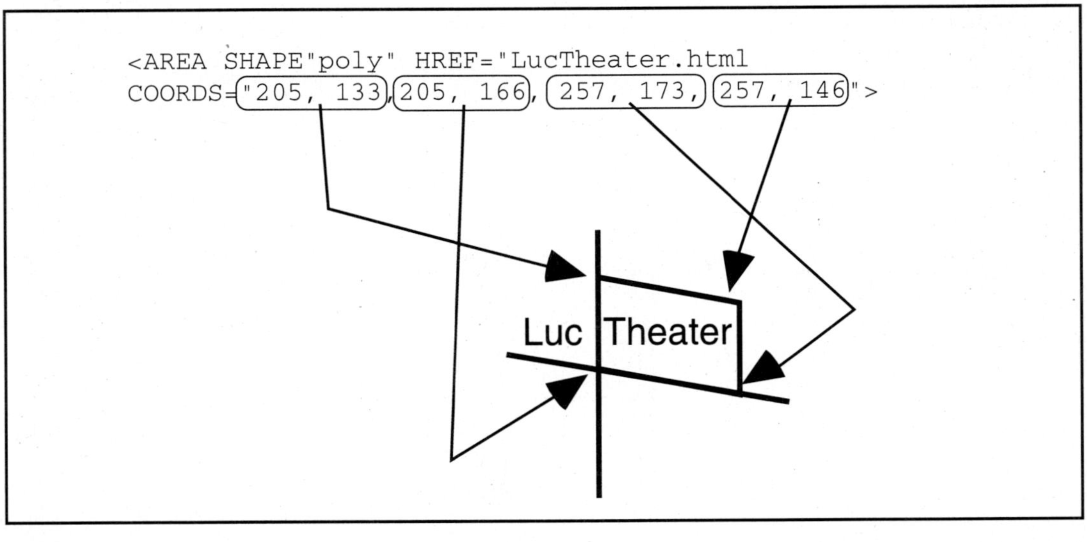

Figure 3.19

If the value of the `SHAPE` attribute is "default" then a click on the image outside of any of the other shapes triggers the display of the document whose `URL` appears in the `HREF` attribute.

Locating the coordinates of regions within image maps

Determining the coordinates of key points in an image requires software that will display the x and y coordinates in pixels. There are a number of programs available for Macintosh, Windows, and Unix platforms.

We have provided a Java applet that can be used for this purpose. You can use it by pointing your browser at the HTML document called MapWiz.html (located on the CD-ROM) and following the directions on that page.

Not all browsers support clickable images and there are now browsers for people who are visually handicapped which allows the text to be spoken. In order to let all users still have the ability to link to the appropriate Web pages, it's a good idea to provide conventional text links immediately below the image. In our example, we have placed these four links on one line with the '|' character between each link so that the user can see that there is more than one link. The resulting file is shown in Figure 3.20 and the way in which it is rendered by the browser is shown in Figure 3.21. It's worth pointing out the use of the `CENTER` tag to make sure that the image and the line of links are centered on the browser window. This is more visually pleasing than having everything left-justified.

File: `townMap.html`

```
<HTML>
<!--File: townMap.html-->
<!--Project: image maps-->
<!--See the ADDRESS tag below for additional information-->
<HEAD>
<TITLE>Our Town</TITLE>
</HEAD>
<BODY BGCOLOR="white" TEXT="blue" LINK="green" VLINK="lime"
ALINK="red">
<P>
<CENTER><H2>Our Town</H2></CENTER>
<P>
<CENTER>
<IMG SRC="graphics/townMap.gif" USEMAP="#townMap">
</CENTER>
<P>
<MAP NAME="townMap">
<AREA SHAPE="rect" HREF="BrentsRestaurant.html"
   COORDS="109, 60, 136, 82">
<AREA SHAPE="rect" HREF="cowboyMuseum.html"
   COORDS="302, 82, 328, 108">
```

```
<AREA SHAPE="circle" HREF="westCircle.html"
   COORDS="109, 150, 16">
<AREA SHAPE="poly" HREF="LucTheater.html"
   COORDS="205, 133, 205, 166, 257, 173, 257, 146">
</MAP>
<P>
<CENTER>
<A HREF="BrentsRestaurant.html">Brent's Restaurant</A>
 |
<A HREF="cowboyMuseum.html">Cowboy Museum</A>
 |
<A HREF="westCircle.html">West Circle</A>
 |
<A HREF="LucTheater.html">Luc Theater</A>
</CENTER>
<P>
<ADDRESS>
<FONT SIZE="-1">
   Programmer:
   <A HREF="mailto:avila@web-archipelago.com">
   J. Avila</A><BR>
   Last modified: 5/24/98<BR>
   Copyright &copy; J. H. Avila, 1998.<BR>
   All rights reserved.
</FONT>
</ADDRESS>
</BODY>
</HTML>
```

Figure 3.20

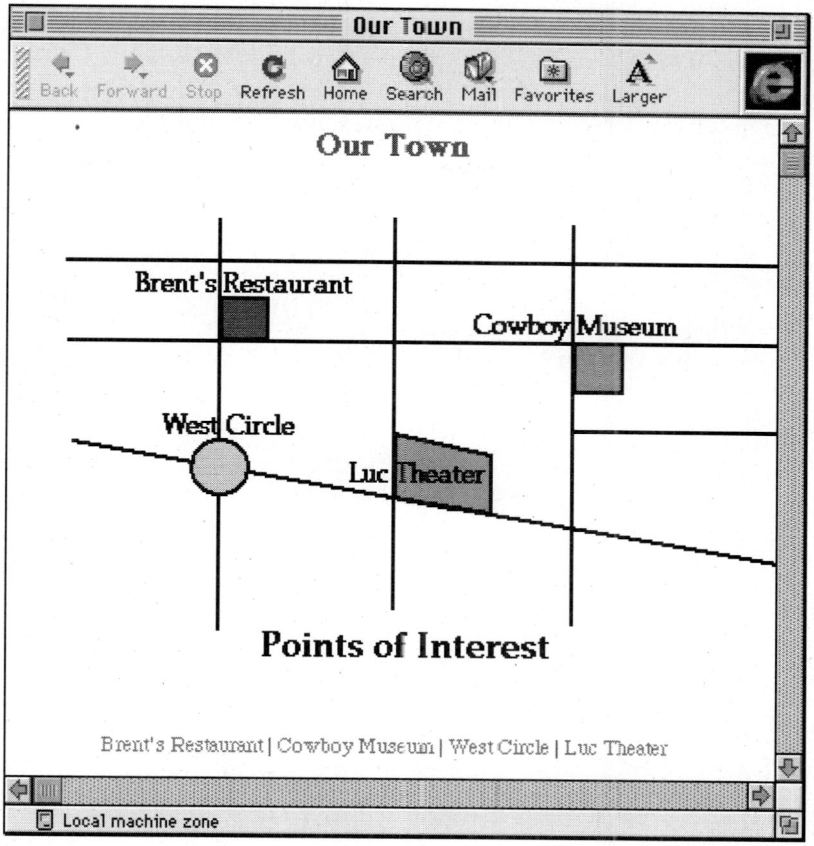

Figure 3.21

Server-side image maps

In the older style server-side image maps, the browser is told that the image is "clickable" and that the server should be given the coordinates of the mouse if a user clicks within the image. This is done using a combination of the `A` tag and the `IMG` tag.

For example, suppose the image shown in Figure 3.14 is in a file named `townMap.gif`. Assume also that there is another file which we will describe shortly named `townMap.map` with information about the hot-spots on the image. Then the HTML statement that we need to place in our document is given as follows:

```
<A HREF="graphics/townMap.map">
   <IMG SRC="graphics/townMap.gif" ISMAP>
</A>
```

Notice that the inner tag identifies the clickable image file using the `IMG` tag. The presence of the `ISMAP` attribute within the `IMG` tag tells the browser that there is a file with a map of the clickable regions (this attribute doesn't take an assigned value, its presence or absence is what matters to the browser). The outer tag then identifies the map file with the information that the server needs to translate mouse click coordinates into an appropriate `URL`.

There is some variability as to how servers support these clickable images. One of the first servers for HTML documents was developed at the National Center for Scientific Applications (NCSA) and was known by the name "httpd" (hypertext transfer protocol daemon). It was freely available and was the server software of choice for several years. We describe the format for clickable images first supported by the httpd server from NCSA and we assume a version of 1.5 or later. We'll describe some of the differences for other servers below.

The map file is just a text file. Figure 3.22 shows the map file for a server-side implementation of the clickable image of Figure 3.14.

map file for server-side implementation of clickable images

```
#Map file in NCSA format for townMap.gif

#rectangle for Brents Restaurant
rect ../BrentsRestaurant.html 109,60 136,82

#rectangle for the cowboy museum
rect ../cowboyMuseum.html 302,82 328,108

#a circle for the west circle
circle ../westCircle.html 109,150 124,150

#a polygonal shape for the Luc Theater
poly ../LucTheater.html 205,133 205,166 257,173 257,146
```

Figure 3.22

The rules for this file are as follows:

Syntax rules for NCSA map files

Lines beginning with # are comments and are ignored by the server. (Remember that these NCSA map files are not HTML documents. HTML-style comments do not apply here.)

Other lines are of the following form:

```
region_type URL x1, y1  x2, y2  ...  xn, yn
```

The choices of `region_type` and the meaning of the `x, y` coordinates are as follows. The coordinate system is the same as for client-side image maps.

`circle`

`x1, y1` are the coordinates of the center
`x2, y2` are the coordinates of a point on the edge of the circle.

`rect`

`x1, y1` are the coordinates of the upper left corner of a rectangle
`x2, y2` are the coordinates of the lower right corner.

`poly`

`x1, y1 ... xn, yn` are coordinates of corner points around the edge of a polygonal region—a region formed by connecting adjacent corner points with straight line segments. There can be at most 100 points

`point`

`x1, y1` are the coordinates of a single point.

`default`

no coordinates are supplied for this option.

The URL can either be a relative

```
../cowboyMuseum.html
```

or a full URL

```
http://web-archipelago.com/textBook/ch03/cowboyMuseum.html.
```

Notes:

(1) It might be tempting to think that the circle would be specified by the center of the circle and the radius of the circle but you must supply the coordinates for **two** points: the center and any point on the rim of the circle.

(2) There are commas between the x and y coordinates for a point, but only spaces between points.

You should be aware of some rules used by the server when it tries to match the coordinates of a mouse click to the information in a map file.

First of all, the default region is used if the coordinates of a mouse click do not fall within any other region. A point "region" is used if the mouse click does not fall within another region type. The point closest to the click then is chosen. Unfortunately, even if you have a default region, the point takes precedence and regardless of where you click (as long as it is outside of one of the other region types) you will trigger the `URL` for the point region.

If you click outside any region and there are neither point regions nor a default region, nothing happens.

The server compares the coordinates of the mouse click with the regions in the order in which they appear in the map file.

Since the regions are examined in the order in which they appear, if you had a circle within a rectangle, you would usually want to have the circle shape appear before the rectangle shape. The situation is shown in Figure 3.23. Users who click on the circle expect to get information about the special offer. In Map file #1, since the rectangle appears first, they will instead go to the homePage document. In Map file #2, since the circle appears first, users will get the correct `specialOffer` document.

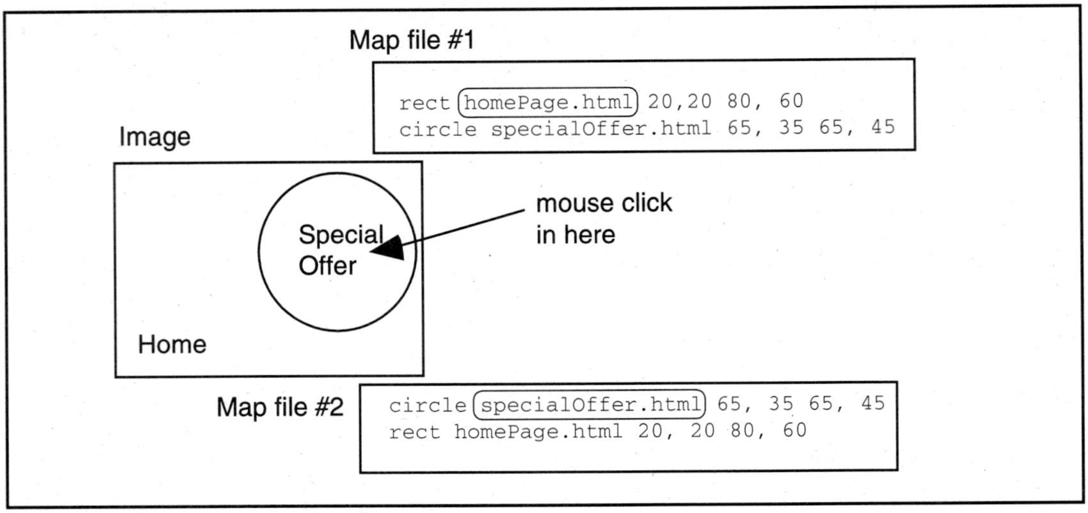

Figure 3.23

A very important note concerns `URL`s as they appear in the map file. If a relative `URL` is used instead of the full `URL`, then the question arises: relative to what? The HTML tags appear in one document in a particular location, the map document may be in a different directory and neither may be in the directory containing the clickable image. Which of these should be used as the starting point in the directory information for a relative `URL` appearing in the map file?

The answer is that, at least for the NCSA httpd software, the base is the location of the map file. Relative `URL`s appearing in the map file have the directory of the map file as the directory base. For example, assuming that the full `URL` of the map is

```
http://web-archipelago.com/textBook/ch03/graphics/townMap.map
```

and that one wished to have one region of the clickable image link to the file

```
http://web-archipelago.com/textBook/ch03/cowboyMuseum.html
```

then the relative `URL` is

```
../cowboyMuseum.html
```

(notice the leading .. which indicates the directory just above the current one in file hierarchy). Of course, one can always use the full URL if there is a problem.

Variations for different servers

Not all servers behave the same with regard to server-side image maps. The earlier versions of httpd (before 1.5) required that you identify a specific executable program (called `imagemap`) and pass along as a parameter the `URL` of the map file. This information was contained as the value of the `HREF` parameter in the `A` tag. We won't pursue this here but the Web master should be aware of these differences if he or she should have to deal with server-side image maps.

The CERN version of the web server software supports server-side image maps but the format of the map file is slightly different. There are many tutorials on the Web that will help you locate information about the CERN server if you ever need to look it up. You can start with the Web-Archipelago site and follow links from there.

Some servers support additional shape regions such as ovals or ellipses. Again, if you are not using NCSA's httpd server software, then check the Web for more information on this topic.

Note some differences between the server-side map format and the client-side map format. First of all for the client-side, the map information is contained within the HTML syntax mechanism of attributes and tags instead of a separate file with the shape information. In addition, there is no "point" shape for client-side image maps. Another difference is that for server-side maps the list of coordinates are of the form `x1, y1 x2, y2` (the commas only between x y pairs for each point but no comma between points). For client-side maps the entire list of coordinates is a comma-separated list (`x1, y1, x2, y2`). Finally, notice that the circle takes the radius of the circle as the third "coordinate" for client-side maps instead of a point on the rim of the circle for server-side maps.

Section review questions

True or false

1. If you are using a clickable image then every portion of the image must correspond to some hyperlink.

2. With server-side image maps, the browser sends the coordinates of a mouse click on a clickable image to the server for determination of a course of action.

3. In client-side image maps, the user's computer does the work of correlating the location of a mouse click with a "hot-spot" in the image.

4. In determining the pixel coordinates for a clickable region, the starting reference point is the lower left corner of the image with x increasing to the right and y increasing to the top.

5. In a server-side image map the default region is any area in the image that is not within a region identified by one of the other region types.

6. In client-side image maps, the `A` tag is not used.

7. If the value of the `USEMAP` attribute of the `IMG` tag is `"#paddington"`, then there must be a `MAP` tag with a `NAME` attribute whose value is `"paddington"`.

8. In a client-side image map, for the polygonal shape, the order of the points is not important as long as the all the "corners" of the shape appear in the list of points.

Multiple choice

9. Server-side image maps are identified by the presence of
   (a) the `ISMAP` attribute within the `IMG` tag.
   (b) an `A` tag containing an `IMG` tag.
   (c) a reference to a file containing information about clickable regions within the image.
   (d) all of the above.

10. If the center of a circular region in an image is located at x = 200, y = 100 and the radius of the circular region is 20 pixels, then which of the following represents the region using the NCSA version of a server-side image map?
   (a) `circle LucTheater.html 200, 100 20`
   (b) `circle LucTheater.html 200, 100 200, 120`
   (c) `circle LucTheater.html 200, 100, 20`
   (d) `circle LucTheater.html 200, 100 220, 120`

11. Suppose we have two clickable regions that overlap, and the user clicks in the overlapped region (server-side or client-side image maps). Then
   (a) the first region listed in the list of clickable regions determines the destination of the hyperlink.
   (b) the last region listed in the list of clickable regions determines the destination of the hyperlink.
   (c) it would be an error to have overlapping regions.

12. With a client-side image map, if the center of a circular hot-spot region is located at the point x = 200, y = 100 and the radius of the circle is 20, then the following AREA tag is appropriate:
    (a) <AREA SHAPE="circle" HREF="circle.html" COORDS="100, 200, 20">
    (b) <AREA SHAPE="circle" HREF="circle.html" COORDS="200, 100 20">
    (c) <AREA SHAPE="circle" HREF="circle.html" COORDS="100, 200, 120, 200">
    (d) <AREA SHAPE="circle" HREF="circle.html" COORDS="200, 100, 20">

13. In a client-side image map, assume we have two concentric circles as hot spots. Their centers are at x = 200, y = 100. The radius of the inner circle is 10 and the radius of the outer circle is 20. If users click on the inner circle we want them to link to one document and if they click in the region outside the inner circle but inside the outer circle, we want them to link to another document. This can be done by
    (a) placing the `AREA` tag corresponding to the outer circle before the `AREA` tag corresponding to the inner circle;
    (b) placing the `AREA` tag corresponding to the inner circle before the `AREA` tag corresponding to the outer circle;
    (c) the result is not predictable.

Short answer

14. Which are more efficient, server-side image maps or client-side image maps? Why?

Short excursion exercises

1. Modify the `IQTravel_3a.html` document by adding a hyperlink near the end of the document. Place the following sentence in the document where the darker type is the clickable portion:

   Find out more about **one of our favorite islands.**

   Locate a "home page" for some island of your choice on the internet and make that the target of the hyperlink.

2. Modify the `IQTravel_3b.html` document by changing the color of the background to black with white as the color of text, yellow as the color of hyperlinks, green as the color of visited hyperlinks and red as the color of active hyperlinks (the `ALINK` attribute). Click on the explicitly anchored hyperlinks and note the change in the color of the text links.

3. If you have access to a printer, print out the document from the previous exercise. Print the original version of the same document and compare.

4. At the end of the `IQTravel_3b.html` place an explicitly anchored hyperlink back to the top of the document by placing the tag
```
<A NAME="top"> </A>
```
right after the `BODY` tag and the appropriate hyperlink at the bottom of the document. (Look up the metacharacter   .)

5. Locate a site containing small icons (you can start from the Web-Archipelago site) and find an appropriate arrow icon that you can use to take you back to the top of the page as in the previous exercise. Turn the icon into an explicitly anchored hyperlink to take you to the top of the page in the `IQTravel_3b.html` Web document. Try the use of the `BORDER` attribute to see the effect.

6. Start with the `IQTravel_3c.html` document and modify the `A` tag within the `ADDRESS` tag so that your name appears and the e-mail will be sent to your e-mail account. View the document with a browser, click on the text with your name and send yourself a message.

7. Modify the `townMap.html` document to provide for a default region in which mouse clicks will result in a link to a document (just create a simple test one) whose name is `neighborhoods.html`.

8. In the previous exercise, add a text version of the hyperlink for the `neighborhoods.html` document along with the others below the image.

Longer voyage exercises

9. Start with the `townMap.html` document and use the coordinates of the clickable regions associated with Brent's Restaurant and the Cowboy Museum in the following way. Suppose the street from the corner on which Brent's Restaurant is located to the corner on which the Cowboy Museum is located is known as Stevens Creek Plaza. In the client-side image map implementation create a narrow rectangular area that contains this street. When the user clicks in this region, link to a test document called `plaza.html`.

   Make sure your implementation works correctly. In particular, let clicks in the restaurant and museum have precedence over the plaza.

10. In this exercise you will develop an HTML notebook where you can keep track of useful Web sites containing material that you can use for your HTML documents.

    (a) Create a table of contents at the beginning of the document (use an ordered list)
    1. HTML language elements
    2. Images and textures
    3. Graphical elements
    4. Useful techniques

[Language elements should be about tag syntax and other things that will help you quickly locate material you need for Web development. Images and textures are either sites where you can get image elements that you can use as background images or links to images themselves that you may have downloaded and placed in a graphics directory. Graphical elements are sites containing collections of things like small icons or perhaps icons themselves that you have downloaded and placed in an icon directory. Useful techniques should be links to sites that contain information about things like forms or techniques for doing interesting things that you might want to use someday.]

(b) Make these topics hyperlinks to explicit anchors within the notebook document.

(c) In each of the sections provide a list of items containing links to locations relating to that topic. Provide a few lines that will tell you what's at the other end of the hyperlink.

For example:

Images and textures

Here's a site from Netscape with a number of texture patterns that vary from marble patterns to more regular patterns in various colors. These can be used for document backgrounds.

This site from company x has a large collection of useful icons such as arrows and colored balls and lines of various types.

11. In the previous exercise, use small icons to identify each list item and make the icon the active element to click.

12. There is software available that will let you create "thumbnail" versions of photographs. If you have access to such software, create thumbnail versions of a set of images (family photos for example) and use the thumbnail versions as links to view the corresponding larger image. (This technique is used to let users decide if they want to see the more detailed but much larger image that may take a long time to download.)

13. Download the image: `stonehenge.gif` from the `textBook` graphics area of the Web-Archipelago. The following figure identifies certain key points in terms of their pixel coordinates relative to the upper left corner of the image.

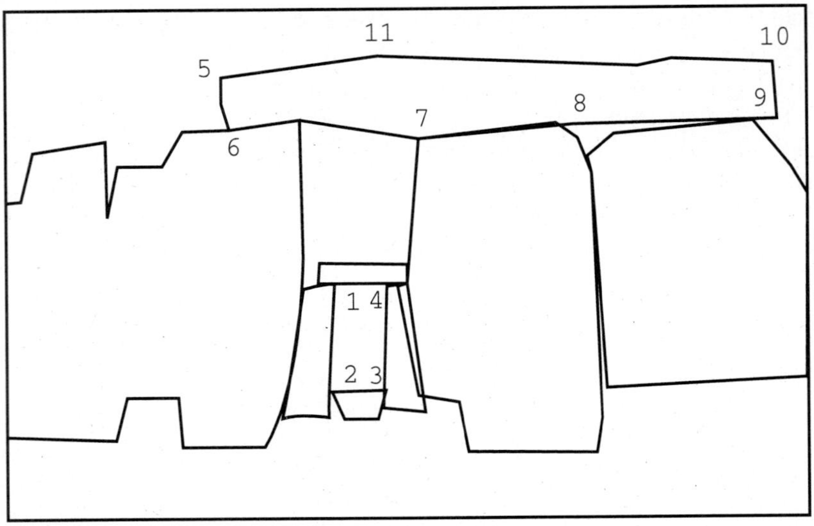

1: (198, 133)	2: (201, 180)	3: (214, 183)	4: (216, 133)	5: (132, 37)
6: (138, 65)	7: (230, 68)	8: (274, 58)	9: (374, 54)	10: (374, 26)
11: (211, 22)				

We'll create a clickable image such as one might use in a computer game. We want to let the region marked by the four points 1 - 4 be a portal into another realm of the game. The dark horizontal stone resting atop the others and marked by the points 5 - 11 is a lethal area. Users who click here will perish. Clicking anywhere else in the image will leave users in a lost state.

First set up a directory called `mystery` in which you will place four HTML documents: (a) an HTML document that will contain the stonehenge picture. Above the picture place the following text as a level 1 header (centered):

Mystery jump

Below the picture, center the following text:

Click in the picture and hyperlink into the mystery.
Beware of the hidden danger!

(b) an HTML document (`perish.html`) that is completely black except for white text (centered—level 1 header)

You have perished

(c) an HTML document (`realm.html`) that is completely white with red text (centered—level 1 header)

Enter into the realm

(d) an HTML document (lost.html) that is gray with black text (centered—level 1 header)

You are lost

Create a client-side clickable image from this image and create links so that users who click in the portal area go to the realm document. Those who click on the dangerous stone go to the perish document and all other clicks go to the lost document.

14. Create a map of your neighborhood or town and produce a `GIF` file with the final product. Produce a clickable map similar to the example in this chapter with your own documents to which hot-spots on the image will link. You might create a restaurant guide in which each destination document can contain information about the restaurant such as its menu or a recent review from the newspaper.

4. Data Gathering and Layout Features: Forms and Tables

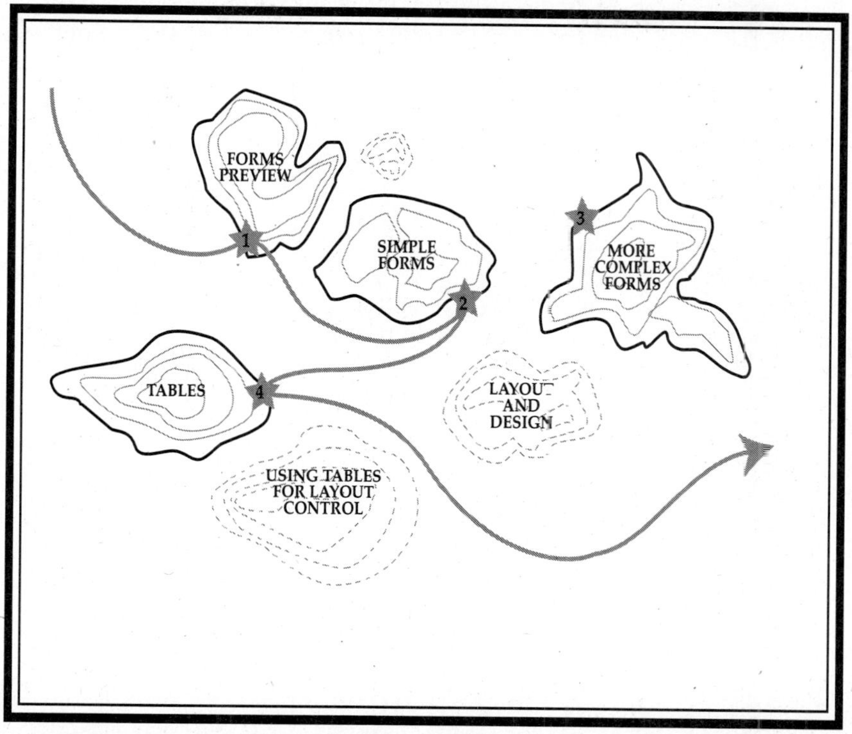

Chapter Preview

4.1 Forms Preview
Web documents with forms allow the user to return information to the server. This allows customers to send in requests or to submit data. We examine what happens behind the scenes when a user enters data into a simple form and presses the return key. The underlying tag that supports this interaction is the `FORM` tag and we examine its syntax.

4.2 Simple Forms
We look at several of the simpler form types that allow the user to type text. This will require that we introduce two new HTML tags, the `INPUT` tag and the `TEXTAREA` tag.

4.3 More Complex Forms
HTML provides for forms that allow users to select from a set of choices. In this section we will examine these form types. We will look at checkbox type forms, pop-up menus, and radio buttons.

4.4 Tables
Tables provide a way to assemble information in a rectangular grid of cells. We start with a simple table to be used as part of the Island Quest Travel Web site. We then build on this simple table to create a slightly more sophisticated version that shows how to create table cells that span several rows or columns. We show how to use tables for page layout such as creating pages with multi-column text.

4.1 Forms Preview

Forms are the mechanism in HTML that allow the user to interact with the Web server. One example is the occurrence of a box into which you can type the name of a keyword when you visit a Web site that will call on a search engine. Figure 4.1 is an example of such a site. The box just above the arrow cursor is ready to receive your keyword. The button (actually a pop-up menu) just to the left indicates that you will be using WebCrawler (one of the major search engines) and the button just to the right of the data-entry box will cause the search to proceed once you click on it.

When you press the Search button, the information that you typed in the box is transmitted back to the server that operates the search engine and is used to locate Web documents that may have the information that you are looking for. The titles of these documents are then displayed to you in a new Web document.

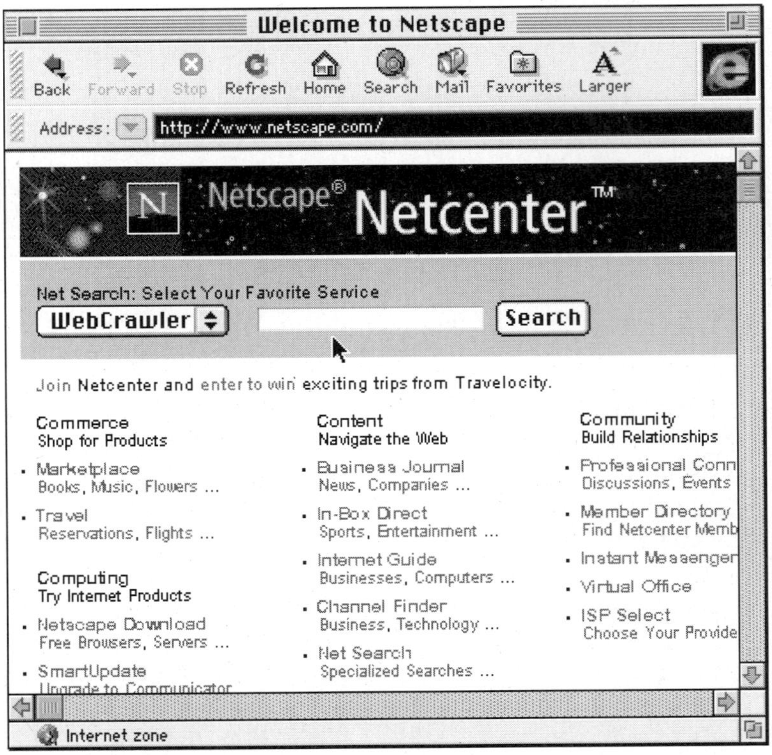

Figure 4.1

The process goes something like the following. You are first presented with a Web page on which a small box appears (usually blank) with some surrounding text that lets you know what information you should enter. You type a phrase or a word and press the Search button. At this point the browser packages your response along with some additional information and transmits this information to an executable program on a server. This program reads this information and carries out its task. The task (in the case of the search engine) is to search a database, create an HTML document using the information extracted from the database, and transmit this HTML document to you to view.

In Figure 4.1 the data entry box, pop-up menu, and button are all HTML elements that you can create with appropriate HTML tags. We learn how to create these forms in this chapter.

The FORM tag

The basis of HTML forms is the `FORM` tag. The general appearance of a `FORM` tag is given by the following:

Syntax: `FORM` tag

```
<FORM ACTION=URL METHOD="get|post">contained elements </FORM>
```

The `URL` value of the `ACTION` attribute identifies the executable file on a Web server that will be sent the data from your form. The value of the `METHOD` attribute can only be one of the two values shown: "`get`" or "`post`." Essentially, each of these refers to the way in which the data in the form will be delivered to the executable program. If the choice is `get` then the data will be delivered through the mechanism of what is known as an environment variable. If the choice is `post` (the more common choice), then the data will be delivered as input data available through the standard input. At this point you don't need to know about environment variables or what the standard input refers to. That will be required knowledge for the programmer who develops the software to process the form data.

If given a choice, you should choose the `post` method over the `get` method—especially if the data being sent is of any length. Both the `get` and `post` methods concatenate the data into one long string. In the `get` method, this string becomes the value of an environment variable which may be subject to arbitrary length restrictions. Data sent via the `post` method are not subject to such restrictions. In any case, unless you are writing the program that will read and respond to the data, you must abide by the choice made by the programmer who wrote the form-processing application.

The contained elements in the `FORM` tag have information that will tell the browser what kind of forms you wish to use. We'll explore these elements in the next two sections.

Section review questions

True or false

1. When form data is sent to the Web server, all the data in the form will be concatenated into one long string.

Multiple choice

2. Form elements are
   (a) one-line boxes into which users can enter data.
   (b) buttons that the user can click to transmit form data to the server.
   (c) buttons that the user can click to erase the contents of all the fields in a particular form document.
   (d) all of the above.

3. When you enter data in an HTML form, the data is processed by
   (a) the server computer.
   (b) the client computer.
   (c) either the client or the server computer, depending on the developer of the Web document.
   (d) none of the above.

4. The `ACTION` attribute of the `FORM` tag is used to
   (a) identify the HTML document to display after the data is received.
   (b) determine the method used to transmit the data to the server.
   (c) identify an executable program on the server that generated the HTML document that contains the form.
   (d) identify an executable program on the server that processes the data from the form.

5. The value of the `METHOD` attribute of the `FORM` tag should be
   (a) "`post`" unless the amount of form data is small.
   (b) "`get`" unless the amount of form data is small.
   (c) "`post`" if the amount of form data is large.
   (d) "`get`" if the amount of form data is large.
   (e) (a) and (c)
   (f) (b) and (d)

4.2 Simple Forms

The opening portion of the `FORM` tag announces to the browser that there are fields of data that will appear subsequently. The closing portion of the `FORM` tag announces to the browser that all data fields associated with this form have been provided. Between the opening and closing portion may appear items that are not directly related to the form and, in fact, often most of the body of an HTML document may appear as contained elements in a `FORM` tag.

The presence of a FORM item among the non-FORM elements is signaled by one of several tags. The most common is the INPUT tag.

Syntax: The INPUT tag for FORM fields

```
<INPUT TYPE=fieldType  NAME=fieldName  otherAttributes >
```

The value of the TYPE attribute identifies the field as one of several different types. There are simple one-line fields, menu fields with multiple items, checkboxes, and radio buttons among the various types. We will examine some of these.

The value of the NAME attribute gives an identifier to each of the fields. This allows the program on the server that will receive the form data to distinguish one field from another. We will see in a couple of instances that the NAME attribute is not used. In these cases, there is no data associated with the tag. If there is data associated with the tag, then there must be a NAME attribute.

The other attributes include things like SIZE to set the size of the input box that is shown on the Web document or VALUE to specify a default value that will be displayed when the document is presented by the browser. We will examine these and other attributes below.

Let's look at a simple example. Assume that a supporting Web page for Island Quest Travel will contain a request for information from the user. Suppose we want the user to be able to request information on places to travel. In order to get information back to him or her we will request the user's name and e-mail address. Often, soliciting information about the user (such as name and e-mail address) will allow us to develop a database that we can use later to notify the user about promotional offers or new features about our Web site.

We will give the user three boxes in which to type in the requested information. Each of these boxes will collect one of the three items mentioned above. Figure 4.2 shows the HTML document with this first example. Figure 4.3 shows what this document looks like in the browser window.

File: RFI.html

```
<HTML>
<!--File: RFI.html-->
<!--Project: forms-->
<!--See the ADDRESS tag below for additional information-->
<HEAD>
   <TITLE>Request for Travel Information</TITLE>
</HEAD>
<BODY BGCOLOR="silver" TEXT="blue">
<P>
```

```
  <CENTER><H2>Request for Travel Information</H2></CENTER>
<P>
  <FORM ACTION="http://web-archipelago.com/cgi-bin/Echo"
  METHOD="post">
  Please fill out the items below and we will get information
  back to you about the travel information you requested.
<P>
<HR>
<P>
  Your name:
  <INPUT TYPE="text" NAME="name" SIZE="30">
<P>
  Your e-mail address:
  <INPUT TYPE="text" NAME="email" SIZE="30">
<P>
  Places about which you would like travel information:
<BR>
  <INPUT TYPE="text" NAME="places" SIZE="50">
<P>
  <INPUT TYPE="reset" VALUE="Clear form">
  <INPUT TYPE="submit" VALUE="Send Request">
</FORM>
<P>
<HR>
<P>
<ADDRESS>
  <FONT SIZE="-1">
     Programmer: J. Avila<BR>
     <A HREF="mailto:avila@web-archipelago.com">
        <B>J. Avila</B>
     </A><BR>
     Last modified: 3/26/98<BR>
     Copyright &copy; J. H. Avila, 1998.<BR>
     All rights reserved.
  </FONT>
</ADDRESS>
</BODY>
</HTML>
```

Figure 4.2

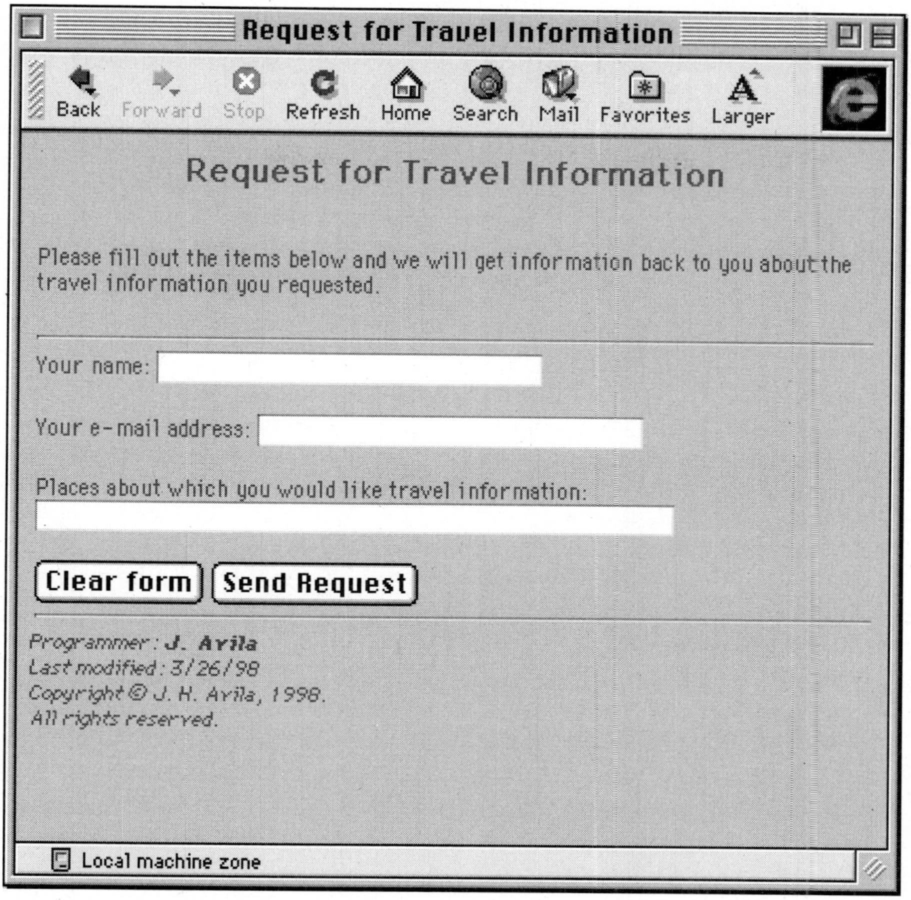

Figure 4.3

Let's look closely at the file shown in Figure 4.2. We've seen the `FORM` tag in the previous section. As you can see in the value of the `ACTION` attribute, the data from this form will be sent to the executable program named "Echo" on the named server.

The first of the fields is announced by the `INPUT` tag with the `TYPE` attribute set to "text"tags: `INPUT: TYPE="text"` and with the NAME attribute set to "name." The value of 30 for the `SIZE` attribute will result in a fill-in box with the ability to display 30 characters. Notice that we have the text: "Your name:" appearing before the `INPUT` tag. As you can see in Figure 4.3, this results in that text appearing just before the fill-in box on the screen. It's always important to let the user know exactly what you expect as input in a field. You can do this by placing the accompanying text close to the fill-in box.

Incidentally, the choice of 30 characters is somewhat arbitrary and only determines the size of the fill-in box on the screen. If the user types in more characters, they are not lost and the field will scroll left to accommodate the input.

The next two `INPUT` tags result in two additional fields being displayed in the Web page. Note that additional text and tags necessary to determine the layout of the text and boxes do not interfere with the form fields and are in fact necessary to accurately display the text that lets the user know what's expected as input for each field.

The next two `INPUT` tags produce the clickable buttons seen on the Web page. These `INPUT` tags do not take `NAME` attributes since they will not carry data that must later be associated with a particular field. The first one with `TYPE="reset"` will reset all the fields of the form to whatever values they had when the form was first displayed if the user clicks on the associated button. The text value of the `VALUE` attribute is the text displayed on the button.

The last `INPUT` tag is of type "submit." Just as in the reset button, this also will result in a clickable button with the string assigned to the `VALUE` attribute displayed on the button. When the user clicks on this button, the data in all the field boxes will be assembled by the browser and transmitted to the program named in the `ACTION` attribute of the `FORM` tag. In this case, we have written a server-side application that when executed will simply return an HTML document with the name of each of the fields in your form together with the value associated with each name. In this way you will be able to see the information that is received by the server. Incidentally, if there is only one text field in the form, then the user need only press the enter or return key after typing in the appropriate information in order to transmit the data.

The `VALUE` attribute can be used with the other `INPUT` types. If present, the value of this attribute becomes the default string shown in the input box when the user first sees it. The user can then simply take the default value or change the value to something else.

Password and hidden fields

There are other field types. The value of the `TYPE` attribute can be "password". A field of password type will hide the characters typed by the user as they are typed. This allows the user to type something like a password without worrying about someone reading it off the screen over his or her shoulder. An example of the use of a password might be to require that a user supply a previously-given password before he or she could receive requested information. An example of such a field would be

```
<INPUT TYPE="password" NAME="password" SIZE="8">
```

It is possible to use the `VALUE` attribute with the password. The result would be that a default password would be there for the user. This is not recommended because anyone can view the source HTML file and any such text would not be secure. There are no special precautions taken with the transmission of the data that the user types.

There is an additional field type obtained by setting `TYPE="hidden."` This field type will produce no fill-in box into which the user would type text but it will contain text that will be transmitted to the server along with the other fields. As an example, the following field would do nothing except send the `NAME` value and the `VALUE` value to the program on the server named in the `ACTION` attribute of the `FORM` tag.

```
<INPUT TYPE="hidden" NAME="message" VALUE="JHAvila">
```

Why would one do this? Suppose the HTML document were generated "on-the-fly" by a program on the server. In particular, suppose the user fills in a preliminary form. Based on the input, the server sends back a secondary HTML document with a form to acquire additional data. When the server receives the new form, how is it to know which earlier form to associate with the current data? After all, there might be many persons filling out preliminary forms and secondary forms. The hidden field is a way that the server can embed information in a form that will allow the server to carry information from the earlier form to the next. The `VALUE` parameter in this example might carry over the name of the original user to the new form.

The `TEXTAREA` tag

Often a single line is inadequate to record all the information that the user needs or wants to supply. For example, suppose the user is asked for comments about the Web page or perhaps the user is asked to describe a problem they have been experiencing with their new product. In these instances, we want to provide room for multiple lines of text. The `TEXTAREA` tag serves this purpose. It's general syntax is given by

```
<TEXTAREA NAME=fieldName ROWS=rows  COLS=cols >
   default text
</TEXTAREA>
```

The `NAME` attribute has the same purpose as in the earlier `INPUT` tags. The value of the `ROWS` and `COLS` attributes determines the size of the fill-in box. The default text can be omitted. If it is present, then the fill-in box will appear with the default text shown in the box. Note that you cannot use markup tags in the default text.

Figure 4.4 shows a portion of an HTML document using the `TEXTAREA` tag.

Creating a textarea field

```
...
   Let us know what difficulty you are experiencing with
   our product
<P>
   <TEXTAREA NAME="feedback" ROWS="5" COLS="40"></TEXTAREA>
<P>
   and we will attempt to correct the problem.
<P>
...
```

Figure 4.4

You can see the result of this `TEXTAREA` tag in Figure 4.5 which shows the file named `textarea.html`.

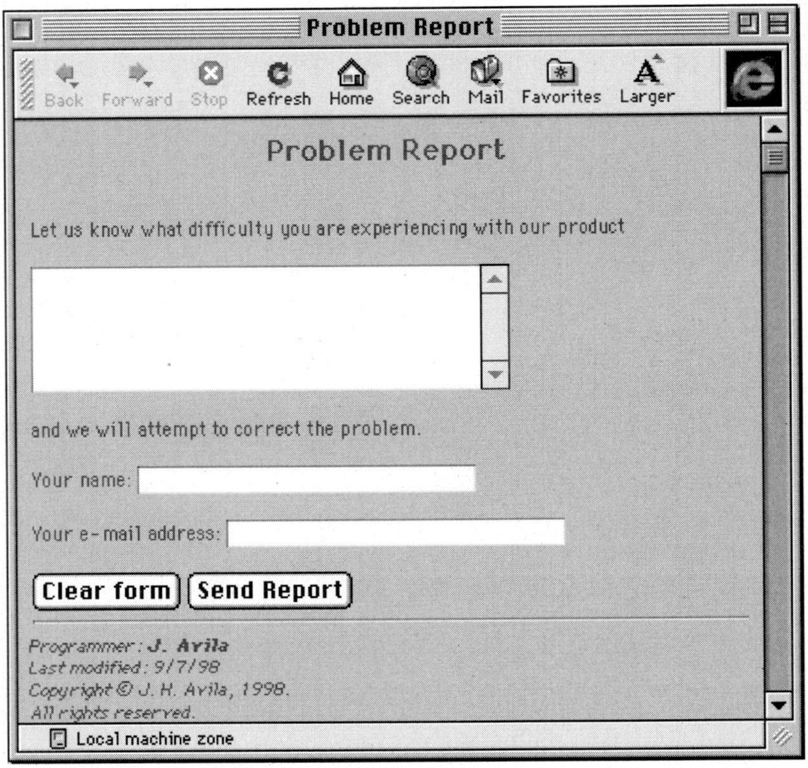

Figure 4.5

Incidentally, text will **not** be automatically wrapped at the end of each line. The user can type more lines than are given in the `ROWS` attribute; the text scrolls to accommodate the additional lines.

Section review questions

True or false

1. The material between the opening `FORM` tag and the closing portion of the `FORM` tag must contain only `FORM` elements such as text fields, checkboxes, pop-up menus, etc.

2. The value of the `NAME` attribute of the `INPUT` tag must be different from the value of the `NAME` attribute of any other `FORM` field.

3. The NAME attribute associated with any of the FORM data fields is useful but not necessary for processing the data.

4. Unless a submit button is present, there is no mechanism for sending FORM data to the program that will process it.

5. If you use the VALUE attribute with a data field, then its value will be displayed in the text area on the form.

6. A hidden field will display nothing in the browser window.

7. A hidden field is no longer useful for HTML and is just a "left-over" from earlier versions of HTML.

8. Hidden fields can be used to carry information from the server to itself at a later time.

9. Password field data are encrypted by the browser.

10. Although the TEXTAREA field allows scrolling in the vertical direction, the user must remember to press the return key at the end of each line or lose the text beyond the edge of the field area.

Multiple choice

11. The value of the SIZE attribute of the INPUT tag
    (a) is used essentially for alignment of similar data fields on the form.
    (b) must be large enough to accommodate the largest number of characters that the user may ever enter into the field.
    (c) can be set to 0 which then will let the browser choose the field size.
    (d) can be any positive value.

12. The INPUT tag with TYPE="reset" will (when clicked by the user)
    (a) reset all data fields to their default values.
    (b) set all data fields blank.
    (c) reset just the fields preceding the reset button in the HTML document.
    (d) none of the above

13. TEXTAREA fields
    (a) are not scrollable.
    (b) cannot contain more rows of data than are specified in the ROWS attribute.
    (c) can contain default text in italics or bold provided you use the appropriate tags.
    (d) none of the above.

4.3 More Complex Forms

Pop-up menus

Often it is more appropriate to offer a set of choices to the user than to require that he or she type a string into a text box. Let's suppose the Island Quest Travel people have a number of islands to which they offer tour packages. We can create a Web page that will allow users to select one from a list of island names when they send in their request for information about these tours.

The `SELECT` tag allows us to place a pop-up menu in a form. The syntax for the `SELECT` tag is as follows:

Syntax: `SELECT tag`

```
<SELECT NAME=fieldName >
   <OPTION VALUE=optionName >display text </OPTION>
   <OPTION VALUE=optionName >display text </OPTION>
   . . .
   <OPTION VALUE=optionName >display text </OPTION>
</SELECT>
```

The opening portion of the tag contains a `NAME` attribute which serves the same purpose of uniquely identifying a field as in the other form fields. Within the contents of the `SELECT` tag, one places one or more `OPTION` tags. Each `OPTION` tag contains a text string which will be displayed as one of the choices in the pop-up menu. Each `OPTION` tag also has a `VALUE` attribute whose value will be the data transmitted to the server as the choice of the `SELECT` field. One of the `OPTION` tags must have a `SELECTED` attribute. This indicates that this option is the default if the user doesn't select a specific choice.

Let's see how we would incorporate a pop-up menu for the Island Quest Travel site in Figure 4.6.

Creating a pop-up menu

```
<SELECT NAME="islands">
   <OPTION VALUE="cayman">Grand Cayman</OPTION>
   <OPTION VALUE="fiji">Fiji</OPTION>
   <OPTION VALUE="molokai">Molokai</OPTION>
   <OPTION VALUE="aruba" SELECTED>Aruba</OPTION>
   <OPTION VALUE="lucia">St.Lucia</OPTION>
</SELECT>
```

Figure 4.6

We have incorporated this pop-up menu in the file `islandChoice_a.html`. This file is a modification of the earlier user request form shown in Figure 4.3. The new version is shown in Figure 4.7.

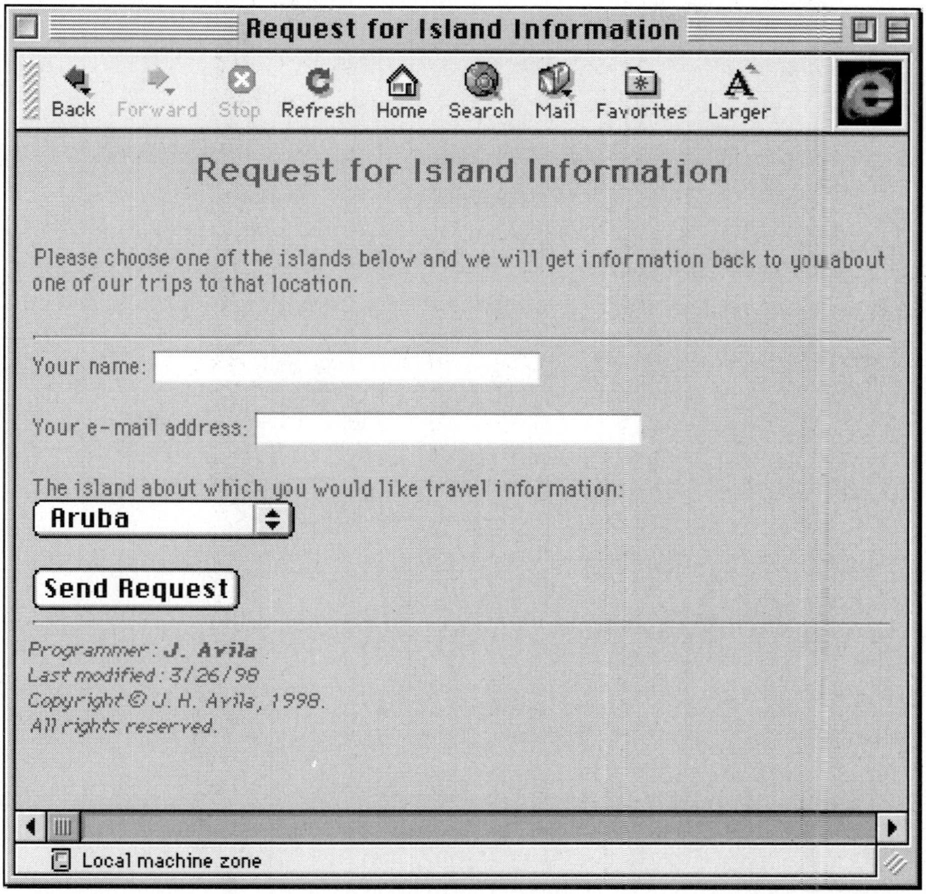

Figure 4.7

Checkbox forms and radio buttons

Another form type is the familiar checkbox. This uses the `INPUT` tag which we have seen before. Now we set `TYPE="checkbox."` The user can toggle between having chosen a particular option or not. For example, to continue with the previous Island Quest Travel Web page that allows users to request information about various travel locations, we can add a checkbox that allows the user to let us know that they would be interested in receiving information about any new sites that Island Quest may offer in the future. The section of the Web page containing the appropriate `INPUT` tag is shown in Figure 4.8. The result (in the file `islandChoice_b.html`) can be viewed in Figure 4.9.

Creating a checkbox form

```
<P>
   <INPUT TYPE="checkbox" NAME="letMeKnow">
   Yes, let me know about any new island packages that you
   may offer in the future.
<P>
```

Figure 4.8

For the checkbox field type, there is a `CHECKED` attribute. If the attribute is present (it doesn't take a value) then the default value of the field is that it is checked or selected.

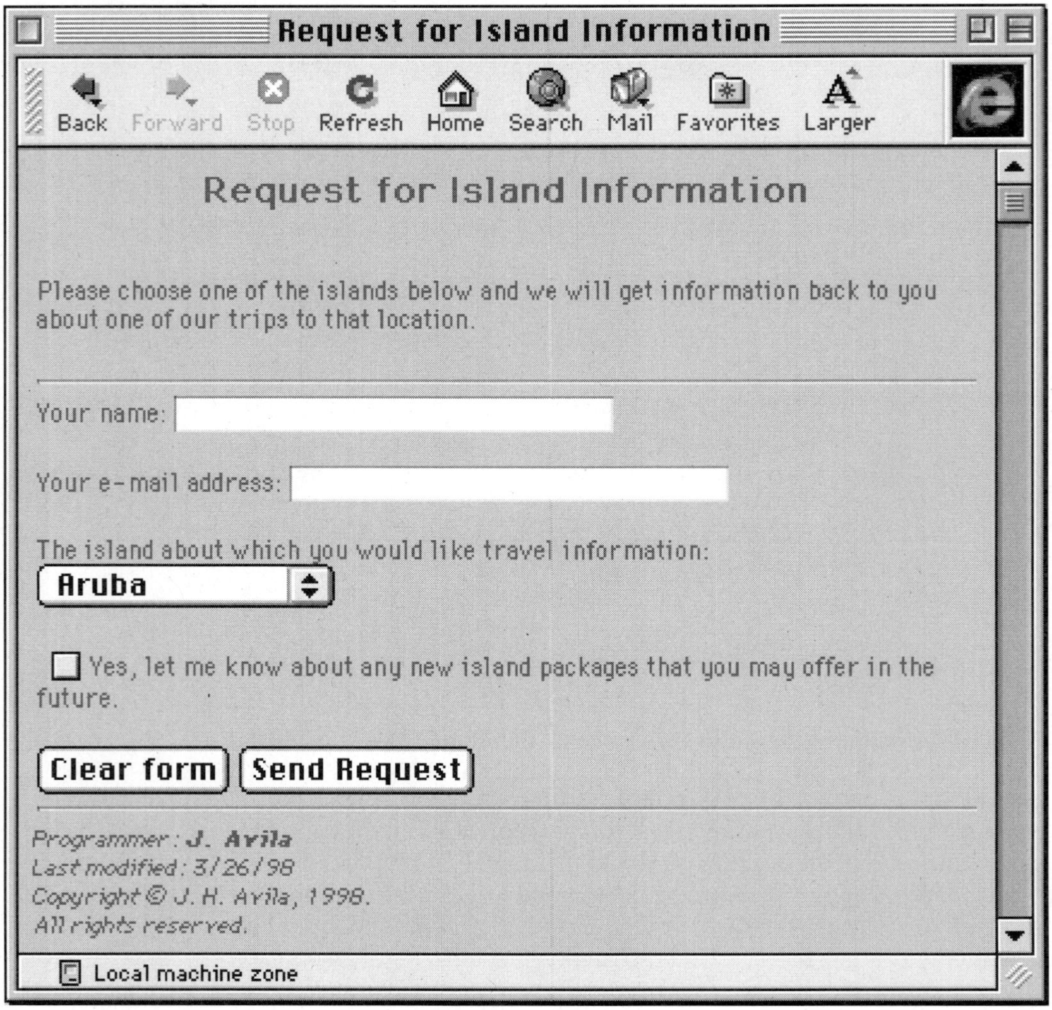

Figure 4.9

The last form field type that we describe is the radio button type (`INPUT` tag with `TYPE="radio"`). With this field type we can create a set of choices for the user such that selecting one de-selects the others. As an example, suppose we add to the Request for Island Information page by letting the user tell us which season he or she would prefer to travel and the length of trip he or she would be interested in. We add the text shown in Figure 4.10 to the HTML document. The entire document is `islandChoice_c.html`.

Creating radio button elements

```
<P>
   I would prefer to travel during:
<BR>
   <INPUT TYPE="radio" NAME="season" VALUE="spring"
          CHECKED>Spring
   <INPUT TYPE="radio" NAME="season" VALUE="summer">Summer
   <INPUT TYPE="radio" NAME="season" VALUE="fall">Fall
   <INPUT TYPE="radio" NAME="season" VALUE="winter">Winter
<P>
   I am interested in trips of length:
<BR>
   <INPUT TYPE="radio" NAME="length" VALUE="oneWeek"
          CHECKED>One week
   <INPUT TYPE="radio" NAME="length" VALUE="twoWeek">Two weeks
<P>
```

Figure 4.10

Notice that all the `INPUT` tags with the same `NAME` attribute value become part of one family. Selecting one of the circles on the Web page de-selects any other of the choices *in that family*. The two families that are shown in Figure 4.10 are completely independent. Notice also that in each family we have marked one of the buttons as `CHECKED`. This is required and specifies which of the buttons is in the selected state when the Web page is first displayed. (See Figure 4.11.)

It is crucial that each separate choice within a family have a different value for the `VALUE` attribute. Each family will contribute a single item of data to the form data. The value for the `VALUE` attribute is this item of data and the only way the server-side application can distinguish which choice is selected by the user.

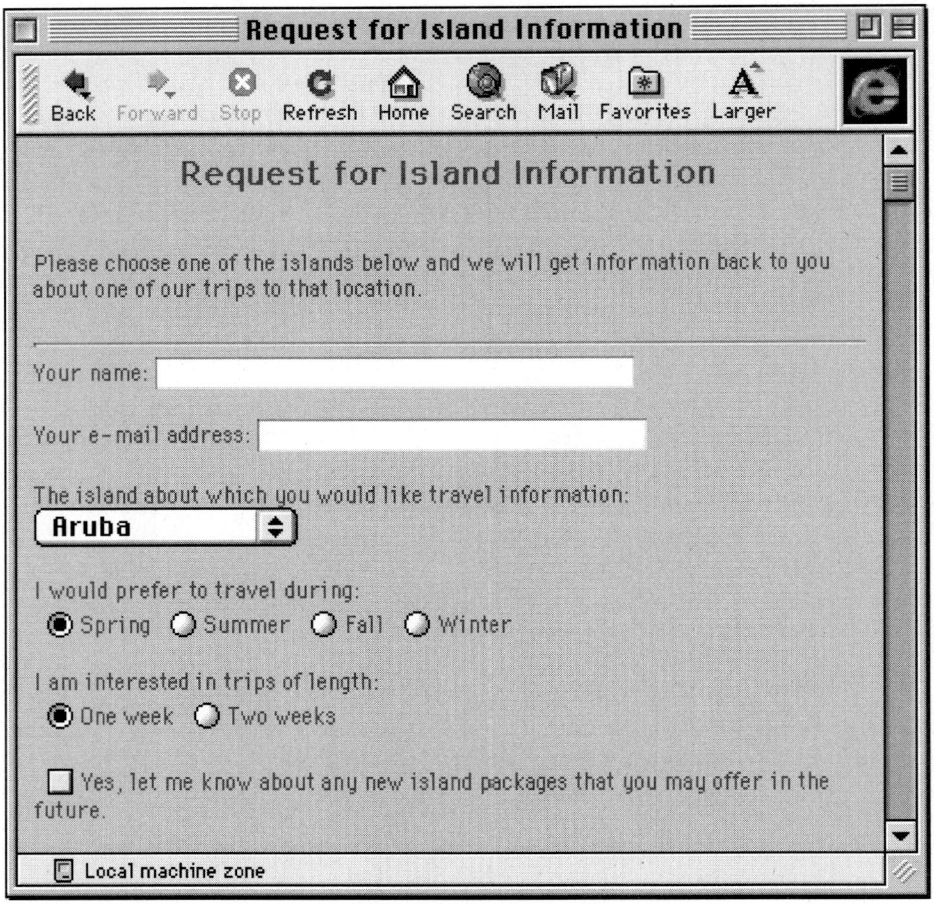

Figure 4.11

Section review questions

True or false

1. The `SELECT` tag is used to create menu items that will appear in the menu bar at the top of the browser window.

2. Pop-up menus will appear in the page at the location determined by the `SELECT` tag in relation to the other elements in the HTML document.

3. There is no way to display the checkbox field in an initial state in which it is "checked."

4. The checkbox field type doesn't need a `NAME` value because the field doesn't contain any user-typed data.

5. Radio buttons belonging to the same family must have the same value for the `NAME` attribute.

6. Any number of radio button families are allowed in a single form.

7. Having the same value for the `VALUE` attribute for a family of radio buttons will pose no problem.

8. You can mix radio buttons and pop-up menus in a single form.

Multiple choice

9. Pop-up menus
   (a) can have essentially any number of items.
   (b) will have only one item showing when the user first sees the form.
   (c) can have any of the items chosen to be the one that appears when the user first sees the form.
   (d) all of the above.

10. Radio buttons
   (a) must have one of the buttons pre-selected.
   (b) can occur in only one family in a form.
   (c) must all share the same value for the `VALUE` attribute.
   (d) can have different `NAME` values to correspond to different buttons.

Layout and Design

Layout is the visual organization of blocks of information.

In designing a Web page, it is easy to forget that the purpose is to communicate. We have become sophisticated viewers. If it's boring, we move on. Communicating effectively with people requires that we use all the tools that we have available.

On a Web page, the layout is often as important as the information itself. If the viewer is not attracted to the information, then communication will not occur.

Uniform blocks of text are efficient ways of using the available space. Each paragraph is a separate block. Each section is preceded by a header to announce the topic. The content of this box so far is a good example of this. Books are usually written in this style.

Breaking the pattern can be a way of presenting information in a more engaging way. Look at Figure 4.12

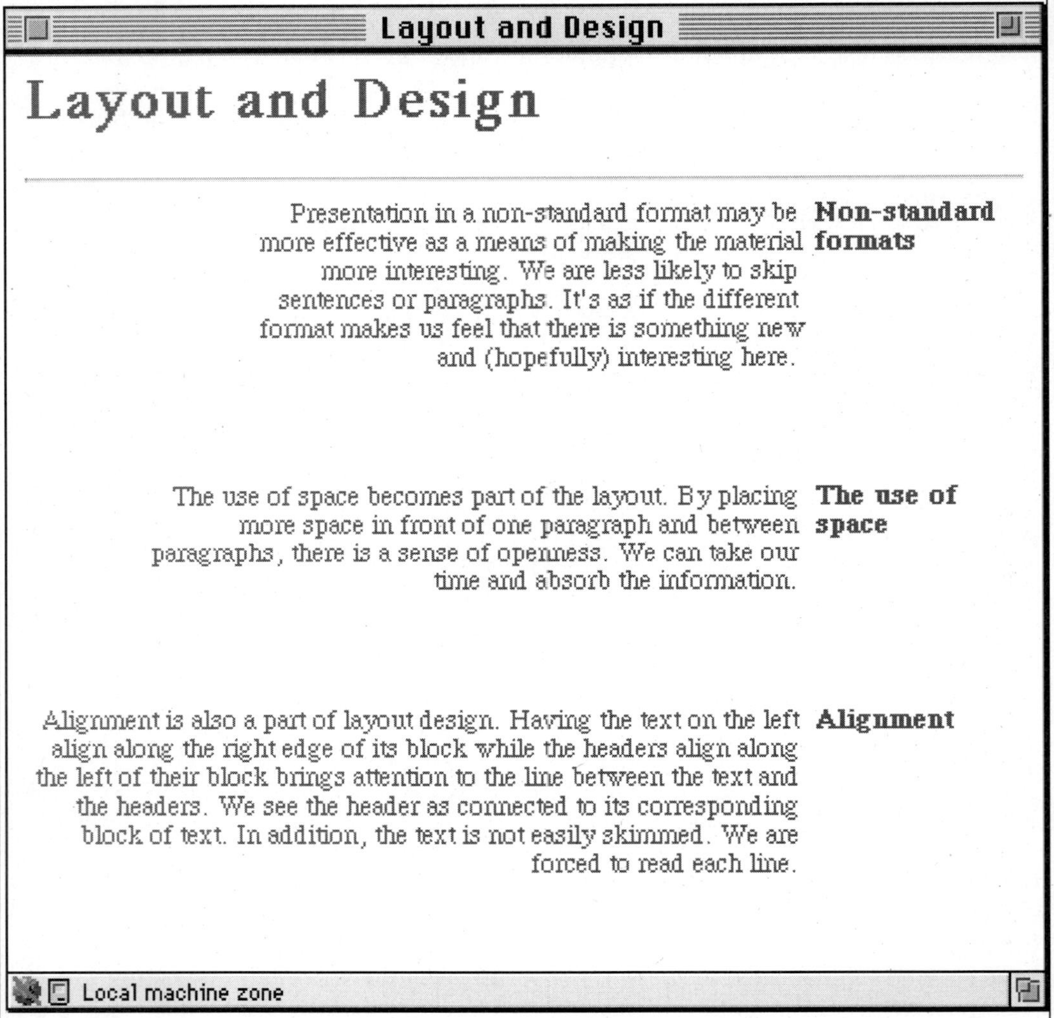

Figure 4.12

The next section of this chapter will give you the tools to be able to put together Web documents that let you incorporate layout into their design.

After you have read and understood the material in the next section, view the file `layout_design.html` found in the HTML folder for Chapter 4 in the enclosed CD-ROM. This file contains the HTML for the document displayed in Figure 4.12.

4.4 Tables

Tables allow us to display information in a rectangular grid of cells. The contents of the TABLE tag determine the layout and content of this grid. The attributes that we will consider for the TABLE tag are WIDTH and BORDER. The general syntax of the TABLE tag is:

Syntax: TABLE tag

```
<TABLE WIDTH=width  BORDER=pixels >
   Table contents
</TABLE>
```

For example, the following HTML text will create a table whose width will be 100% of the width of the browser window and will have a border of 4 pixels around the table.

```
<TABLE WIDTH="100%" BORDER="4">
   Table contents
</TABLE>
```

The presence of the BORDER attribute will also place a border around each cell in the table although the number of pixels for those borders are fixed and independent of the value of BORDER. Leaving out the BORDER attribute or setting its value to 0 will produce a table without any border around either the table itself or any of the cells.

The WIDTH attribute can actually be given in pixels as well as percent. If you want to use percent, then the '%' character is necessary. We have found that the percentage option is generally more useful. If the value is less than 100% then you may want to place the TABLE tag within the contents of a CENTER tag to center the table on the screen.

A simple table

Tables can have captions. A caption is identifying text that is placed either just below or just above the table to tell the reader what the table represents. Captions are inserted by placing a CAPTION tag somewhere within the opening and closing TABLE tags. The syntax is:

Syntax: CAPTION tag for Tables

```
<CAPTION ALIGN=alignment >
   table caption
</CAPTION>
```

Captions are centered and usually rendered in a way to emphasize them. The value of the ALIGN attribute is either "top" or "bottom" depending on whether you want the caption above or below the table.

Tables are assembled row by row. Each row is contained between an opening and closing `TR` tag:

Syntax: TR tag for Tables

```
<TR>
   Contents of a table row
</TR>
```

Each row is made up of cells. There are two types of cells denoted by the `TH` (table header cells) and the `TD` (table data cells) tags. The header cell is denoted by

Syntax: TH tag for Tables

```
<TH attributes >
   Contents of a header cell
</TH>
```

Table header cells are usually used at the top of a column of a table and often contain things like labels that identify the other items in that column. For that reason text content is often displayed in boldface and centered within the cell. The contents of a header cell, however, can be virtually anything including other tables.

One possible attribute for the `TH` tag is `NOWRAP` which takes no value and will force the browser to make the cell wide enough to accommodate the longest line in the contained text. Lines will be identified with the `BR` tag. Generally, this is not a good idea because the user may have to scroll the window horizontally to view the entire table which is often inconvenient and annoying.

Other attributes include options for allowing cells to span across more than one column or row. We'll explore these attributes below.

The other cell type is denoted by the `TD` tag with essentially the same syntax as the `TH` tag:

Syntax: TD tag for Tables

```
<TD attributes >
   Contents of a data cell
</TD>
```

In addition to the NOWRAP attribute mentioned above for the TH tag, there is also an ALIGN attribute whose value can be "left," "right," or "center" and determines how the contents of the cell are to be displayed within the cell. There is also a VALIGN (for vertical alignment) which takes values of "top," "middle," and "bottom." We'll examine the use of these table tags in an example.

Let us assume that the Island Quest Travel site is going to have a Web page with a table showing all the island tours planned for the year. The first column will denote the island, the second column will have the dates the tours start, the third column will let the user know the length of the tour (either one week or two weeks) and the last column will be the price of the tour.

Figure 4.13 shows the full TABLE tag with its content. The document tourInfo_a.html containing this table is shown in Figure 4.14 as it is rendered by a browser.

Let's examine the contents of the TABLE tag. The first tag is the CAPTION tag which results in a caption for the table. The default location is to place the caption above the table (ALIGN="top"). The choice of ALIGN="bottom" places the caption below the table. We decided to make the caption in boldface type so we have enclosed it in the B tag.

The remaining tags determine the layout and content of the table cells. The TR tag encloses the contents of a table row. There are two possible attributes, ALIGN (for horizontal alignment) and VALIGN (for vertical alignment), although we have taken the defaults and omitted these attributes. Note the use of indentation in the HTML document to allow us to quickly identify the extent of a table row.

If you view the tourInfo_a.html file you will see that, as described above, the header cells contain text which labels the contents of the corresponding columns and is usually rendered in boldface and centered within the cell.

The TD tag contains the contents of a cell. The number of cells in a row is simply determined by the number of TD tags within a TR tag. Likewise the number of rows is determined by the number of TR tags within a TABLE tag.

Creating a table

```
<TABLE BORDER="4" WIDTH="100%">
   <CAPTION ALIGN="bottom"><B>Island Tours for this
   year</B></CAPTION>
   <TR>
      <TH>Island</TH>
      <TH>Start date</TH>
      <TH>Tour length</TH>
      <TH>price</TH>
   </TR>
```

```
    <TR>
       <TD>Grand Cayman</TD>
       <TD>Feb 5, Apr 19, Jul 8, Oct 7</TD>
       <TD>One week</TD>
       <TD>$1800</TD>
    </TR>
    <TR>
       <TD>Fiji</TD>
       <TD>Jan 3, Mar 18, May 28, Jul 5</TD>
       <TD>Two weeks</TD>
       <TD>$4100</TD>
    </TR>
    <TR>
       <TD>Molokai</TD>
       <TD>Feb 18, Apr 20, Nov 8, Dec 12</TD>
       <TD>One week</TD>
       <TD>$2100</TD>
    </TR>
    <TR>
       <TD>Aruba</TD>
       <TD>Jan 18, Mar 3, Nov 20, Dec 27</TD>
       <TD>One week</TD>
       <TD>$1900</TD>
    </TR>
    <TR>
       <TD>St. Lucia</TD>
       <TD>Jan 21, Mar 1, Apr 8, Oct 8</TD>
       <TD>Two weeks</TD>
       <TD>$3000</TD>
    </TR>
</TABLE>
```

Figure 4.13

We have not used the `NOWRAP` attribute in the `TH` or `TD` tags. The default is to wrap the text if the width of the cell is insufficient to contain the text on one line.

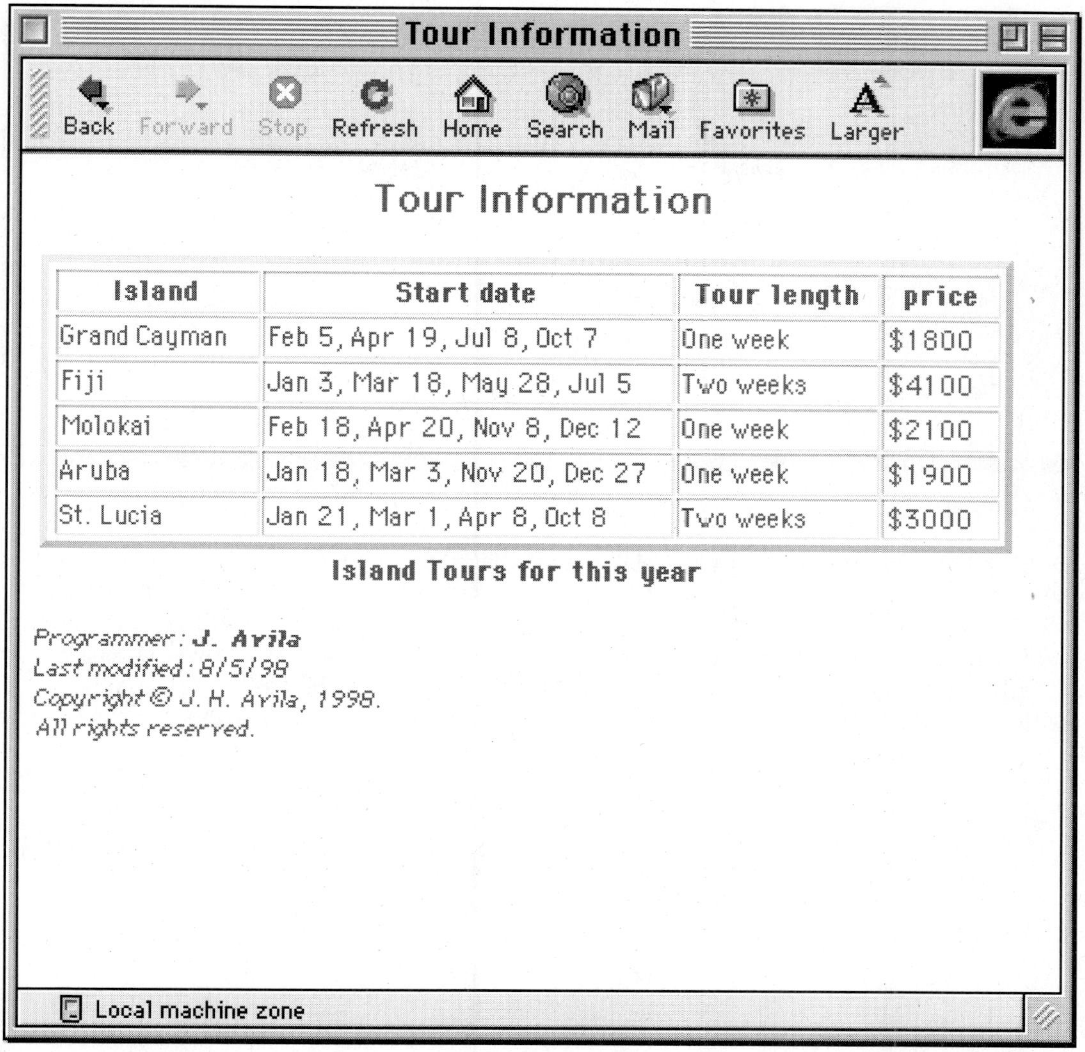

Tour Information

Island	Start date	Tour length	price
Grand Cayman	Feb 5, Apr 19, Jul 8, Oct 7	One week	$1800
Fiji	Jan 3, Mar 18, May 28, Jul 5	Two weeks	$4100
Molokai	Feb 18, Apr 20, Nov 8, Dec 12	One week	$2100
Aruba	Jan 18, Mar 3, Nov 20, Dec 27	One week	$1900
St. Lucia	Jan 21, Mar 1, Apr 8, Oct 8	Two weeks	$3000

Island Tours for this year

Programmer: ***J. Avila***
Last modified: 8/5/98
Copyright © J. H. Avila, 1998.
All rights reserved.

Figure 4.14

The other attributes for the `TH` and `TD` tags that we will consider are the `ROWSPAN` and `COLSPAN`. These are used to allow a cell to span more than a single row or column. An example will help clarify the idea. Suppose that we wish to modify the table of Figure 4.13 so that we show two-week tours to Aruba as well as the present one-week tours. Instead of having two rows with Aruba as the named island, we want to simply let the cell containing the name Aruba to span two rows. This is done by modifying the appropriate row as shown in Figure 4.15.

Creating a table with overlapping cells

```
<TR>
   <TD ROWSPAN="2">Aruba</TD>
   <TD>Jan 18, Mar 3, Nov 20, Dec 27</TD>
   <TD>One week</TD>
   <TD>$1900</TD>
</TR>
<TR>
   <TD> Apr 9, May 10</TD>
   <TD>Two weeks</TD>
   <TD>$3000</TD>
</TR>
```

Figure 4.15

Now we have two rows. The first row has `ROWSPAN="2"` in the first cell to indicate that this cell will span two rows. We continue with the remaining `TD` tags for this row. In the next row we now only provide the `TD` tags for the cells following the first since the place of the first is being occupied by the cell in the previous row that spans two rows. Thus there are only three `TD` tags for this row instead of the four for each of the other rows. The resulting table is in the file `tourInfo_b.html` and is shown in Figure 4.16.

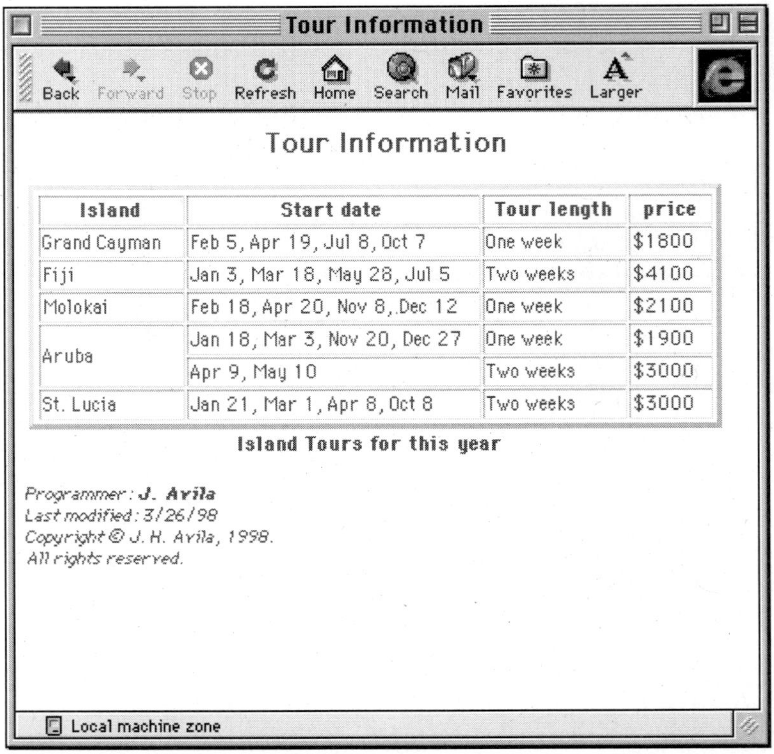

Figure 4.16

Tables are quite flexible and we will examine their use in the following box as well as in the exercises.

Using tables for layout control

Tables can be used to achieve better layout control when you want to obtain certain effects. Since table cells can contain essentially any HTML element, we can place images as well as text more accurately on the page by the use of tables. As an example, suppose we want to get an effect like that shown in Figure 4.17. Without tables it would not be possible. With tables, it is not difficult.

Figure 4.17

The way is to map out a cell structure as shown in Figure 4.18. We have a grid of two rows and three columns. The first cell of the first row will span two columns and the third cell will span two rows. Earlier we saw the use of the `ROWSPAN` attribute. There is a `COLSPAN` attribute that works in a similar way. We will use that in this example.

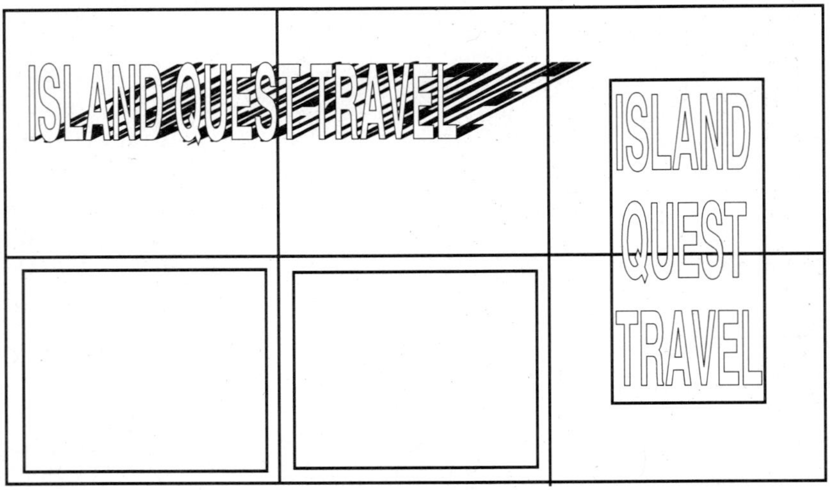

Figure 4.18

The HTML to accomplish this is shown in Figure 4.19 (see `islandLog.html`). It's important to make sure you have the right number of cells in each row (taking any cells that span rows or columns) or the effect may be quite strange. The other thing that is important to remember is to set the value of the `BORDER` attribute to 0 so that the underlying cell structure doesn't intrude on the visual effect.

It's important to realize that there is a downside to the use of tables in this way. For those users without a browser that supports tables the result will be a Web page that will bear little resemblance to the look that you were trying to achieve. Since both Netscape and Internet Explorer support tables and since tables are included as part of HTML 3.2, this should not be a serious problem.

```
<TABLE WIDTH="100%" BORDER="0">
<TR>
   <TH COLSPAN=2><H2><I>Island Quest Travel</I></H2></TH>
   <TD ROWSPAN="2"><IMG SRC="Graphics/IQTravel_vert.gif"></TD>
</TR>
<TR>
  <TD>
  <I>Island Quest Travel </I>can take you to exotic locations
  where you can walk in the footsteps of buccaneers and adven-
  turers from the past. We can take you to places that are just
  dots on the map.
  </TD>
```

```
   <TD>We'll fly you there and back and even provide guides for
   special treks into jungles. Or if you prefer the sailing
   adventure, we will gather a crew and a ship and let you
   cruise mysterious islands.
   </TD>
</TR>
</TABLE>
```

Figure 4.19

Section review questions

True or false

1. The number of rows and columns in a table is determined by the value of the `ROWS` and `COLS` attributes.

2. The `WIDTH` attribute of the `TABLE` tag allows us to determine the percentage of the total browser window width that will be occupied by the table.

3. The `BORDER` attribute of the `TABLE` tag allows you to eliminate a border around the cells in a table.

4. If `ALIGN="top"` for the `CAPTION` tag, then the table caption will be placed just above the table on the page.

5. If the following appears within the contents of a `TABLE` tag

```
<TR>
      <TH> Level 1 </TH>
      <TH> Level 2 </TH>
      <TH> Level 3 </TH>
</TR>
```

then the table will have at least three columns when it is displayed on the screen.

6. In order to get a cell to "overlap" the adjacent cell in the same row, use `ROWSPAN="2"`.

7. In order to get a cell to "overlap" the adjacent cell in the same column, use `ROWSPAN="2"`.

8. If a cell in one row overlaps its neighbor in the same row, then one should have one fewer `TH` or `TD` tag in that row than the number of columns in the table.

9. If we use the `TABLE` tag for layout control, then we may use the `ROWSPAN` or `COLSPAN` attributes.

Multiple choice

10. The `NOWRAP` attribute of the `TH` or `TD` tag will force all items in the cell to be displayed on
    (a) one line.
    (b) one line unless this would cause the table to be wider than the browser window.
    (c) one line unless this would cause the cell contents to be wider than the browser window.
    (d) one line unless you use the `BR` tag.

11. You can achieve a two-column text format on a Web document by
    (a) using the `TABLE` tag with each row cell having `COLSPAN="2"`.
    (b) using the `TABLE` tag with one row and two columns with each cell containing one column of text.
    (c) using the `TABLE` tag with one column but with `COLSPAN="2"` in each cell.
    (d) none of the above.

Short excursion exercises

1. Create a simple HTML document with a `FORM` that has only a submit button. Use `http://web-archipelago.com/cgi-bin/Echo` for the value of the `ACTION` attribute. What data (if any) get transmitted to the Web server?

2. Modify the `RFI.html` document so that instead of just allowing a single line for the "places" field, the user has a space consisting of three lines into which to type a response.

3. Change the submit button in the `RFI.html` document so that the text on the button is "Request Info."

4. Pretend the request for information required that the user supply a password. Place a password field in the document shown in `RFI.html` with additional information asking the user to supply their Island Quest Traveler's password.

5. Place a hidden field in the document with the data "user number: 1234". Make sure the data is correctly transmitted to the Web server by using the Echo program as before in the `ACTION` attribute of the `FORM` tag.

6. Experiment with the form in the document `textarea.html`. In particular, what happens if you enter data into the `TEXTAREA` field that extends beyond the right edge

of the text entry box? Does text wrap? What happens if you enter more lines than the number originally created in the `TEXTAREA` tag?

7. In the file `islandChoice_a.html` modify the pop-up menu to add two more islands: Tahiti and Curacao. Make Curacao the default.

8. Modify the `islandChoice_a.html` file so that there is one more menu item which reads "select an island". Make this the default. Pick an appropriate `VALUE` for this selection and view the data received by the Web server by using the Echo program in the `ACTION` attribute.

9. Add another checkbox to the `islandChoice_b.html` file which asks the user if he or she would like to receive information on travel insurance.

10. Modify the `islandChoice_c.html` file so that the "length" family of radio buttons is placed vertically (one above the other).

11. Modify the `islandChoice_c.html` file so that the "season" family of radio buttons is placed on two lines. The Spring and Summer buttons are on the first line, and the Fall and Winter buttons are on the next line.

12. Add another row to the table in `tourInfo_a.html`. This row will advertise trips to Victoria Island starting on June 15, July 1 and July 30, each of one-week length. The cost is $1200.

13. Add another column to the table in tourInfo_a.html. This column will contain the number of persons each trip can handle. Let the column heading be "Persons." Then make up numbers for each of the islands and place these numbers in the last column of the table.

14. Start with the file `tourInfo_b.html` and add one-week trips to Fiji starting Feb 3, May 1 and June 6. The cost is $2500. Be sure that the cell containing the island name extends across the two rows containing the data for that island.

15. Earlier in the book we mentioned a number of rules that Roger Black listed as things you should do in your Web pages. Well, he also has a list of things you should not do. Here are a few. For each one, find an example on the Web where the developer has not followed the suggestion.

    1. *Don't confuse the viewer.* Viewers should be able to move about your Web site and know that they are still in the same site. Don't change the background from one page to the next. A navigational bar may be the same on each page instead of having different navigational aids on different pages.

    2. *Don't make oversize pages.* Lots of people use laptops to view the Web Not everyone has a 17-inch monitor. If they have to scroll (especially horizontally), viewers will simply walk away. The rule of thumb is to design for 480 x 640 pixel monitors.

3. *Don't use big, slow graphics.* We displayed graphically in an earlier chapter the amount of time that it takes to download an image as a function of its size. The bottom line is that any delay is annoying and big graphics images mean a big delay. People are not patient on the Web.

4. *Don't have a lot of text.* People want their facts quickly. Books are for reading, Web pages are for obtaining information quickly. Give viewers the opportunity to go right to what they want to read without having to read what they're not interested in.

Longer voyage exercises

16. Create a simple HTML document with a form that asks the user for their name and address. Use the `Echo` program in the `ACTION` attribute of the `FORM` tag to view the data received by the server. Do you think that a `TEXTAREA` field is better for the name and address or a series of `TEXT` fields?

17. Take the previous HTML document or create a new HTML document with at least two form fields and alter it so that two fields have the same `NAME` attribute. What do you observe about the data returned to you from the server? Try changing the order of the fields in the document and see if there is any effect.

18. Create an HTML form document which will be a "guest book." Let the user supply his or her name. Solicit comments about the Island Quest Travel Web site. Place a link to the guest book page in one of the Island Quest Travel Home page examples.

19. Put together an HTML form document that you might use for a student registration form. Ask the student for his or her name and student ID number. Use a pop-up menu to determine the student's grade level in school. Instead of picking one of the possible values (Freshman, Sophomore, etc.) as a default, add an extra menu item labeled "Pick your grade level" and make it the default.

20. Create a registration form for the Island Quest Travel Web site. What information will you need in order to be able to communicate with the customer later? Be sure not to ask for information that is sensitive such as a social security number. You should also collect information that will help you tailor your mailings to your customer. Find out if the customer is interested in cruises or in land excursions, for example. Find out if the customer is interested in family excursions or in small "adventure groups."

    Use your imagination.

21. Assume you have a customer named *Lampoon* that sells a number of items:
    desk lamp model D-3
    desk lamp model D-5
    table lamp model T-2
    table lamp model T-4

Put together an HTML form document that is an order form. The `SELECT` tag allows the attributes of `SIZE` and `MULTIPLE` (in addition to the one examined in the chapter). The value of the `SIZE` attribute determines the number of options visible to the user (the default is one). If the `MULTIPLE` attribute is present (it doesn't take a value), then the user can select more than one of the options. Use these attributes to allow the user to view all the lamp models and to be able to order any (or all) of them.

22. Add to the previous exercise the ability for the user to indicate how many of each lamp model he or she wants to buy.

23. Put together an HTML document that will let the user take the following multiple-choice exam. Be sure to get the name of the user.

    For each question respond (a) if you agree, (b) if you don't have an opinion on the matter, or (c) if you disagree.

    a. If you like computers, you will do well as a Web developer.
    b. Some people have a natural ability to develop computer software.
    c. Education only unlocks the potential in what was "destined" to be a good Web developer.
    d. Anyone can learn to program a computer at some level.

24. Develop an HTML form document to let a user fill in the following questionnaire.

    Name:
    Check all those that apply.

    a. I exercise regularly.
    b. I have colds frequently.
    c. I am almost never sick.
    d. I have good eating habits.
    e. I eat too much "junk food."
    f. I drink fruit juices at least once a day.
    g. I drink fewer than 3 cups of coffee a day.

25. Build a Web page for a customer who wants to sell rugs. Your page will contain a table where the first column is the rug pattern, the second is the available dominant color and the third is the size. The contents of the table should be as shown below.

Rug types

Pattern	**Dominant color**	**Size (in feet)**
Leaf and flower	green	8 x 10
hexagonal	deep blue	12 x 18
interlocking ovals	maroon	6 x 10
spiral weave	off-white	10 x 12

26. Create a Web page that will display sample text in each of the 16 named colors given in Section 2.2. Use a table with four columns and use the `FONT` tag with the `COLOR` attribute to display the color name in the appropriate color. Place a caption below the table to indicate the contents of the table.

27. In this exercise we will use the `COLSPAN` attribute accompanying the `TD` or `TH` tags. Change the table for the Island Tour Information page so that instead of a column indicating Tour Length, there are two columns (entitled "One week" and "Two weeks") with the X character placed in the appropriate column for each set of tours.

28. Assume that Figure 4.20 represents a cross-section of a downtown three-story building. Use a table to represent this on a Web page. Let each cell be linked to a section in a separate Web page that contains a description of each of the businesses. Provide that separate page with six sections of text for the six businesses with the appropriate anchor tags.

City View Restaurant		
Jackson & Franks Law Office	H. Nguyen Graphics Design	
Ray's Guitar Shop	Sergio's Web Services	Ellie's Sidewalk Cafe

Figure 4.20

29. Aligning form fields can be difficult, especially if they are not up against the left margin of the document. Create an HTML form document or modify one used in this chapter so that the form fields are placed in a table. In particular, make the table so that the fields are aligned in a right-most column with the text explaining the form to the left of each field.

30. Modify `islandChoice_c.html` so that two families of radio buttons appear vertically side-by-side as in the following diagram.

I would prefer to travel during:	I am interested in trips of length:
◉ Spring ○ Summer ○ Fall ○ Winter	◉ One week ○ Two weeks

To get the alignment, you will have to use a table. Remember that essentially any HTML element can be placed in a table cell.

31. Create an HTML document that will serve as a reference of the different form types and how they appear when displayed. Use a table with two columns. Each row will correspond to one of the form types. In the first cell, place the HTML code for the form. In the second cell, display the results of the HTML in the first cell. As an example, here's one of the rows as it would be rendered by the browser. How can you preserve the indentation and text alignment in the left cell? Re-read the material on metacharacters in Section 2. 2.

<table>
<tr>
<td>Sample HTML:<pre>

      <INPUT TYPE="radio" NAME="season"
              VALUE="spring">Spring
      <INPUT TYPE="radio" NAME="season"
              VALUE="summer" CHECKED>Summer
      <INPUT TYPE="radio" NAME="season"
              VALUE="fall">Fall
      <INPUT TYPE="radio" NAME="season"
              VALUE="winter">Winter
</pre></td>
<td>What it looks like:

○Spring ◉Summer ○Fall ○Winter</td>
</tr>
</table>

5. Dynamic Content and Extensions: Applets and Frames

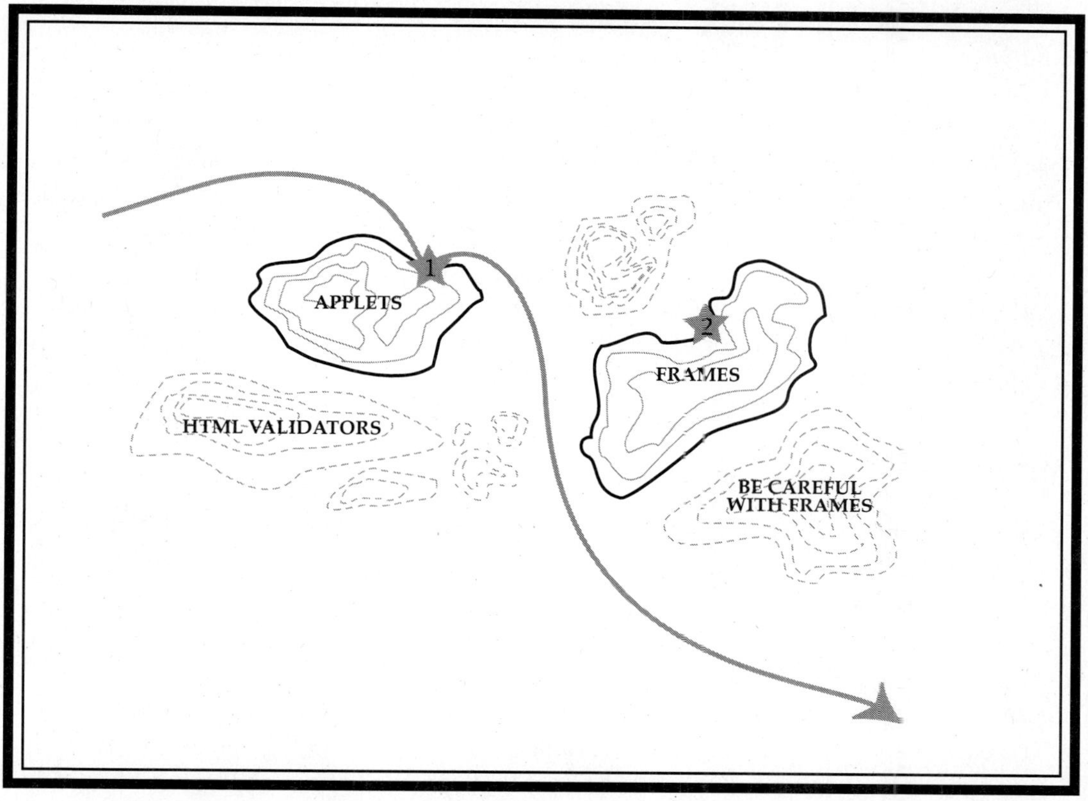

Chapter Preview

5.1 Applets
We start by examining the nature of an applet—what it is and how it works with browsers. We also consider some of the concerns about downloading executable code to your machine from an unknown server. Finally, we show how to access applets from your Web documents.

5.2 Frames
The frames concept is an HTML extension that allows the browser window to be divided into sub-windows (frames) each displaying their own HTML document. We learn how to do this using the tags used by Netscape and Microsoft. We also examine the downside of working with frames.

5.1 Applets

Introduction to applets

So far we have seen that HTML documents provide a means of presenting text and graphics to a user. Hyperlinks extend the ability of the user to move from one document to another in a non-linear way. Forms allow the user to return information to a server where server-side applications can process the information. With applets, the capabilities of Web documents are extended even further so that executable applications can be downloaded from a server to run on the user's machine using the browser as an intermediary.

Creating applets is beyond the scope of this book. Here we are looking at how to execute existing applets from Web pages that we create. It is important to have an overview of what applets are and how they work.

What are applets?

Applets are written in a language called Java. They are executable programs that can do most things that programs in any other language can do. There are certain features of Java, however, that make these programs especially suited to the Web.

In Figure 5.1 we give a very simplified picture of traditional software development. Most programs (in any language) are written with a text editor. The resulting text file is read and processed by a program called a compiler to produce a file containing machine code. The file produced by the compiler is the application that you execute usually by double-clicking on an icon or entering its name in a window. The machine code consists of instructions that your particular computer will recognize. For example a program written in the C++ language may be compiled to be run on an Intel Pentium processor. This compiled version of the program cannot run on a Macintosh PowerPC processor or a Sun Microsystems SPARC processor. To get a version of the same program for one of the other platforms requires a different version of the program instructions in the text file and a different compiler.

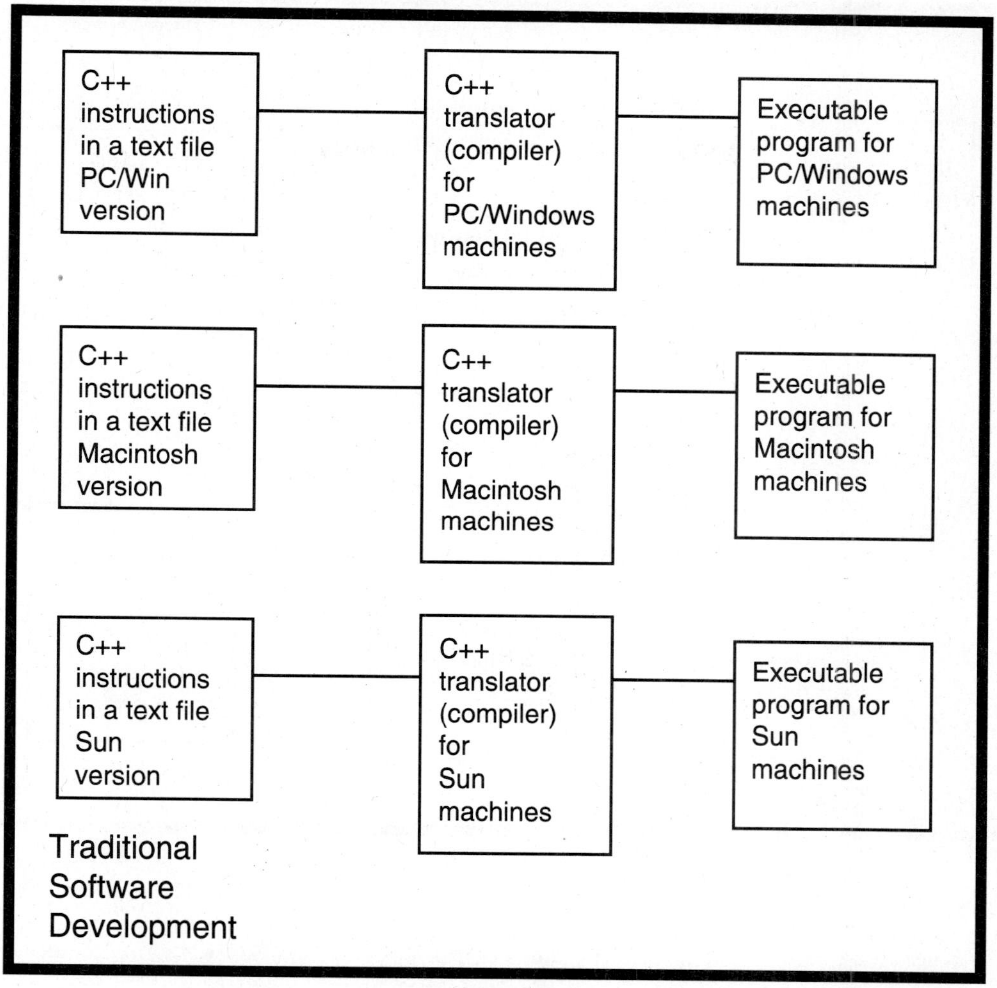

Figure 5.1

The developers of Java decided to modify this approach in the following way (see Figure 5.2). They created a *virtual* processor with its own instruction set. Virtual processors are conceptual, not physically implemented in hardware (although they could be). The instruction set for this virtual machine is similar to that of most modern processors but is not specific to any processor. The machine code for this virtual machine has been named *byte code*. Java compilers convert text files with Java language statements into byte code. The conversion from byte code to the local machine language for an Intel Pentium or a Macintosh PowerPC or other processors is not difficult and Java-capable browsers do this for you when you download a Java applet. The end result is that Java applets in their byte code form (on the server) can be downloaded to your local processor and converted to run on your local processor regardless of the type. Suddenly one can write applications once that will execute on any processor that supports a Java-capable browser.

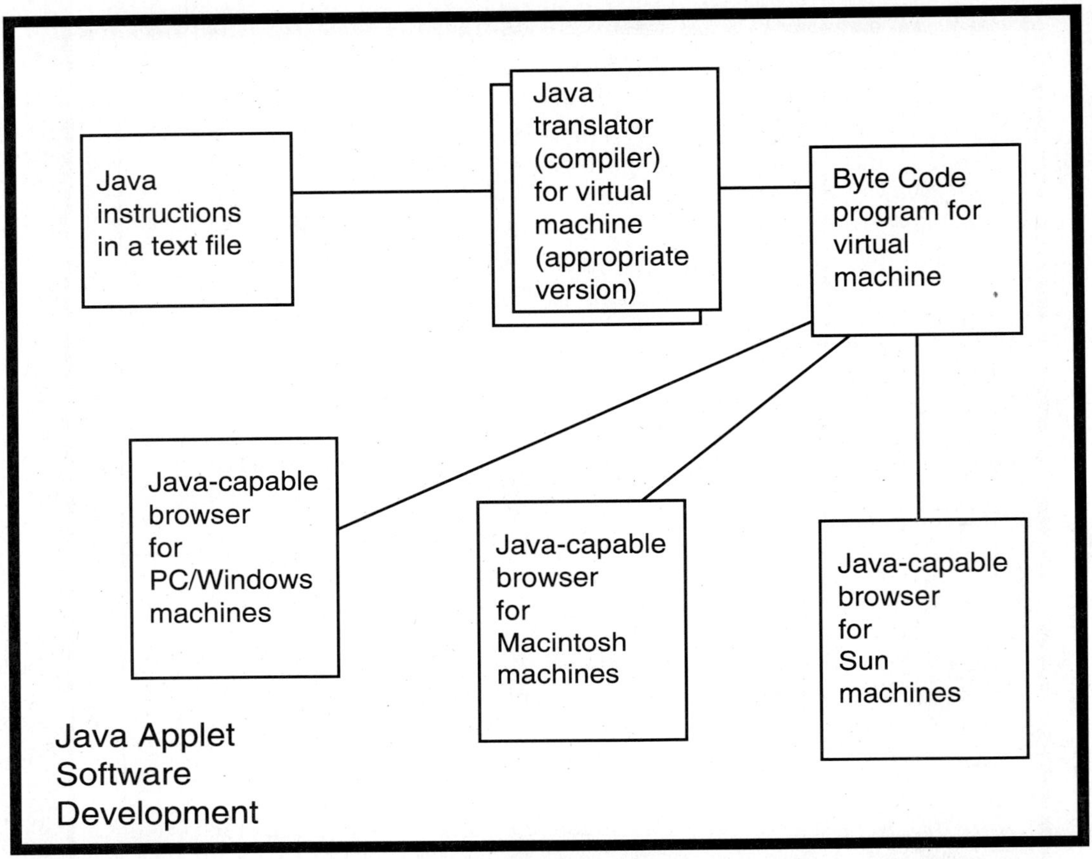

Figure 5.2

Security concerns

What about security? Generally, it is not a good idea to download executable code to your computer from an unknown source. Sadly, there are people who could probably contribute to society positively who are instead unable to direct their talents in that direction. They write software that may just type a "Gotcha" message on your screen or may trash the data on your hard disk.

The developers of Java have anticipated concerns about such software and written the language with the intention of making it as difficult as possible for malicious software to find its way to your machine. Java does not support certain features that are exploited by hackers. Moreover, not only does the compiler enforce the language rules that make Java very secure but the Java software "engine" that runs the byte code within the browser tests to make sure the code has not been tampered with at the byte code level. The end result is a language that has been made extremely safe.

Running a Java applet

HTML supports Java applets by means of the `APPLET` tag This tag has several attributes. For example, the following shows how you would include a particular applet in an HTML document. This applet will produce the image shown in Figure 5.3. The assumption here is that the `ZoomText.class` file named in the `CODE` attribute is located in the same directory as the HTML document in which the `APPLET` tag appears. (The `ZoomText.class` file is located on the enclosed CD ROM or via the Web-Archipelago site.)

```
<APPLET CODE="ZoomText.class" WIDTH=400 HEIGHT=100>
  <PARAM NAME="text" VALUE="Island Quest Travel">
  <PARAM NAME="backGroundColor" VALUE="black">
  <PARAM NAME="fontSize" VALUE="36">
  <PARAM NAME="fontName" VALUE="Helvetica">
  <PARAM NAME="fontBGcolor" VALUE="cyan">
  <PARAM NAME="fontFGcolor" VALUE="red">
   This applet is viewable only with a Java-capable browser.
</APPLET>
```

Figure 5.3

The `APPLET` tag has several attributes. `CODE`, `WIDTH`, and `HEIGHT` are required. These tell the browser the location of the byte code for the applet (the value of the `CODE` attribute), and the width and height (in pixels) of the area in the browser window used to display the applet.

Some applets such as this one can accept parameters from the HTML document that called them. The name of these parameters and their acceptable values are determined by the writer of the applet. The parameters and their values appear in `PARAM` tags within the contents of the `APPLET` tag. Each parameter requires a separate `PARAM` tag.

This particular applet is capable of displaying zoom text of many colors. The `NAME-VALUE` pairs for this applet allow any user to define the text to be displayed and to set the window's background color. In addition, the user can specify the font name and size and the color of the text itself. One color for the "zoomed" portion as well as another color for the text at the "top" of the zoomed text.

Programmer Note

The colors recognized by the ZoomText applet are:

black	blue	cyan	darkGray
gray	green	lightGray	magenta
orange	pink	red	white
yellow			

Finally, the plain text within the contents of the `APPLET` tag (after the last `PARAM` tag) is only displayed if the browser being used is not Java-capable. This is the only way to let the user know that the empty space he or she is looking at should have contained an applet but that the browser is not able to display it.

Another applet

The previous applet can be used as a utility by a Web master. In fact, we will explore its use in the exercises. Many applets are just fun "eye candy" that can provide something that will capture the attention of the user (usually involving animation). The next applet falls into this category. The `APPLET` tag is now

```
<APPLET CODE=Origami.class WIDTH=100 HEIGHT=100>
If you had a Java-capable browser, you could see
some cool graphics here.
</APPLET>
```

In this one the only choice the person writing the HTML document has is how big a window to provide. In this applet, the user will see what appears to be a piece of colored paper folded so that it appears to be three connected triangles with different colors on each side of each triangle. The colored triangles fold and rotate in the window and get progressively smaller as the applet runs. Two snapshots of the Origami applet are shown in Figure 5.4. The applet itself can be found on the enclosed CD or on the Web-Archipelago site.

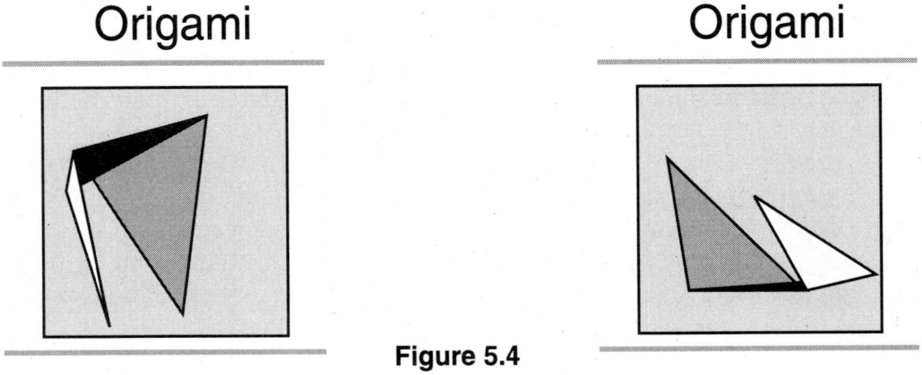

Figure 5.4

As an indication of how small some of these applets can be, the Origami applet file contains about 3K bytes and the ZoomText applet above is contained in a file of less than 3K bytes. Given that image files that appear on typical HTML documents are often ten times that size, it gives you an appreciation of the power of such applets.

What are the restrictions on applets?

Applets can do most things that any other programs can do. Text and graphics can be displayed, for example, and users can interact with such programs. For security reasons, however, an applet downloaded by a browser and running on a user's machine cannot

- read or write a file on the user's local system,
- get file information (such as directory information),
- delete a file, or
- run another program on the user's local system.

Applets can, however, communicate with the server that delivered the applet (the host server). In particular, an applet can have a program run on the host server as well as read and write files on the host server. Figure 5.5 illustrates the access available to a Java applet.

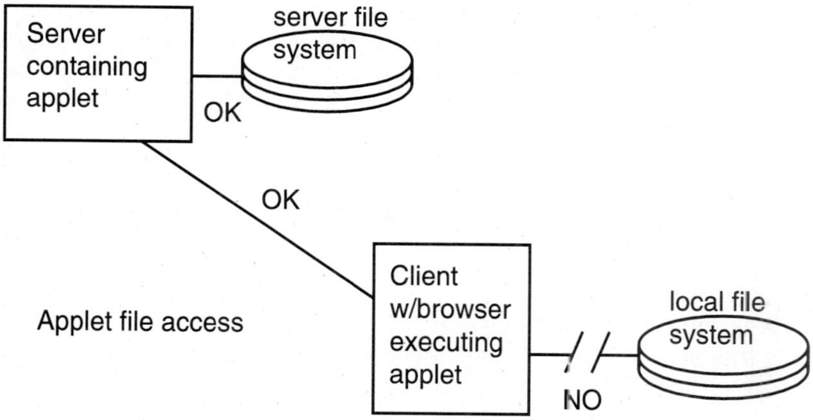

Figure 5.5

The applets that we've examined here only give a small demonstration of the capabilities of this feature for HTML documents.

What do you need to supply applets in your HTML documents?

Putting it all together, if you want to provide an applet within a Web page, you need the following:

1. A `.class` file containing the byte code for the applet. This byte code can only be produced by a Java compiler. This is the file that the Java code developer will give to you.
2. An `APPLET` tag within the HTML document with the `CODE` attribute set to the

name of the class file. This file name can be relative to the location of the HTML document or can be an absolute `URL` anywhere on the internet.
3. Appropriate values for the `WIDTH` and `HEIGHT` attributes of the `APPLET` tag.
4. `PARAM` tags for each parameter that the applet expects to obtain from `APPLET` tag contents. This requires the correct `NAME` attribute with appropriate `VALUE` settings.
5. On the client side: a Java-capable browser that can execute the Java byte code.

Where can you get applets for your HTML documents?

There are a number of sites on the Web where you can get applets to download and use. Some of these require that you reimburse the author. Some are generously provided by applet authors. Usually these applets are supplied as byte code. That is, they are "ready to use."

A great place to start looking for applets is `http://www.gamelan.com/` where you will find a wide variety of Java applets to try out.

HTML Validators

Now that we've examined the major features of HTML it's important to point out that HTML is a dynamic language that is continually being modified to incorporate new features. Partly fueling this constant change is the "browser war" primarily between Netscape and Microsoft to gain market share. Each vendor wants to have the most attractive features for the documents that its browser can support.

If you incorporate features in your HTML documents that are only viewable by users with a particular browser, then you will limit the audience that can view those documents.

Since each browser is committed to supporting the most recent HTML standard, one way to verify that your documents are viewable by anyone with the major browsers is to make sure that the HTML features that you use are supported by the standard.

There are HTML *validators* available to check your HTML documents. These validators are programs that are accessible through the Web and allow you to supply the URL of the document you want to check. Then the validator fetches your document, checks it out against the HTML rules and reports back to you on the results of the check. Check the Web-Archipelago site for locations of HTML validators.

Most validators require that you supply an additional line at the very beginning of your HTML document (**before** the `<HTML>` opening tag). The line has the following form

```
<!DOCTYPE HTML PUBLIC "-//W3C//DTD HTML 3.2 Final//EN">
```

This somewhat cryptic line identifies the standards body (World Wide Web Consortium—W3C) as well as the version of HTML against which your document will be tested.

Section review questions

True or false

1. Applets are elements supplied with the browser somewhat like a software library.
2. One of the direct benefits of Java is that only one version of the program needs to be written despite the computer types on which the program will execute.
3. Java applets need to be downloaded only from trusted locations since they can easily contain viruses.
4. Java applets are checked by the software that executes these programs in the browser to make sure they have not been altered in their byte code form to introduce viruses.
5. The appearance of the output of a Java applet is determined by the programmer and cannot be altered by the HTML author.
6. The `PARAM` tag is used to set parameter values within an applet.
7. If we change the size of the font in the ZoomText applet, then we probably will have to change the value of the `WIDTH` and `HEIGHT` attributes of the `APPLET` tag.
8. We can select alternate `NAME` values for the `PARAM` tag if we don't like the ones that are originally given.
9. The value of the `CODE` attribute must always be the name of the file containing the byte code for the applet.
10. The file containing the byte code for the applet must reside in the same directory (folder) as the one containing the HTML document in which the `APPLET` tag appears.
11. Some applets do not require `PARAM` tags.
12. Unfortunately Java applets will take a long time to download because they are rather large files.
13. Java applets cannot read or write files on your hard disk but they can get information about the names of files and directories.
14. Java applets cannot delete files on your hard disk but they can read their contents.

15. Java applets can send data back to the server from which they came.

16. The only applets that you can use with your HTML documents are ones for which you have acquired the byte code versions.

Multiple choice

17. Applets
    (a) can be written in any programming language.
    (b) can only execute on the server.
    (c) must be written in the Java programming language.
    (d) none of the above.

18. Byte code
    (a) is the name of the machine code for a Java virtual machine.
    (b) is an intermediate form for Java programs that must later be translated into local machine code for particular computers.
    (c) is processed and executed within a Java-capable browser.
    (d) all of the above.
    (e) none of the above.

19. The `APPLET` tag
    (a) is the mechanism by which the Java applets are downloaded and executed as part of an HTML document.
    (b) determines the location within an HTML document where the output from a Java applet will be displayed.
    (c) will cause browsers that are not Java capable to "crash".
    (d) (a) and (b).
    (e) none of the above.

20. To convey a message to the user of a non-Java-capable browser that an applet cannot run,
    (a) add a `MSG` attribute to the `APPLET` tag with a value which will be a message to be displayed in the browser window.
    (b) place the message as part of the content of the `APPLET` tag.
    (c) add a `PARAM` tag within the content of the `APPLET` tag whose `NAME` value is "message" and whose `VALUE` is the message itself.
    (d) none of the above.

21. In order to provide an applet in one of your HTML documents, you must
    (a) embed the byte code in the HTML document.
    (b) place the byte code in the same directory as the HTML document.
    (c) be sure that the user will have a Java-capable browser.
    (d) select values for the `WIDTH` and `HEIGHT` attributes of the `APPLET` tag.
    (e) none of the above.

22. Validators are
    (a) programs that you can download to check your HTML documents for compliance with the HTML standards.
    (b) programs that are accessible on the Web that will let you test to see if you are using Java applets correctly.
    (c) programs that are accessible on the Web that will let you submit the URL for any HTML document that you want to check for compliance with the HTML standards.
    (d) none of the above.

5.2 Frames

Frames are an extension of HTML although both Netscape's browser and Microsoft's Internet Explorer support them. Using this extension, one can divide the browser window into "sub-windows," each displaying its own HTML document. With the introduction of frames there are two types of HTML documents. There are the usual documents which are called *body documents* which contain text and graphics for display. These are the ones we have been creating up to this point. In addition, there are *frameset documents* that tell the browser how to partition the browser window and which documents to display in each sub-window. Figure 5.6 illustrates the relationship between these two types of HTML documents. The frameset document establishes the layout of the individual sub-windows which are called frames. In addition it determines the initial documents to be placed in each frame.

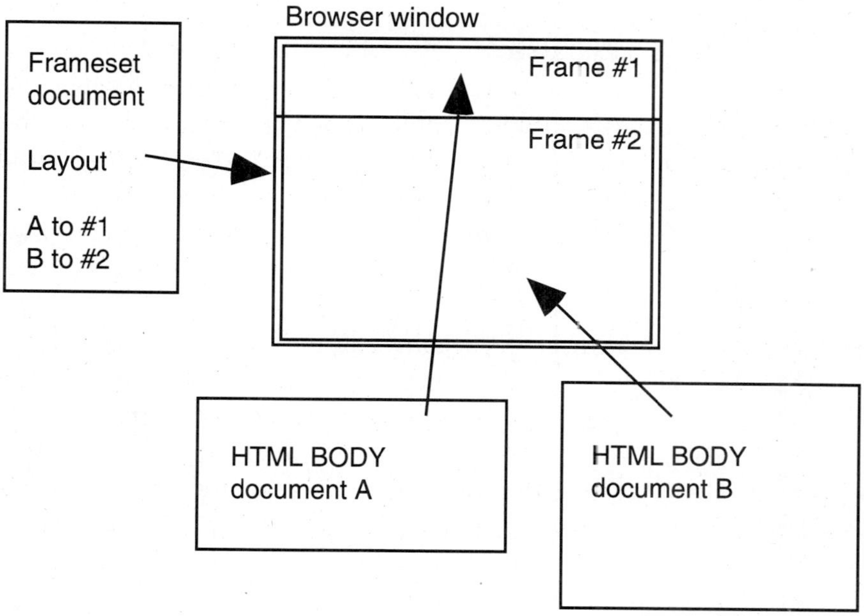

Figure 5.6

In order to clearly understand the concepts, we will re-do the Island Quest Travel site to use frames. We will partition the browser window into a narrow window on top and a second below occupying the rest of the "real estate" (see Figure 5.7). The upper window will contain an image and three text hyperlinks immediately below the image. The lower window will contain one of three different HTML documents depending on which link the user chooses in the upper window.

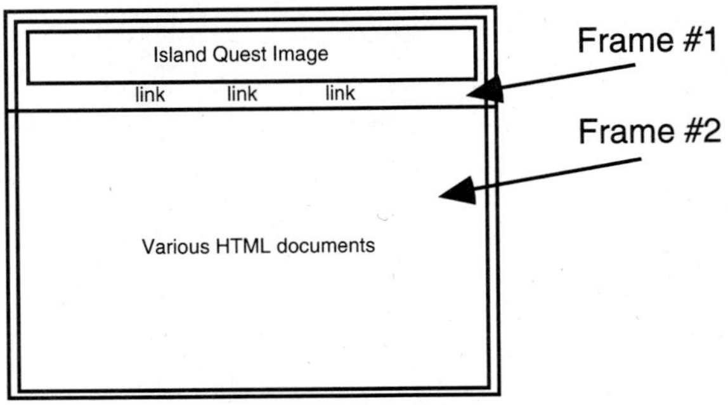

Figure 5.7

Notice that we will be clicking on a text link in the upper window and changing the contents of the lower window. This is one of the powerful features of frames. Let's see how to put this together.

Frameset documents

The frameset document tells the browser how to divide its window and what to place initially in each frame. In a frameset document, the `BODY` tag is replaced by the `FRAMESET` tag. Figure 5.8 shows the frameset document for the Island Quest Travel site and Figure 5.9 shows how it is rendered by the browser. The opening `FRAMESET` tag shows the attribute `ROWS` with a value equal to a two-item list. The fact that `ROWS` is the attribute (see the Syntax rule following Figure 5.9) tells the browser that the window should be divided horizontally.

The fact that there are two elements in the item list tells the browser that there are two sub-windows. If the attribute had been `COLS` then the window would be partitioned vertically. The number of elements in the value list determines the number of partitions.

Finally, the values of 80 and * tell the browser to use 80 pixels for the height of the upper portion and to let the lower window take up the rest of the space (again, see the Syntax rule).

File: IQTravel_frameset.html

```
<HTML>
<!--File: IQTravel_frameset.html-->
<!--Project: frames-->
<!--See the comment below for additional information-->
<HEAD>
   <TITLE>Island Quest Frameset document</TITLE>
</HEAD>
<FRAMESET ROWS="80, *">
   <FRAME SRC="IQTravel_head.html"
          SCROLLING="no"
          MARGINHEIGHT="0" MARGINWIDTH="0">
   <FRAME SRC="IQTravel_home.html" NAME="content">
</FRAMESET>
<!--
   Programmer: J. Avila<BR>
   Last modified: 8/5/98<BR>
   Copyright &copy; J. H. Avila, 1998.<BR>
   All rights reserved.
-->
</HTML>
```

Figure 5.8

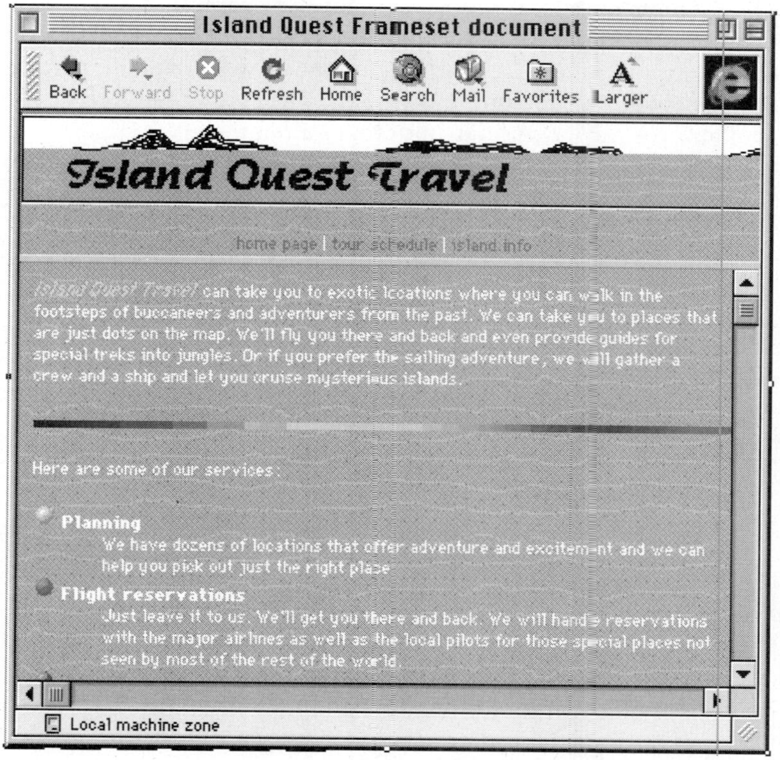

Figure 5.9

Syntax rule

The `FRAMESET` tag takes one of two attributes: `ROWS` or `COLS`. If `ROWS` is present, the browser window is divided into horizontal sub-windows, if `COLS` is present, the browser window is divided into vertical sub-windows.

The value of either the `ROWS` or `COLS` attribute is a comma-separated list of items. The number of items in the list determines the number of partitions into which the browser window is to be divided. Each item denotes the space allocated to each partition.

Each item is one of the following forms:

- an integer (e.g. 80) indicating number of pixels
- a percentage (e.g. 50%)
- the * character which tells the browser to allocate an equal amount of area to each partition not assigned values using an integer or percentage. (For example, if there are four partitions and one of them has been given the value of 50 pixels, another has been given the value of 30%, and the * character is used for the remaining two partitions. The browser takes what's left after the first two partitions and assigns half of this remaining area to the third and the other half to the fourth partition.)

The contents of the `FRAMESET` tag, for our example, consist of two `FRAME` tags. The first one will correspond to the upper sub-window; the second will correspond to the lower sub-window. The `FRAME` tag will tell the browser what to place in each of the frames initially when the document is viewed. The syntax rule below describes the attributes available for the `FRAME` tag and their values.

Syntax rule

The `FRAME` tag will accept six attributes:

- `SRC=`"*url*" where *url* corresponds to the HTML (body document) that will be displayed in the designated frame initially.
- `NAME=`"*frame_name*" where *frame_name* is any string that uniquely identifies the frame. This name will be used to allow links in one frame to have actions in other frames.
- `NORESIZE` The presence of this attribute tells the browser that the frame is not allowed to be re-sized by the user.
- `SCROLLING=`"*value*" where value is either "yes," "no," or "auto." If "yes" then the sub-window for this frame will be scrollable, if "no" then the sub-window will not be scrollable. If "auto" then the window will be scrollable if necessary to accommodate the contents.
- `MARGINHEIGHT=`"*value*" or `MARGINWIDTH=`"*value*" where *value* is the number of pixels that should be used for the margin between the content of the frame sub-window and the edge of the frame itself.

As we see in Figure 5.8 the upper frame will initially contain the HTML document, `IQTravel_head.html`, it will not have a scroll bar and there will be no margin between the content of the frame and the border. The lower frame will initially contain the document `IQTravel_home.html` and will have the name "content" associated with that frame. It is this initial state that we see in Figure 5.9.

Hyperlinks in frame documents

Examine the document in Figure 5.10. This was named in the `FRAME` tag in Figure 5.8 as the document to be displayed in the upper sub-window.

File: IQTravel_head.html

```
<HTML>
<!--File: IQTravel_head.html-->
<!--Project: frames-->
<!--See the comment below for additional information-->
<HEAD>
  <TITLE>Island Quest Header</TITLE>
</HEAD>
<BODY>
<CENTER>
  <IMG SRC="graphics/island_horizon.gif">

  <A HREF="IQTravel_home.html" TARGET="content">home page</A> |
  <A HREF="IQTravel_tours.html"
     TARGET="content">tour schedule</A> |
  <A HREF="island_RFI.html" TARGET="content">island info</A>
</CENTER>
<!--
  Programmer: J. Avila <BR>
  avila@web-archipelago.com<BR>
  Last modified: 8/5/98<BR>
  Copyright &copy; J. H. Avila, 1998. <BR>
  All rights reserved.
-->
</BODY>
</HTML>
```

Figure 5.10

In each of the three hyperlinks we have an attribute `TARGET` whose value must correspond to the name placed in the `NAME` attribute of a `FRAME` tag. In fact, if you examine Figure 5.8 you will see that the `FRAME` tag that identifies the initial contents of the lower sub-window has "content" as the value of the `NAME` attribute. The value of the `TARGET` attribute tells the browser which sub-window to update as a result of the mouse click on the link.

Notice that in this case we have replaced the ADDRESS tag with information about the author and file modification date with a comment. This is so that the upper frame will not contain any distracting information. The choice of 80 pixels for the height of the window will probably not allow the user to see any information below the three hyperlinks but users are free to alter the font size which will affect what can be seen in those 80 pixels.

Getting fancy

The FRAME tag can name a frameset document instead of a body document in the SRC attribute. Suppose, for example, you wished to have a fixed sub-window at the top of your Web document and to split the lower sub-window into a left and right sub-window.

One way to do this would be to have the FRAME tag in the first frameset document (such as Figure 5.8) reference a second frameset document in which a FRAMESET tag would allocate the real estate of the lower sub-window such as in Figure 5.11. The situation is illustrated in Figure 5.12.

Frames within frames

```
...
<FRAMESET COLS="50%, 50%">
   <FRAME SRC="url_for_left_half_of_sub-window"
          NAME="lower_left">
   <FRAME SRC="url_for_right_half_of_sub-window"
          NAME="lower_right">
</FRAMESET>
...
```

Figure 5.11

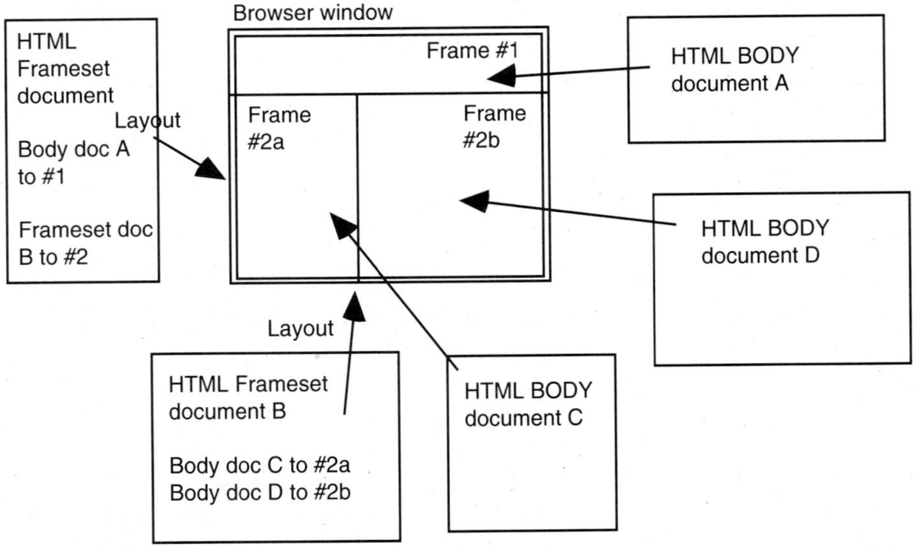

Figure 5.12

Hyperlinks in any of the frames can refer to any of the sub-windows. The key element is to make sure that the `TARGET` attribute has the correct value.

There are four special values that can be assigned to the `TARGET` attribute. These are:

`_self`	the default value
`_parent`	this tells the browser to update the parent frame
`_top`	this tells the browser to update the entire browser window regardless of the current frame layout
`_blank`	this tells the browser to display the new document in an entirely new window.

For example, assume we have subdivided the lower sub-window into left and right sub-windows as in Figure 5.12. In the left lower sub-window we have an anchored hyperlink:

```
<A HREF="url_to_replace_lower" TARGET="_parent">
   Replace lower two windows with single document
</A>
```

Then when the user clicks on the link, the left and right sub-windows will be replaced by a single sub-window in which the named document will appear.

Clearly, there are many things that you can do and you should experiment to gain familiarity with how frames work. We will explore some of these in the exercises.

Be careful with frames

As already mentioned, frames are an HTML extension. This means that not all browsers support them. Since Netscape and Internet Explorer each support frames, most users will be covered, but you should be careful anytime you artificially limit your audience. One tactic that some authors use is to have a non-frames opening page on a Web site from which the user can select a frames version of following pages or a non-frames version. This (at least) doubles the work of the Web developer but in some instances may be crucial for your customer's needs.

Since a frame is an HTML extension, the implementation of the syntax for the required tags and attributes may change. This will necessitate changing any previously written frames documents. The likelihood of major changes is quite small given that the two major players in the browser market get to set the standards by virtue of their dominance.

Another issue to keep in mind as a Web developer is that the browser window is limited in size. Not everyone has a 21-inch monitor with a lot of real estate to allocate to sub-windows. For users with small screens (e.g. laptop computers) anything more than two sub-windows on the screen will render the small windows essentially useless and certainly annoying.

Section review questions

True or false

1. The frames idea involves partitioning the browser window into sub-windows.

2. Frames can be implemented with the `TABLE` tag if a particular browser doesn't support frames.

3. In an HTML document using frames, it is possible to retain the content of one frame in the browser window while replacing the content of another.

4. A frameset document cannot refer to another frameset document.

5. A hyperlink in a body document appearing in one frame can cause the contents of another frame to be replaced.

6. A single frameset document can be used to subdivide a browser window horizontally and vertically.

7. The `FRAME` tag is used to determine the content of a subwindow only initially. The content may be replaced later as a result of user action.

8. Any of the valid HTML documents we have seen before this could be used as body documents.

Multiple choice

9. The presence of the * character in value of a `COLS` attribute tells the browser
   (a) to allocate the same amount of horizontal space to each subwindow.
   (b) to allocate the same amount of horizontal space to each subwindow from the amount remaining after allowing for those subwindows with specific allocations.
   (c) to allocate the horizontal space as "it sees fit" to best accommodate the content.
   (d) none of the above.

10. If a frame document contains two horizontal subwindows (as in the Island Quest Travel example) and the value of the `TARGET` attribute is `_parent` in a document appearing in one of the subwindows,
   (a) then the browser will replace the content of the other subwindow.
   (b) then the browser will replace the content of the subwindow containing the particular hyperlink.
   (c) then the browser will replace the entire two-subwindow frames document with the new content.
   (d) none of the above.

Short answers

11. What is the purpose of a frameset document?

12. How does the browser know from a frameset document whether to divide a window horizontally or vertically?

13. What is the purpose of the `NAME` attribute in the `FRAME` tag?

14. What is the difference in purpose between the `FRAMESET` tag and the `FRAME` tag?

15. What is the purpose of the `TARGET` attribute used with the `A` tag in frame documents?

Short excursion exercises

1. Create a simple HTML document containing an `APPLET` tag to execute the ZoomText applet. What happens if the values of the `WIDTH` and `HEIGHT` attributes are not sufficient to completely display the text?

2. Modify the HTML document created in the previous exercise and make the backGroundColor parameter the same as the background color of the rest of the document. (Use the `BGCOLOR` attribute of the `BODY` tag.)

3. Again modify the HTML document created in Exercise 1 to display the ZoomText applet. This time, repeat the `APPLET` tag three times. Each time display just one of the three words in the string: "Island Quest Travel". You will want to modify the values of the `WIDTH` and `HEIGHT` attributes as appropriate.

4. In the ZoomText applet try using white as the background font color as well as the background color for the document and the font foreground color. See if you can get similar results by playing with the colors in other ways.

5. Start with a simple HTML document to display the Origami applet. Modify the value of the `WIDTH` and `HEIGHT` attributes so that each is 200. Then set the value of each to 50. Use a watch to time how long each case runs until the applet screen area goes black. Does there appear to be a difference in the running time?

6. Use the HTML document from the previous exercise and modify it so that the `APPLET` tag appears twice. Then view the Origami applet. What do you notice?

7. Pick an HTML document from an earlier exercise. Place the line
   <!DOCTYPE HTML PUBLIC "-//W3C//DTD HTML 3.2 Final//EN">
   at the very beginning of the file and place the document into a directory that can be accessed from the Web. Now use the Web to locate an HTML validator and check your document.

8. Start with the a copy of the frameset document IQTravel_frameset.html and modify it so that the value of 80 pixels in the ROWS attribute is set to *. This demonstrates the need to specify the pixel values in particular applications.

9. In a copy of the frameset document IQTravel_frameset.html add a SCROLLING="no" attribute to the second FRAME tag. Now view the document. Why is this not a good idea?

10. Use the browser to open the frameset document. Place the mouse over the bar between the upper and lower frames and drag the bar by holding down the mouse button as you move the mouse. What do you observe?

    Now in a copy of the frameset document IQTravel_frameset.html use the NORESIZE attribute in each FRAME tag. Then repeat the experiment. What does your browser do?

11. In a copy of the IQTravel_head.html document, modify the value of the TARGET attribute for the middle hyperlink (tour schedule) so that it has the value _parent. Now view the frame document and click on the middle hyperlink. What do you find? Click on the browser button to take you back to the previous document. What do you find?

12. In a non-frames HTML document, place a TARGET attribute with a value of _parent in one of the A tags. View the document and click on the hyperlink. What do you find?

13. In a non-frames HTML document, place a TARGET attribute with some value such as "bogus" in one of the A tags. Now view the document and click on the hyperlink. What do you find? (This may not be consistent across different browsers.)

Longer voyage exercises

14. Locate the ZoomText applet in the Web-Archipelago site. Write a small HTML document to display your name in zoom text. You must specify all the parameters. Once you have viewed the result in your browser, modify the HTML document by changing colors and selecting the "Reload" button. What happens? Try exiting the browser and re-starting it and loading the modified HTML document. Now what happens? Why do you think this happens?

15. What happens if the value of the `WIDTH` or the `HEIGHT` attributes are set too small to view the text? Try an experiment by modifying the HTML document to view the applet and observe the results. Unfortunately, the size of the window allocated for the applet cannot be modified from within the applet itself so if you will have to do some trial and error work to get the sizes right for your application.

16. Start at the Web site `www.gamelan.com`. Locate an applet on the Web that you can download. Remember that the file with the `.class` extension is the one with the byte code and the one that you want. Place the file in the same directory as an HTML document that you create so you can view the applet.

    You can place your applets in a directory other than the one containing the HTML document referring to the applet. See the HTML reference in Appendix B and place your downloaded applet in a separate directory from the one containing the HTML document that references it. In particular, see the `CODEBASE` attribute of the `APPLET` tag.

    Another alternative to downloading the applet to your site is to refer to it in the applet tag in the location in which it is currently located. Use the `CODEBASE` attribute to reference directly (without downloading the applet) one of the applets that you locate on the Web. Why is using `CODEBASE` in this way not a good idea?

17. Start with your HTML notebook document that you developed in the exercises for Chapter 3 (or you can simply develop the version called for in this exercise). In this exercise, you will create a `FRAMES` version of your notebook.

    a. Divide up the browser window into two vertical frames.

    b. Make the left frame smaller than the right frame (you decide what looks best).

    c. The left frame will contain a table of contents (use the four items identified in Chapter 3 plus the one listed below in item e).

    d. The right frame will contain the items corresponding to the table of contents. Make a separate HTML document for each of these items (instead of putting them all in one document).

    e. Add another item in the table of contents about `FORMS`. Have this item point to a document that you will develop that has examples of each of the form types.

    f. The `FORMS` document must utilize `TABLES` so that each form type appears in a separate row of the table. Here's an example of the sort of thing you should have for one row of the table when it is displayed:

Sample HTML:

```
<BR>
     <INPUT TYPE="radio" NAME="season"
            VALUE="spring">Spring
     <INPUT TYPE="radio" NAME="season"
            VALUE="summer" CHECKED>Summer
     <INPUT TYPE="radio" NAME="season"
            VALUE="fall">Fall
     <INPUT TYPE="radio" NAME="season"
            VALUE="winter">Winter
```

What it looks like:

○Spring ●Summer ○Fall ○Winter

g. Re-write the hyperlinks to pages not on your site and have them displayed in the right frame.

6. Cascading Style Sheets

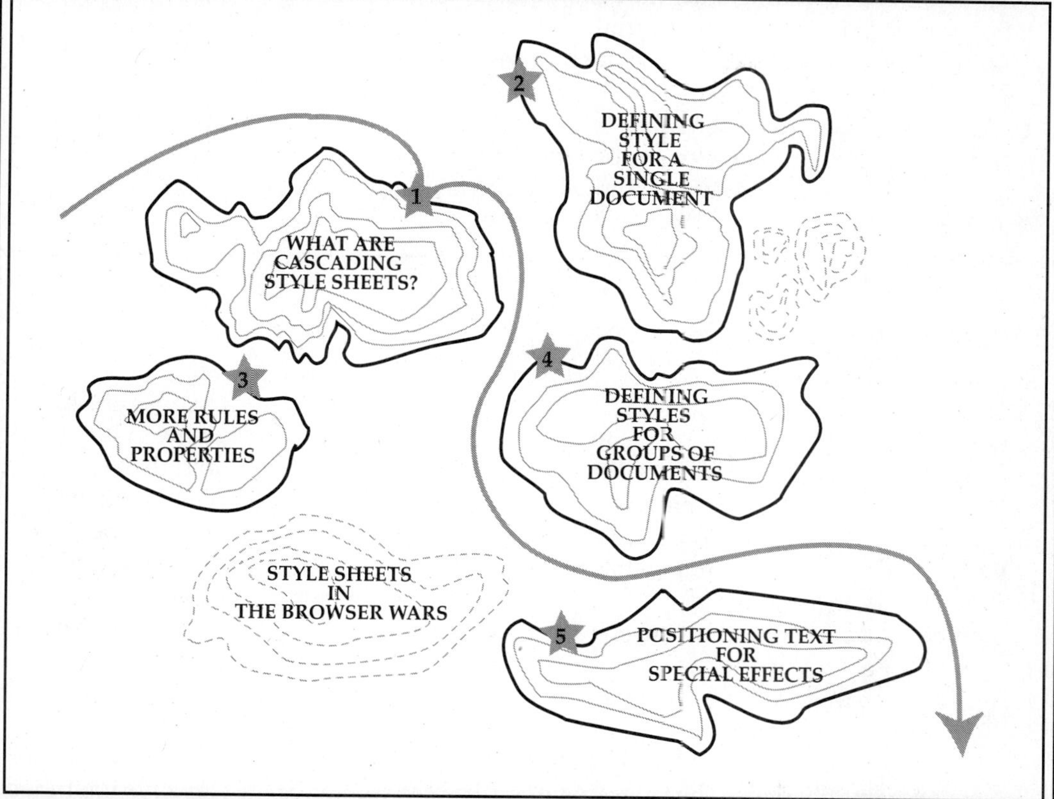

Chapter Preview

6.1 What are Cascading Style Sheets?
The standards group for HTML has given us a tool that gets us back to the original reason for markup languages. CSS allows us to set up rules that will provide a consistent look and feel for groups of HTML documents. In this section we examine the basic ideas.

6.2 Defining a Style for a Single Document
We start with defining a style for a single document. There is some basic terminology that we will need. In this section we introduce these terms and give some examples that will clarify the concepts.

6.3 More Rules and Properties
Now that we have the basic idea, let's look at some of the details for creating the style rules and some of the properties that are available for us to work with. Along the way we will explore the little-used `DIV` tag from HTML.

6.4 Defining Styles for Groups of Documents
What is it that's cascading and what are those sheets? Here we look at how we can define style rules that apply to a number of different documents. We also need to examine how the browser decides which rules to apply if there is an apparent conflict.

6.5 Positioning Text for Interesting Effects
Text positioning gives one of the most interesting aspects of CSS, but it has its problems. We look at some examples of how to place text in pre-planned locations on the Web page, and produce overlapping text.

6.1 What are Cascading Style Sheets?

HTML is a member of a family of SGML (Standard Generalized Markup Language) languages. This family (a meta-language) was developed originally at IBM in the 1970s. The concept was to allow you to specify *what* an element of a document was and then tie that element to some rule that determined how to render it on paper. Back in Chapter 2 we made the distinction between logical and physical tags. SGML is a language for specifying logical tags. The idea is to separate what something *is* (like a paragraph or a section heading) from the way it will be displayed (e.g. 14pt Helvetica font and blue). Large government agencies latched on to this concept because this would allow people from all over the country who were working for the same agency to create documents that had the same "look and feel" as their colleagues anywhere else in their agency.

The HTML language is a version of SGML with rules specifying the tags that we have seen in the previous five chapters. The rules that describe how to render the elements identified by the HTML tags are part of the browser. The introduction of physical tags (see Section 2.2) in HTML took back some control but left most of the rules about how to display Web documents with the browser. With Style Sheets, we are moving back to the notion of using HTML as a language for telling the browser what an element is and then having a different mechanism (style sheets) for determining how to render (display) that element.

Every browser has what could be called a default style sheet. That is, it has a set of rules that tells it how to display everything from `Hn` headers to text embedded in the content of `P` or `I` or `B` or `EM` tags. Style Sheets that we write are mechanisms for substituting the rendering rules that the browser uses for ones that we pick ourselves. The idea is to assign properties to HTML (logical) elements telling the browser how to render them. There are a few more bells and whistles and added features and we'll get to these later. Style sheets allow us to decide that every time we use the `H1` tag, for example, it will be rendered in 14pt New York font and in red. We can do that now with the `FONT` tag but style sheets allow us to specify our rule once and then have it apply everywhere in a particular document or, in fact, a group of documents.

We still haven't said what "cascading" has to do with this. Cascading is the idea of allowing multiple style sheets so that one with general rules combines with other style sheets with more specific rules for more specific cases. One of many uses for this cascading idea is to have style sheets provided by readers as well as ones provided by the authors of the Web documents. Reader-supplied style sheets could override more general rules to determine that text elements should be rendered as spoken text. This would be particularly useful for someone who was visually impaired or dyslexic. A more descriptive term instead of "cascading" might have been "layered" but we'll go with the conventional term. We'll examine how to use style sheets in the remainder of this chapter.

Finally, it's important to know that Cascading Style Sheets (CSS) are only supported by versions 4.0 (and later) of the major browsers, Netscape Communicator and Internet Explorer. Older browsers will ignore the style sheet commands. Moreover, even the 4.0 versions of the browsers are still somewhat flaky with some of the features of CSS. The good news is that you will be ahead of the curve when the browser developers get the bugs out of their software. The bad news is that some things just won't work "as advertised." Welcome to the "bleeding edge."

We don't try to cover all (or even most) of CSS. You will have the idea of how style sheets work, you will see interesting examples of how to use them, and with that you can readily pick up whatever additional information you find that you need.

Section review questions

True or false

1. SGML is a language for specifying physical tags.
2. The rendered version of a document is the version you see on your browser window.
3. Style sheets tell the browser how to display HTML elements.
4. Style sheets allow the author of an HTML document to specify how the browser is to render HTML elements.
5. CSS are supported by Netscape 4.0 and later versions and by Internet Explorer 4.0 and later versions.
6. CSS apply only to single documents.

Multiple choice

7. SGML is
   - (a) a subset of the HTML language.
   - (b) an HTML-like language for working with printed documents.
   - (c) a family of languages of which HTML is a member.
   - (d) an ancestor of HTML.

8. The term "cascading" refers to
   - (a) the ability to have multiple sets of rendering rules with general rules being superseded by more specific rules.
   - (b) allowing multiple sets of rendering rules that group together into blocks or cascades.
   - (c) the ability of rendering rules to provide for spoken text.
   - (d) all of the above

6.2 Defining a Style for a Single Document

As described in the previous section, styles are really designed to apply to multiple Web documents. They can be defined for a single document, however, and that's a good place to begin to understand how to use them.

We'll start by going back to an early version of the Island Quest Travel home page. One of the annoying things about `H1` headers has been that generally they are rendered much larger than we want. In fact, earlier we used `H2` and `H4` headers and ignored `H1` headers simply to get the size to be more consistent with the default font size in the Web document. In keeping with the notion of using the tags to describe *what* something is, we should use the `H1` header for the highest level header, then `H2` for the next level, etc. Now we can have our cake and eat it too! We'll be able to decide how `H1` headers are rendered by the browser using styles.

Styles are defined by *rules*. Rules are put together in certain precise ways. For example, the rule that all `H1` headers are to be rendered by letting the characters be 150 percent of the default font size can be stated as

```
H1 {font-size:150%}
```

The beginning portion before the { character is known as a *selector*. It is usually an HTML tag but not always. The portion between the opening and closing braces is called the *style definition*. The style definition is made up of one or more *declarations*. A declaration is made up of a *property* (e.g. `font-size`) and its *value* (e.g. 150%). The two are separated by a colon. Multiple declarations are separated by a semi-colon. We illustrate this in Figure 6.1. There we also show that we can specify things such as the color to be used to render a particular element. We'll see that there are lots of properties over which we have control.

Just as in HTML, the spacing and alignment of rule elements is irrelevant to the browser but not to humans, and we will use indentation and alignment of symbols as appropriate to make style rules more easily read.

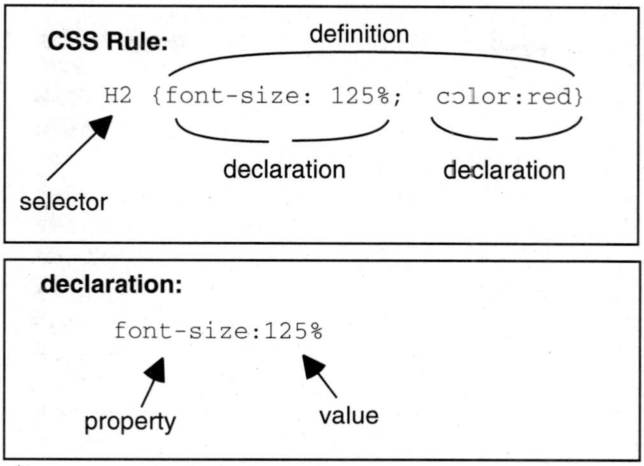

Figure 6.1

A style sheet consists of a series of rules. How do we tell the browser about a style sheet? The first way we consider is to use an HTML tag for this purpose. The `STYLE` tag is placed in the `HEAD` portion of a Web document. Here's how we would specify that the `H1` and `H2` tags are to be rendered so that `H1` headers are 150 percent as large as the default font size and `H2` headers are 125 percent of the default font size.

```
<STYLE TYPE="text/css">
   H1 {font-size:150%}
   H2 {font-size:125%}
</STYLE>
```

The `TYPE` attribute for these styles is always "text/css". (The only other possible value that is currently recognized by browsers that support the `STYLE` tag is related to Netscape's JavaScript language which is not part of this textbook.)

In Figure 6.2 we see the complete file with the embedded `STYLE` tag. The `STYLE` tag is placed in the `HEAD` portion of the document and appears before any other tags relating to the format of the document.

There is a difference, however, from the `STYLE` tag contents shown above. It looks like the contents are an imbedded HTML comment! This is a precaution in the event that a browser that doesn't understand about the `STYLE` tag tries to process this HTML document. If the comment tag was not present, then such a browser would ignore the `STYLE` and `/STYLE` tags themselves (as you would expect) but render the contents as text according to its usual rules. With the comment tag even the contents will be ignored. For those browsers that understand the `STYLE` tag, it turns out the rules will be processed and understood even if they are contained in an HTML comment tag.

File: IQTravel_6a.html

```
<HTML>
<!--File: IQTravel_6a.html-->
<!--Project: Island Quest Travel Site-->
<!--Programmer: J. Avila-->
<!--Last modified: 7/12/1998-->
<!--Copyright J. H. Avila, 1998. All rights reserved.-->
<HEAD>
<STYLE TYPE="text/css">
  <!--
  H1 {font-size:150%}
  H2 {font-size:125%}
  -->
</STYLE>
<TITLE>Island Quest Travel</TITLE>
</HEAD>
<BODY BGCOLOR="white" TEXT="blue">

<H1>Island Quest Travel</H1>
<P>
<EM>Island Quest Travel</EM> can take you to exotic locations
where you can walk in the footsteps of buccaneers and adventur-
ers from the past. We can take you to places that are just dots
on the map.  We'll fly you there and back and even provide
guides for special treks into jungles. Or if you prefer the
sailing adventure, we will gather a crew and a ship and let you
cruise mysterious islands.
<P>
<HR>
<P>
Here are some of our services:

<H2>Planning</H2>
<P>
We have dozens of locations that offer adventure and excitement
and we can help you pick out just the right place.

<H2>Flight reservations</H2>
<P>
Just leave it to us. We'll get you there and back. We will
handle reservations with the major airlines as well as the
local pilots for those special places not seen by most of the
rest of the world.
```

```
<H2>Sailing accommodations</H2>
<P>
For the buccaneer, we can charter sailboats and crews who will
fix your meals and take you to those hidden island coves where
perhaps treasure is hiding in a nearby cave.

<H2>Guide services</H2>
<P>
Islands often have jungles and we have the guides to take you
to some of the temples from forgotten civilizations. These
guides will provide everything you need in the way of meals and
accommodations.

</BODY>
</HTML>
```

Figure 6.2

In Figure 6.3 we see how the browser renders the text with no style rules. In Figure 6.4 we see the result of using the style rules shown in Figure 6.2. As mentioned earlier, if we use the default style rule, the headers seem disproportionately large in comparison to the rest of the text on the page.

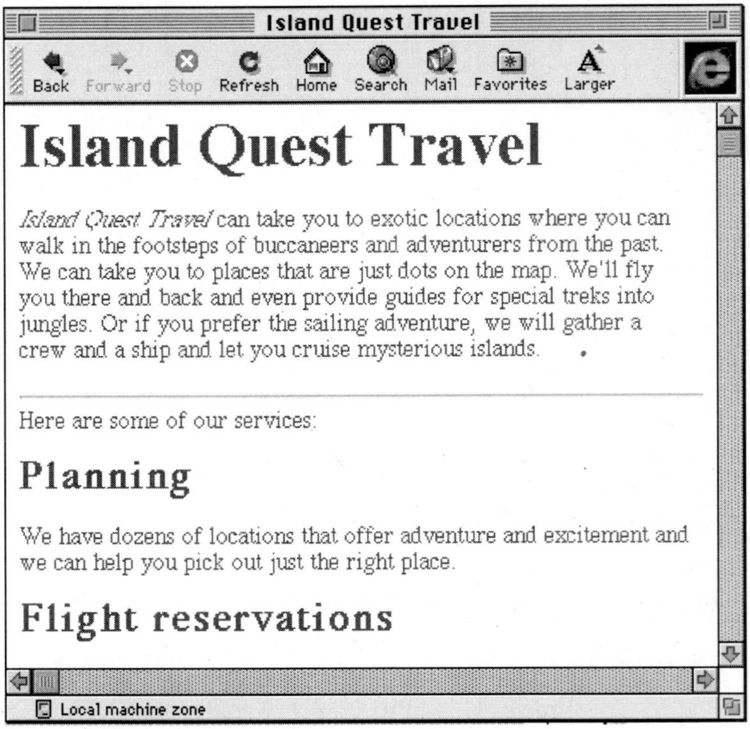

Figure 6.3

Figure 6.4

The use of styles is not restricted to the header tag. We can decide that we want to have all emphasized text (using the EM tag) to be rendered in red and 10 percent larger than the default font size. In order to include this feature in our document shown in Figure 6.2, all we need to do is to add the rule

```
EM {font-size:110%; color:red}
```

to the contents of the STYLE tag so that it will now read

```
<STYLE TYPE="text/css">
   <—!
   H1 {font-size:150%}
   H2 {font-size:125%}
   EM {font-size:110%; color:red}
   -->
</STYLE>
```

The result of this style can be seen in the file IQTravel_6b.html and in Figure 6.5.

Figure 6.5

Section review questions

True or false

1. Styles are made up of rules that tell the browser how to render HTML elements.

2. The style definition part of a style rule can have only one declaration.

3. Style rule declarations are made up of a property and its value.

4. Color is an example of a property.

5. The `STYLE` tag is used to tell the browser about style rules.

6. The `STYLE` tag may be placed anywhere in an HTML document.

7. Style rules in the `STYLE` tag will apply only within the `HEAD` portion of the document.

8. Style rules appearing in a `STYLE` tag cannot override the default style rules that the browser uses.

Multiple choice

9. A selector is
   (a) usually an HTML tag.
   (b) the leading part of a style rule and is followed by a style definition.
   (c) the value associated with a property.
   (d) (a) and (b).
   (e) none of the above.

10. Which of the following is a properly formed style rule?
   (a) `H3 (color : yellow; font-size: 110%)`
   (b) `H1 { font-size 150%; color blue }`
   (c) `H2 {font-size: 130% color: red }`
   (d) all of the above
   (e) none of the above

11. The use of the HTML comment within the body of a `STYLE` tag
   (a) is there to prevent browsers that do not support the `STYLE` tag from displaying the style rules.
   (b) is there so that browsers that do not support the `STYLE` tag will still get the desired rendering rules.
   (c) may cause problems with browsers that do not support the `STYLE` tag.
   (d) is only to help the human reader of the HTML document.

12. Which of the following style rules will cause the contents of the `STRONG` tag to be rendered in red and 20 percent larger than the default type size?
(a) `STRONG { font-size: 20%; font-color: red }`
(b) `STRONG { font-color: red; font-size: 20%}`
(c) `STRONG { color: red; size: 120% }`
(d) `STRONG { font-size: 120%; color: red }`

6.3 More Rules and Properties

So far we have seen how to set the size and color of fonts in headers and in emphasized text. Styles are capable of much more. In this section we will explore some of the possibilities available to us.

In style rule declarations we have assigned values to certain properties. Unlike the attributes associated with HTML tags, properties are not specific to particular selectors. For example, the font-size property is not restricted to `Hn` or `EM` selectors. In most cases (where it makes sense) properties can be assigned values for any selector. We can specify the font-size property, for example, for most HTML tags such as `P`, `BODY`, `STRONG`, and so forth.

Font properties

The properties available to us in building our styles are grouped into several categories. The first category is font properties. The particular properties in this category are displayed in the following box.

CSS Font properties

property	values
`font-family`	family name (e.g. `Helvetica`) or a generic family (e.g. `sans-serif`)
`font-style`	`"normal"` or `"italic"` or `"oblique"`
`font-variant`	`"normal"` or `"small-caps"`
`font-weight`	`"normal"` or `"bold"` or `"bolder"` or `"lighter"`
`font-size`	absolute size (`"xx-small"` or `"x-small"` or `"small"` or `"medium"` or `"large"` or `"x-large"` or `"xx-large"`) relative size (`"smaller"` or `"larger"`) percentage (e.g. `"150%"`) actual point size (e.g. `"10pt"`)

As an example of the use of these, Figure 6.6 shows the `HTML file Demo_6a.html` containing a sampling of the use of some of the font properties. We should point out that the use of an actual font size value such as 6pt will make your Web document rather dependent on the medium in which it is viewed. On small screens the type may be unreadable, for example.

File: Demo_6a.html

```
<HTML>
<!--File: Demo_6a.html-->
<!--Project: CSS-->
<HEAD>
<STYLE TYPE="text/css">
  <!--
  H1 {font-family:Arial; font-style:oblique;
      font-size:x-large}
  H2 {font-family:Helvetica; font-style:italic;
      font-size:large}
  H3 {font-family:Courier; font-style:normal;
      font-size:medium}
  ADDRESS {font-family:New York; font-variant:small-caps;
          font-size:6pt}
  -->
</STYLE>
<TITLE>Demo</TITLE>
</HEAD>
<BODY BGCOLOR="white" TEXT="blue">

<H1>Arial font family in oblique style and x-large</H1>
<P>
<H2>Helvetica font family in italic style and large</H2>
<P>
<H3>Courier font family in normal style and medium size</H3>
<P>
<ADDRESS>
  New York font family, small caps font variation and 6pt
  type<BR>
  Programmer:
  <A HREF="mailto:avila@web-archipelago.com">J. Avila</A><BR>
  Last modified: 7/26/98<BR>
  Copyright &copy; J. H. Avila, 1998.<BR>
  All rights reserved.
</ADDRESS>
</BODY>
</HTML>
```

Figure 6.6

The rendered version of Demo_6a.html is shown in Figure 6.7.

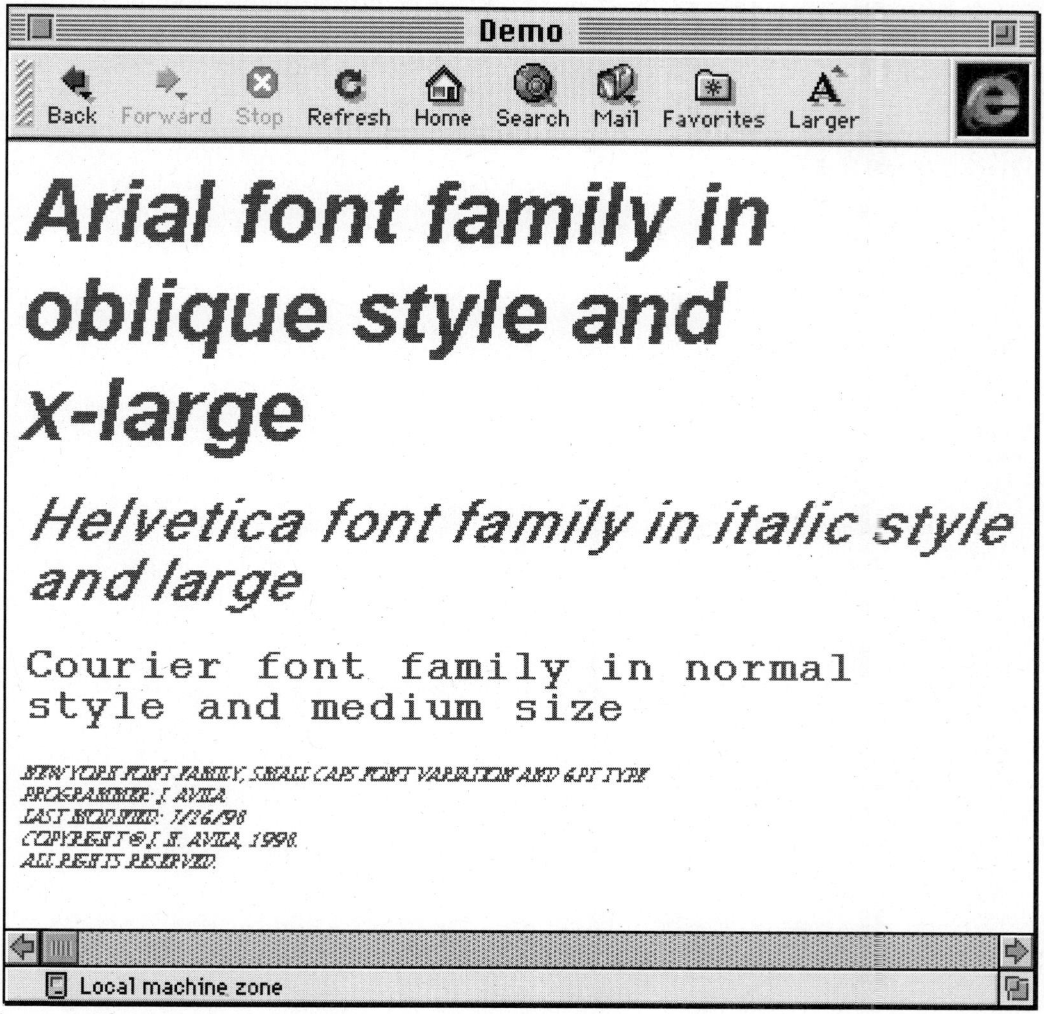

Figure 6.7

Color and background properties

Selectors can appear in more than one rule and more than one selector can appear in a single rule. Here's an example that also shows us a new property. Suppose we want to have all H1 and H2 headers rendered with a red background. CSS allows us to specify a background color for a particular element (in this case the two header types). We want to keep the relative font sizes the same as before. The following rules accomplish this:

```
H1 {font-size:150%}
H2 {font-size:125%}
H1, H2 {background-color:red}
```

If a selector appears more than once, then the declarations are simply merged together. Let's use this new style with our Island Quest Travel Web document we examined in the previous section. The new document is shown in Figure 6.8. We have retained the earlier rule regarding the `EM` tag. The effect can be very interesting as we see in Figure 6.9.

File: IQTravel_6c.html

```
<HTML>
<!--File: IQTravel_6c.html-->
<!--Project: CSS-->
<HEAD>
<STYLE TYPE="text/css">
  <!--
  H1 {font-size:150%}
  H2 {font-size:125%}
  H1, H2 {background-color:red}
  EM {font-size:110%; color:red}
  -->
</STYLE>
<TITLE>Island Quest Travel</TITLE>
</HEAD>
<BODY BGCOLOR="white" TEXT="blue">
<H1>Island Quest Travel</H1>
<P>
<EM>Island Quest Travel</EM> can take you to exotic locations
where you can walk in the footsteps of buccaneers and adventur-
ers from the past. We can take you to places that are just dots
on the map.  We'll fly you there and back and even provide
guides for special treks into jungles. Or if you prefer the
sailing adventure, we will gather a crew and a ship and let you
cruise mysterious islands.

...same as before

</BODY>
</HTML>
```

Figure 6.8

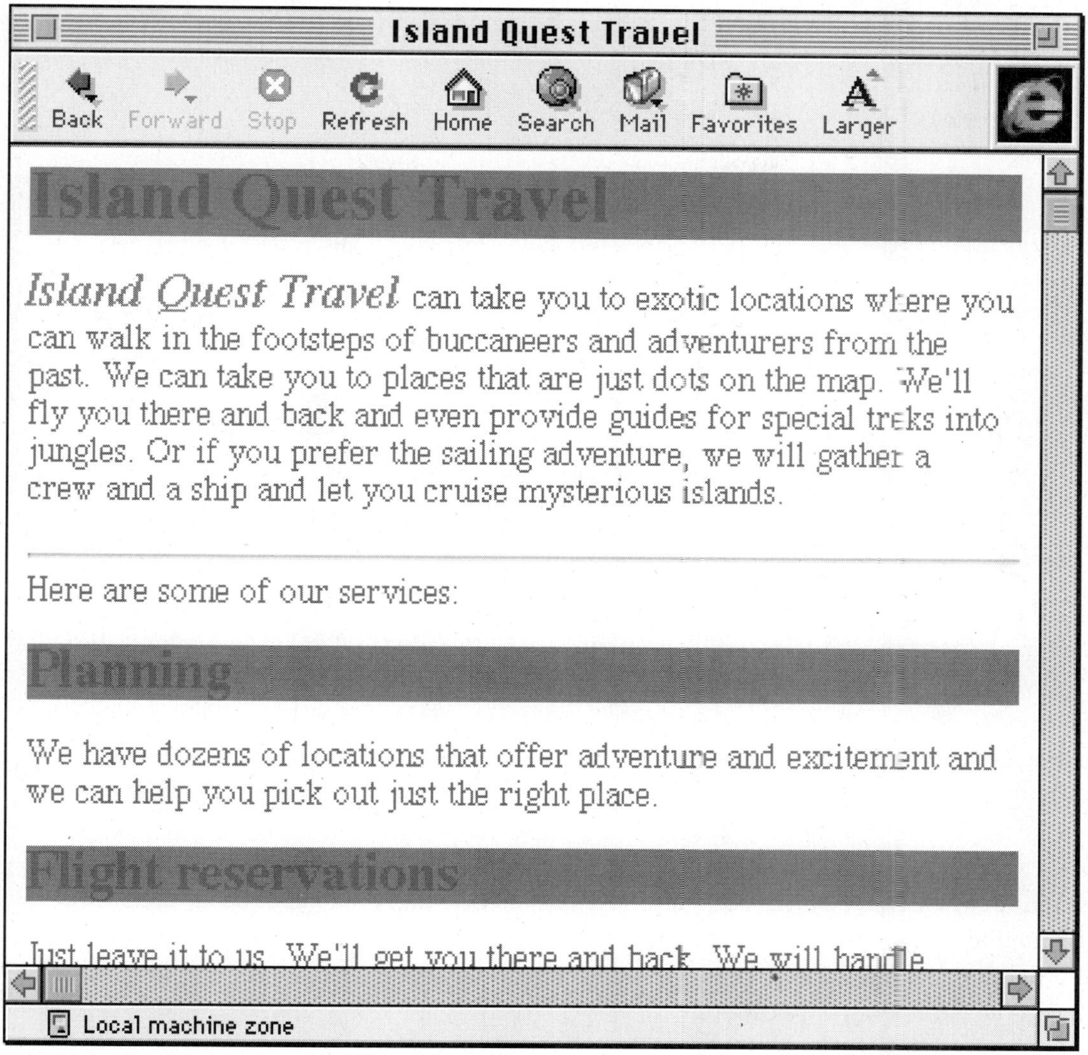

Figure 6.9

CSS provides us with the ability to color an element's background. We have already seen another of this family of properties—the color property which we used in the rule for the EM tag. Here is a list of some of the color and background properties:

CSS Color and Background properties

property	values
color	color value (e.g. "red" or "#ccffff")
background-color	"transparent" or color value (e.g. "red")
background-image	"none" or url (e.g. "url(yellowSqr.gif)")
background-repeat	"repeat" or "repeat-x" or "repeat-y" or "no-repeat"
background-position	"top" or "center" or "bottom" with "left" or "center" or "right" (These can be replaced by percentage values.)

Take a look at the properties in the table and the values that can be used; it's worth pointing out a few things. Notice that we can use 6-digit hexadecimal values for color if the color we want doesn't have a name recognized by the browser. Also notice that the `background-image` property allows us to use an image file for a background instead of a color. This is exactly like the attributes in the `BODY` tag. The syntax for specifying the url is slightly unusual. It requires that the word url be followed by the name of the image file—without quotes—within parentheses.

Recall that with the `BACKGROUND` attribute of the `BODY` tag, the image file is "tiled" over the entire document. That is, it is replicated in the x and y directions until the entire document is filled. With the `background-repeat` property, we have control over the tiling. This has some interesting applications.

Suppose we specify a rule for the `P` tag as follows:

```
P {background-image:url(ltBlueBar.gif);
   background-repeat:repeat-y}
```

This assumes a file named `ltBlueBar.gif` in the same directory as the HTML file (otherwise, we have to supply the full path name). The `background-repeat` property tells the browser to repeat the image as necessary to fill the background for the `P` element but only in the y direction (vertical). If we add this rule to our style above, we have the file shown in Figure 6.10.

File: IQTravel_6d.html

```
<HTML>
<!--File: IQTravel_6d.html-->
<!--Project: CSS-->
<HEAD>
<STYLE TYPE="text/css">
  <!--
  H1 {font-size:150%}
  H2 {font-size:125%}
  H1, H2 {background-color:red}
  P {background-image:url(ltBlueBar.gif);
     background-repeat:repeat-y}
  EM {font-size:110%; color:red}
  -->
</STYLE>
<TITLE>Island Quest Travel</TITLE>
</HEAD>
<BODY BGCOLOR="white" TEXT="blue">
<H1>Island Quest Travel</H1>
<P>
<EM>Island Quest Travel</EM> can take you to exotic locations
where you can walk in the footsteps of buccaneers and adventur-
ers from the past. We can take you to places that are just dots
on the map.  We'll fly you there and back and even provide
guides for special treks into jungles. Or if you prefer the
sailing adventure, we will gather a crew and a ship and let you
cruise mysterious islands.

...same as before

</BODY>
</HTML>
```

Figure 6.10

This file is shown as the browser renders it in Figure 6.11. The light blue bar image is just a simple bar about as tall as a single line. The `background-repeat` property tells the browser to repeat the image in the vertical direction over the entire paragraph element.

The `background-position` property tells the browser where to start either with the background color or the background image. You should specify both the horizontal and vertical values (separated by at least one blank). Currently, this feature seems to be a little buggy, but we'll propose some exercises at the end of the chapter to try this feature on your computer.

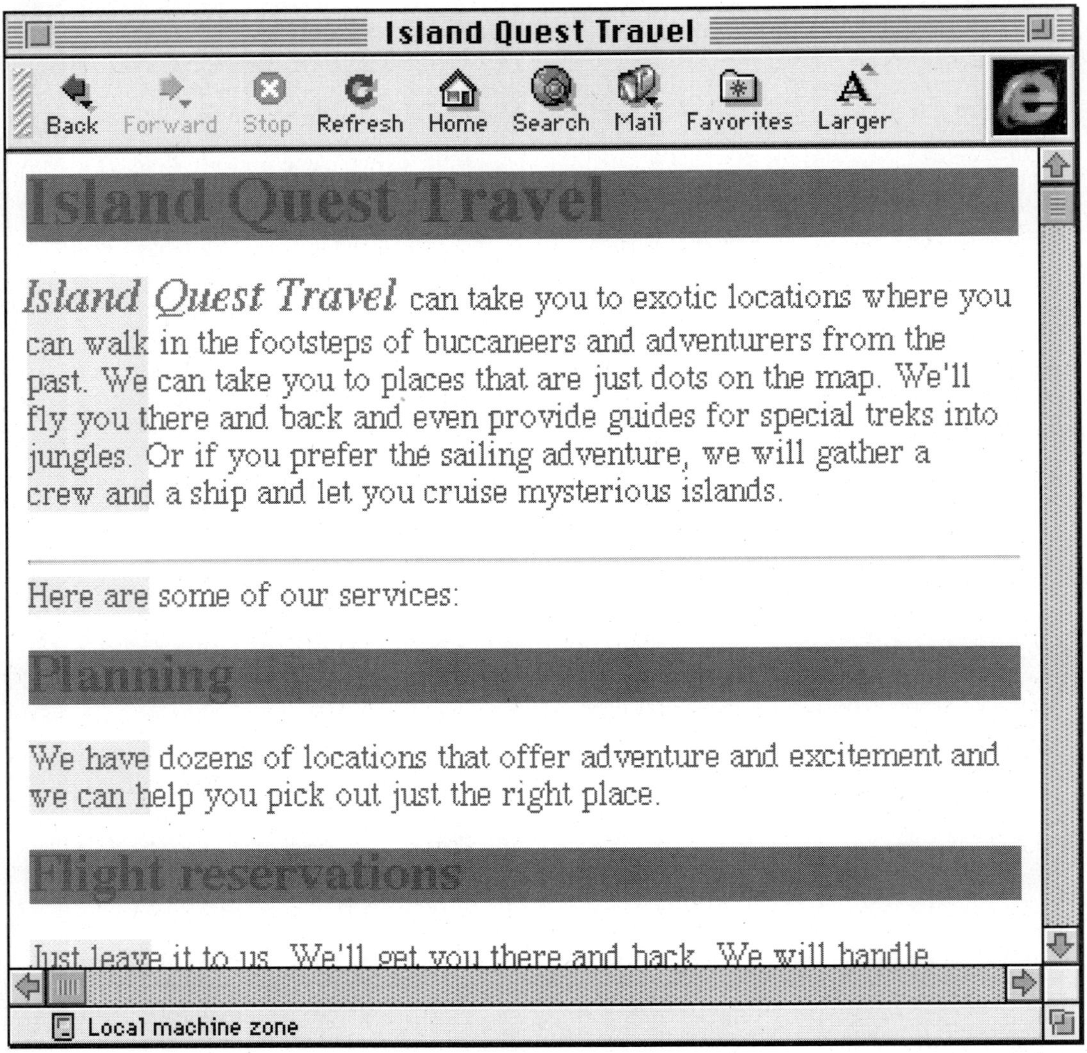

Figure 6.11

Property classes

In this particular example, we would like to utilize the blue highlighting bar only in the paragraphs describing the various services that Island Quest Travel supplies. In particular, we don't want the blue bar in the first two paragraph elements.

There is a way to do this. We can create a class of properties without immediately assigning them to a particular tag and then later pick the class we want for each instance of the tag. Let's see how this works.

In the style rule we identify a class of properties with a name of our choosing preceded by a dot (.) as the selector. For example,

```
.blueBar {background-image:url(ltBlueBar.gif);
          background-repeat:repeat-y}
```

identifies a property class named "blueBar." Then in our document, for each P tag, we can choose to use this class of properties or not as we wish. Figure 6.12 shows this new file. Notice how when we have those paragraphs in which we want the blue bar we indicate that with a CLASS attribute as follows:

```
<P CLASS="blueBar">
```

The file is shown as rendered by the browser in Figure 6.13. Only those paragraphs that we want to have the blue bar now have it.

File: IQTravel_6e.html

```
<HTML>
<!--File: IQTravel_6e.html-->
<!--Project: CSS-->
<HEAD>
<STYLE TYPE="text/css">
  <!--
  H1 {font-size:150%}
  H2 {font-size:125%}
  H1, H2 {background-color:red}
  .blueBar {background-image:url(ltBlueBar.gif);
            background-repeat:repeat-y}
  EM {font-size:110%; color:red}
  -->
</STYLE>
<TITLE>Island Quest Travel</TITLE>
</HEAD>
<BODY BGCOLOR="white" TEXT="blue">

<H1>Island Quest Travel</H1>
<P>
<EM>Island Quest Travel</EM> can take you to exotic locations
where you can walk in the footsteps of buccaneers and adventur-
ers from the past. We can take you to places that are just dots
on the map.  We'll fly you there and back and even provide
guides for special treks into jungles. Or if you prefer the
sailing adventure, we will gather a crew and a ship and let you
cruise mysterious islands.

<P>
<HR>
```

```
<P>
Here are some of our services:

<H2>Planning</H2>
<P CLASS="blueBar">
We have dozens of locations that offer adventure and excitement
and we can help you pick out just the right place.

<H2>Flight reservations</H2>
<P CLASS="blueBar">
Just leave it to us. We'll get you there and back. We will
handle reservations with the major airlines as well as the
local pilots for those special places not seen by most of the
rest of the world.

<H2>Sailing accommodations</H2>
<P CLASS="blueBar">
For the buccaneer, we can charter sailboats and crews who will
fix your meals and take you to those hidden island coves where
perhaps treasure is hiding in a nearby cave.

<H2>Guide services</H2>
<P CLASS="blueBar">
Islands often have jungles and we have the guides to take you
to some of the temples from forgotten civilizations. These
guides will provide everything you need in the way of meals and
accommodations.

</BODY>
</HTML>
```

Figure 6.12

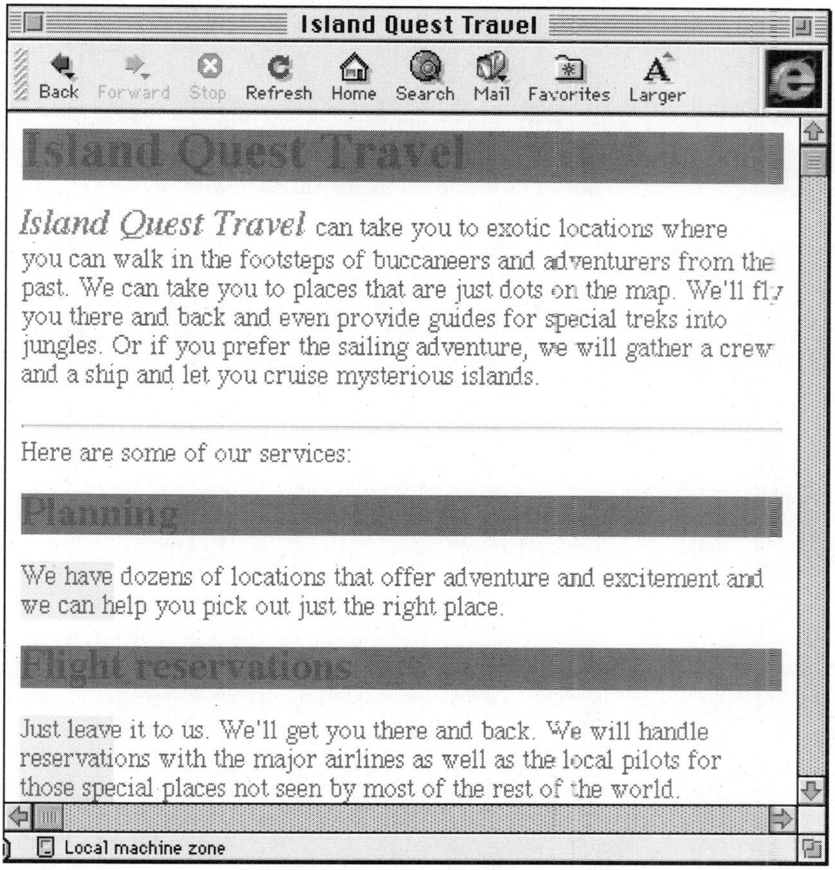

Figure 6.13

Property conflict resolution

Any set of properties can be grouped into classes to be used in this way. The same class may be used for more than one element type. As an example of using a class in more than one context, suppose we add the `CLASS` attribute to the `H1` tag in the previous example and give it the value "blueBar." That is, instead of `<H1>` we use `<H1 CLASS="blueBar">`. The result is shown in Figure 6.14. From a design point of view, this is not an attractive Web page but it does illustrate some points. The first is, as mentioned already, that we can re-use the blueBar class in more than one element. The second involves what we call property conflict resolution. The style rule for `H1` has a background color of red. The blueBar class has a background image consisting of the blue bar image. These two styles conflict. As you can see the class rule won, but why? The way style rules work is that the rule *closest* to the element with conflicting properties wins. The style rule for `H1` is located in the `HEAD` portion of the document. The `CLASS` attribute for the `H1` tag which calls for the use of the blueBar class rule is right with the `H1` tag with the conflicting rules, therefore the class rule wins. We'll have more details on how the browser resolves conflicting style rules in Section 6.4 when we discuss cascading order.

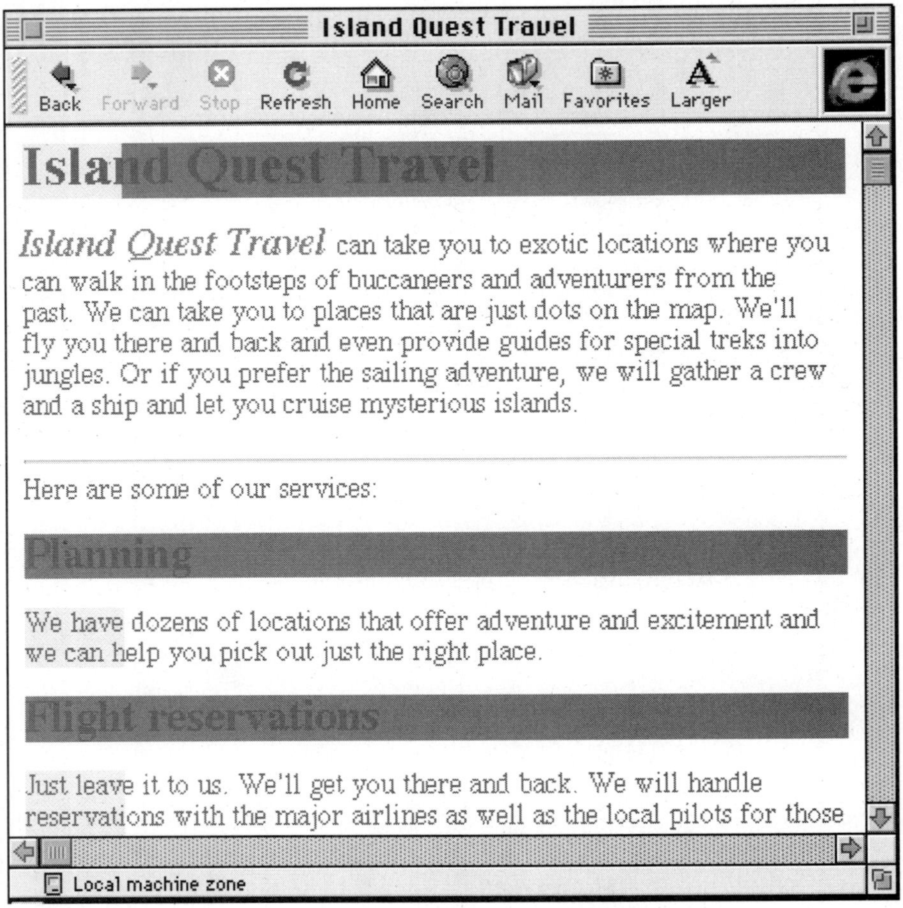

Figure 6.14

Inheritance

In HTML, tags appear within the contents of other tags. The most obvious example is the `BODY` tag which contains all the tags associated with the contents of the Web document. If a property is associated with an "outer" tag, what happens when the browser encounters another tag within its contents? The answer is that the inner tag inherits the properties of the outer tag. Let's look at another example of one of our earlier Island Quest Travel Web documents. Figure 6.15 shows the HTML associated with a document that will display the upcoming tours by Island Quest Travel in a table format. We have defined a style class to place a yellow-green background on some elements. In our case, we use the `CLASS` attribute to place a colored background behind the `H1` tag and alternate rows of the table. That is, we use the `CLASS` attribute to use the `yGreen-color` properties class for the `H1` tag near the beginning of the document and then in every other `TR` tag. All the `TH` tags within the `TR` tag will inherit this background color without having to specifically name that property or class.

Figure 6.16 shows how the browser renders this document.

File: tourInfo_6a.html

```
<HTML>
<!--File: tourInfo_6a.html-->
<!--Project: CSS-->
<!--See the ADDRESS tag below for additional information-->
<HEAD>
  <STYLE>
     <!--
     H1 {font-size:150%}
     ADDRESS {font-size:x-small}
     .yGreen-color {background-color: #00ff99}
     -->
  </STYLE>
  <TITLE>Tour Information</TITLE>
</HEAD>
<BODY BGCOLOR="white" TEXT="blue" LINK="red" VLINK="purple">
<P>
  <CENTER><H1 CLASS="yGreen-color">Tour Information</H1></
  CENTER>
<P>

<TABLE BORDER="4" WIDTH="100%">
  <CAPTION ALIGN="bottom"><B>Island Tours for this year</B></
  CAPTION>
  <TR CLASS="yGreen-color">
     <TH>Island</TH>
     <TH>Start date</TH>
     <TH>Tour length</TH>
     <TH>price</TH>
  </TR>
  <TR>
     <TD>Grand Cayman</TD>
     <TD>Feb 5, Apr 19, Jul 8, Oct 7</TD>
     <TD>One week</TD>
     <TD>$1800</TD>
  </TR>
  <TR CLASS="yGreen-color">
     <TD>Fiji</TD>
     <TD>Jan 3, Mar 18, May 28, Jul 5</TD>
     <TD>Two weeks</TD>
     <TD>$4100</TD>
  </TR>
  <TR>
     <TD>Molokai</TD>
     <TD>Feb 18, Apr 20, Nov 8, Dec 12</TD>
```

```
      <TD>One week</TD>
      <TD>$2100</TD>
   </TR>
   <TR CLASS="yGreen-color">
      <TD ROWSPAN="2">Aruba</TD>
      <TD>Jan 18, Mar 3, Nov 20, Dec 27</TD>
      <TD>One week</TD>
      <TD>$1900</TD>
   </TR>
   <TR>
      <TD> Apr 9, May 10</TD>
      <TD>Two weeks</TD>
      <TD>$3000</TD>
   </TR>
   <TR CLASS="yGreen-color">
      <TD CLASS="white">St. Lucia</TD>
      <TD>Jan 21, Mar 1, Apr 8, Oct 8</TD>
      <TD>Two weeks</TD>
      <TD>$3000</TD>
   </TR>
</TABLE>
<P>
<ADDRESS>
     Programmer: J. Avila<BR>
     <A HREF="mailto:avila@web-archipelago.com">
        <B>avila@Web-Archipelago.com</B>
     </A><BR>
     Last modified: 7/27/98<BR>
     Copyright &copy; J. H. Avila, 1998.<BR>
     All rights reserved.
</ADDRESS>
</BODY>
</HTML>
```

Figure 6.15

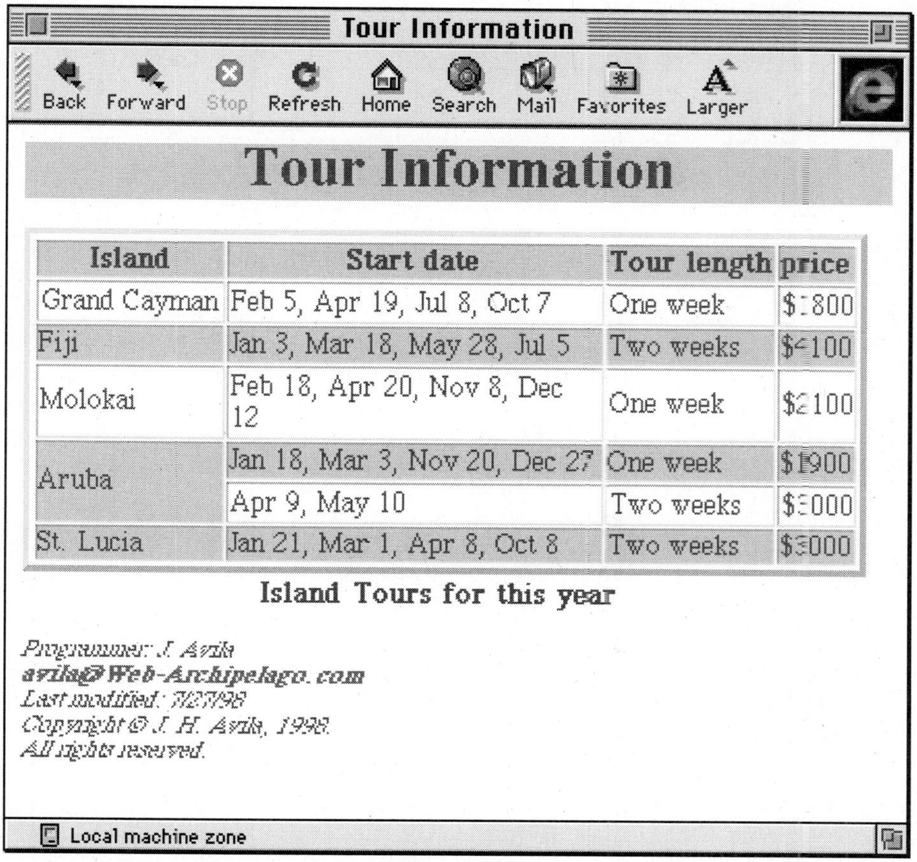

Figure 6.16

As it turns out, because of the double row of entries for Aruba, the last two rows in column one have the same color. We can modify this by overriding the inherited yellow-green color in the first cell of the last row. This can be done in several ways. The first would be to create another style class to set the background color to white and then explicitly associate the first `TD` tag in the last row with this class. Instead we will use this opportunity to demonstrate another way of specifying style rules known as *in-line style definitions*. Here are the tags for the last row of the table modified to set the background color of the first cell to white:

```
<TR CLASS="yGreen-color">
   <TD STYLE="background-color:white">St. Lucia</TD>
   <TD>Jan 21, Mar 1, Apr 8, Oct 8</TD>
   <TD>Two weeks</TD>
   <TD>$3000</TD>
</TR>
```

We have used a `STYLE` attribute for the `TD` tag to specify a style rule for this tag. This mechanism defines a rule that only applies to this specific tag. And since this style rule is attached to the tag, it will supersede the rules defined earlier in the document. The file containing this change is `tourInfo_6b.html` and is shown in its rendered form in Figure 6.17.

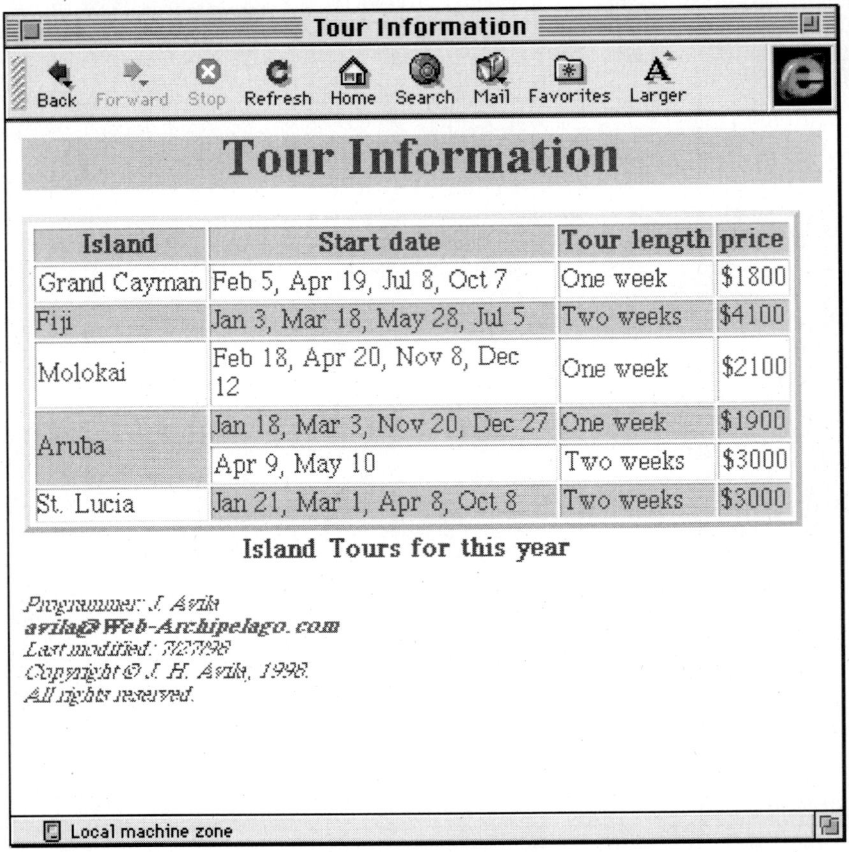

Figure 6.17

Style blocks

Using inheritance as we did in the previous example is an efficient way to manage style rules. That is, we define the style rules that apply generally to a section and let inheritance carry over those rules to all embedded tags. Only when there are exceptions do we have to intervene. A convenient way to establish a section of a Web document for this purpose is to use the `DIV` tag in HTML. This tag identifies a document division or block. By attaching style classes to one of these tags, we will guarantee that every tag within the division inherits the properties we want.

Figure 6.18 shows this technique. The rendered version of this document is shown in Figure 6.19. We've used the `DIV` tag to identify three separate blocks of the Web document. Each block is indented by a certain percentage of the width of the browser window and is associated with a specific background color. Within the block, the `H2` tags have their own background color which overrides the block background color.

Notice that we have taken this opportunity to demonstrate two other properties, the `text-align` property and the `margin-left` property. The first is one of a group of properties known as text properties and the second is one of a group known as box properties. We won't pursue other properties here but check out some of the documentation available through the Web by visiting and following the links from the Web-Archipelago (or from the copy of this page on the CD-ROM).

File: IQTravel_6f.html

```
<HTML>
<!--File: IQTravel_6f.html-->
<!--Project: CSS-->
<HEAD>
<STYLE TYPE="text/css">
  <!--
  H1 {font-size:150%}
  H2 {font-size:125%}
  H1, H2 {text-align: right;
          background-color:blue;
          color:white}
  EM {font-size:110%; color:red}
  -->
</STYLE>
<TITLE>Island Quest Travel</TITLE>
</HEAD>
<BODY BGCOLOR="white" TEXT="blue">

<H1>Island Quest Travel</H1>
<P>
<EM>Island Quest Travel</EM> can take you to exotic locations.

<P>
<HR>
<P>

<DIV STYLE="margin-left: 20%; background-color:#66ff99">
<H2>Planning</H2>
<P>
We have dozens of locations that offer adventure and excite-
ment.
</DIV>

<DIV STYLE="margin-left: 10%; background-color:#ff9966">
<H2>Flight reservations</H2>
<P>
Just leave it to us. We'll get you there and back. We will
```

```
handle reservations with the major airlines as well as the
local pilots.
</DIV>

<DIV STYLE="background-color:#ccff00">
<H2>Guide services</H2>
<P>
Islands often have jungles and we have the guides to take you
to some of the temples from forgotten civilizations.
</DIV>

</BODY>
</HTML>
```

Figure 6.18

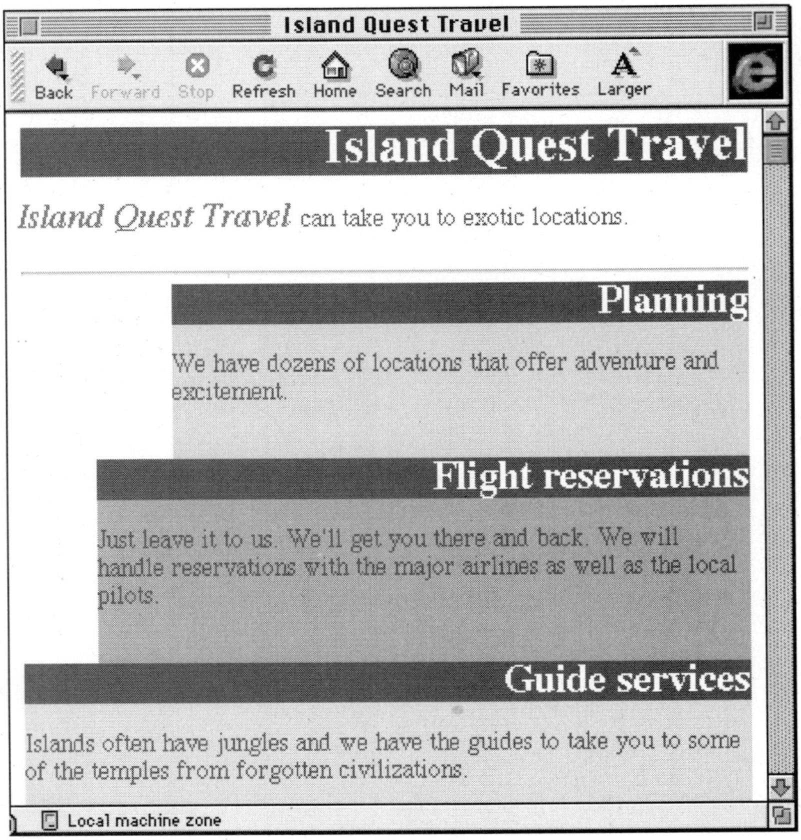

Figure 6.19

Section review questions

True or false

1. Each type of selector has its own set of properties, similar to the attributes associated with HTML tags.

2. Specifying the value of the font-size property in point sizes is discouraged because it is too dependent on the screen size.

3. The style rule
```
H1, H2 { color: blue; font-weight: bolder }
```
will cause `H2` headers to be rendered in blue and in a bolder or "heavier" style but will have no impact on `H1` headers.

4. Color values can only be given as names of colors.

5. Style classes are created by using a dot followed by a name in the place where a selector would appear in a style rule.

6. Style classes can only be used once after they are declared.

7. In order to use a style class, you must use the `CLASS` attribute associated with any of the HTML tags.

8. If a style rule in the `HEAD` portion of a document conflicts with a style rule that is attached to an element using the `CLASS` attribute, then the latter style rule will be the one used by the browser.

9. Assume no style rule for the `EM` tag. If an `EM` tag appears within a paragraph and the `P` tag is associated with the following style rule
```
P { color: red }
```
then the contents of the `EM` tag will be rendered in the default color that the browser would use if the style rule for `P` were not present.

10. In-line style definitions will override styles that are inherited by one tag within the contents of another tag.

11. The `text-align` property allows us to have the text in a paragraph be aligned on the right margin of the paragraph.

Multiple choice

12. The following style rule

```
P { font-size: 90%; font-family: Courier }
```

   (a) will be overridden by the browser's own default style for paragraphs.
   (b) will cause paragraphs to be rendered 10 percent smaller than the default size using the Courier font.
   (c) is illegal.
   (d) will cause paragraphs to be rendered 90 percent smaller than the default size using the Courier font.

13. The following two style rules:

```
H1 { font-size: 150% }
H1 { color: blue }
```

   (a) are equivalent to the following single style rule:

```
H1 { color: blue; font-size: 150% }
```

   (b) are illegal because `H1` can only appear once as a selector.
   (c) are legal but will produce different results because the order of the declarations are not the same.
   (d) none of the above.

14. The following style rule:

```
P { background-image: url(yellowSqr.gif);
    background-repeat: repeat-x }
```

   (a) will cause a yellow stripe to appear along the left edge of all paragraphs.
   (b) will cause the first line of each paragraph to appear in yellow.
   (c) will cause paragraphs to appear with a yellow background.
   (d) none of the above.

15. Defining a property class
   (a) requires that you assign a name to a set of properties.
   (b) doesn't immediately bind any of the class properties to any specific element.
   (c) allows you to bundle together a set of properties that you can then apply to a number of different elements.
   (d) all of the above.

16. Inheritance means
   (a) that tags within the contents of other tags will always be rendered according to the style rule for the outer tag.
   (b) that tags within the contents of other tags will be rendered according to the style rule for the outer tag only if no style rule exists for the inner tag.
   (c) that tags not associated with a style rule will be rendered according to the style tag for the preceding tag in the document.
   (d) none of the above.

17. Assume only the following style rule:

```
P { font-size: 80% }
```

and the following piece of an HTML document:

```
<P> You must be careful to follow
the instructions <EM> exactly </EM>.
```

Which of the following is correct?

(a) All the text will be rendered 80 percent of the default size including the word "exactly".

(b) The word "exactly" will be rendered in the default font size, everything else will be rendered 80 percent of the default size.

(c) The first part of the paragraph will be rendered in a font size 80 percent of the default size. The word "exactly" will be rendered 80 percent of this smaller size.

(d) none of the above.

18. The `DIV` tag

(a) allows us to establish style rules for a section of a document so that they cannot be overridden by tags within the section.

(b) will block out style rules that occur outside that section of a document.

(c) allows us to establish style rules for a section of a document and then to use in-line style definitions to modify the section rules.

(d) none of the above.

Short answers

19. What is the difference between

```
H1 { background-color: red }
```

and

```
H1 { color: red }
```

20. Write the style rule to have the background behind the text in the contents of a `STRONG` tag rendered in yellow.

21. What would be the effect of the following style rule (assume the named file exists and is in the appropriate folder)?

```
P { background-image: url(picture.jpeg) }
```

22. What would be wrong with having the `color` property and the `background-color` property have the same value?

23. Use an in-line style definition to modify the following HTML to have the word *sure* rendered in red.

```
<P> Be <EM> sure </EM> before you buy.
```

6.4 Defining Styles for Groups of Documents

As we explained at the beginning of the chapter, CSS is really a mechanism to allow us to establish a style or "look and feel" that we can utilize for a family of documents. The obvious use is to establish style rules for a Web site. How can we do this?

The way is to place all our rules in a separate document. The convention is to name this document with a `.css` extension. These style sheets, as they're called, become a collection of rules to be applied in each document that refers to them. As an example, let's take our rules that we used for the document shown in Figure 6.19 and place them into the file `IQTstyles.css` shown in Figure 6.20.

File: IQTstyles.css

```
/* Style sheet for Island Quest Travel */
/* File: IQTstyle.css */

  H1 {font-size:150%}
  H2 {font-size:125%}
  H1, H2 {text-align: right;
          background-color:blue;
          color:white}
  EM {font-size:110%; color:red}
```

Figure 6.20

The first two lines are comments. These follow the C language style with an opening `/*` and a closing `*/`. Notice that, except for the comments, there are only rules in this file. No `STYLE` tags or other HTML tags. In the HTML file, we now have to tell the browser about the existence of the style sheet file. This is done with a `LINK` tag which, in our case, looks like this:

```
<LINK REL="stylesheet" TYPE="text/css"
      HREF="IQTstyle.css">
```

This must be placed in the `HEAD` portion of the document in the same location where we formerly had the `STYLE` tag. The resulting file is shown in Figure 6.21. (The result of rendering that file is the same as Figure 6.19.) The `REL` attribute of the `LINK` tag identifies the named file as a CSS style sheet. The `TYPE` attribute always has this same value for CSS style sheets. The `HREF` attribute behaves just like its counterpart in the `A` tag.

File: IQTravel_6g.html

```
<HTML>
<!--File: IQTravel_6g.html-->
<!--Project: CSS-->
<HEAD>
<LINK REL="stylesheet" TYPE="text/css"
      HREF="IQTstyle.css">
<TITLE>Island Quest Travel</TITLE>
</HEAD>
<BODY BGCOLOR="white" TEXT="blue">

<H1>Island Quest Travel</H1>
<P>
<EM>Island Quest Travel</EM> can take ycu to exotic locations.

<P>
<HR>
<P>

<DIV STYLE="margin-left: 20%; background-color:#66ff99">
<H2>Planning</H2>
<P>
We have dozens of locations that offer adventure and excite-
ment.
</DIV>

<DIV STYLE="margin-left: 10%; background-color:#ff9966">
<H2>Flight reservations</H2>
<P>
Just leave it to us. We'll get you there and back. We will
handle reservations with the major airlines as well as the
local pilots.
</DIV>

<DIV STYLE="background-color:#ccff00">
<H2>Guide services</H2>
<P>
Islands often have jungles and we have the guides to take you
to some of the temples from forgotten civilizations.
</DIV>

</BODY>
</HTML>
```

Figure 6.21

We could now use the same style sheet file for all the documents related to this particular Web site. Invariably, however, there will be some style changes that apply to one or two documents within a large group of documents that we want to manage. One solution would be to have several different style sheet files, but CSS has a better solution.

There can only be one `LINK` tag in an HTML document to identify a style sheet but we can have a `LINK` tag and a `STYLE` tag. The `LINK` tag brings in the basic style sheet. Following that we place a `STYLE` tag with additional rules. These rules, being closer to the elements they apply to, will override any rules in the separate style sheet file if any rules conflict.

As an example, let's revisit the example of Figure 6.21 (`IQTravel_6g.html`). Let us assume that for this document we want to alter the text within the paragraphs to be aligned on the right instead of on the left. If we change the `IQTstyle.css` file by adding another rule, then all other Web documents that utilize this style sheet will also be changed, and we only want to change this document. The way to do this is to add a `STYLE` tag after the `LINK` tag with the appropriate new rule. Figure 6.22 shows the `HEAD` portion of the new file (`IQTravel_6h.html`) and Figure 6.23 shows how it is rendered.

File segment from: `IQTravel_6h.html`

```
<HEAD>
<LINK REL="stylesheet" TYPE="text/css"
     HREF="IQTstyle.css">
<STYLE>
  <!--
  P {text-align: right}
  -->
</STYLE>
<TITLE>Island Quest Travel</TITLE>
</HEAD>
```

Figure 6.22

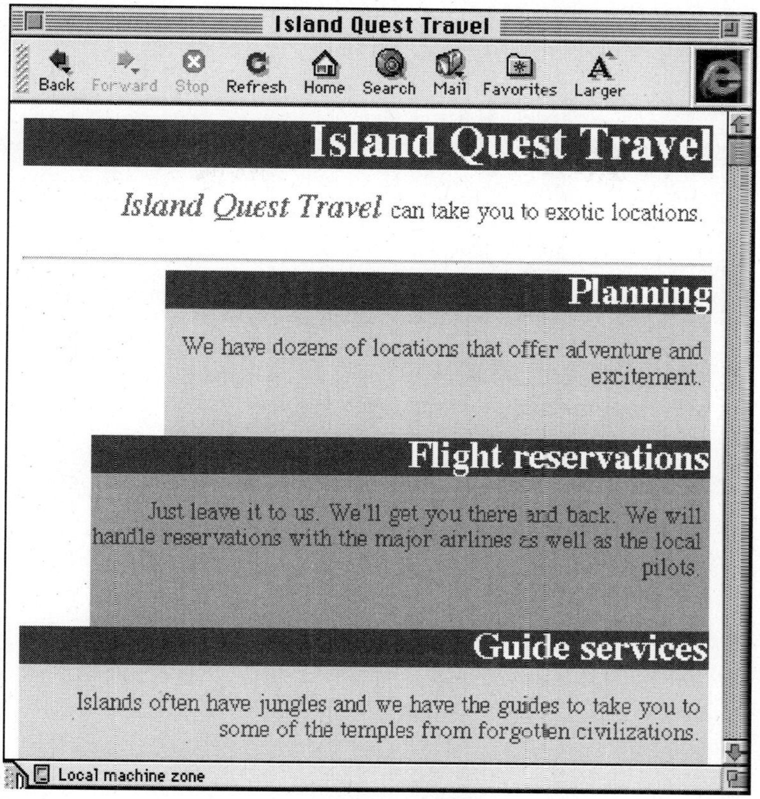

Figure 6.23

Contextual selectors

Selectors can be very specific. We will only mention some simple examples. The idea is that you can specify that certain HTML elements are to be rendered in a particular way but only if they are found within the body of another tag. For example, suppose we are working with lists. We can decide that list items (`LI`) that appear within unordered lists (`UL`) are to be rendered in a small font size and that sub-list items (within other lists) are to be rendered in an extra small font size. The following rules would do this:

```
UL LI    { font-size: small }
UL UL LI { font-size: x-small }
```

List items within ordered lists would not be affected.

Notice that the selectors are listed from the outermost to the innermost using only a space as a separator (no commas).

Let's take this example and use it in a simple demonstration example. Figure 6.24 shows the file `Demo_6b.html` and Figure 6.25 shows its rendered version.

File: Demo_6b.html

```
<HTML>
<!--File: Demo_6b.html-->
<!--Project: CSS-->
<HEAD>
<STYLE TYPE="text/css">
  <!--
  H1 { font-size:150%;
       background-color:red;
       color:white}
  UL LI    { font-size:small}
  UL UL LI { font-size:x-small}
  -->
</STYLE>
<TITLE>Contextual Selectors</TITLE>
</HEAD>
<BODY BGCOLOR="white" TEXT="black">

<H1>Contextual selectors</H1>
<P>

<UL>
  <LI>This is a first-level list item within an unordered list.
  <LI>This is another first-level list item.
  <UL>
     <LI>This is a second-level list item within an unordered
         list.
     <LI>This is another second-level list item.
  </UL>
</UL>

</BODY>
</HTML>
```

Figure 6.24

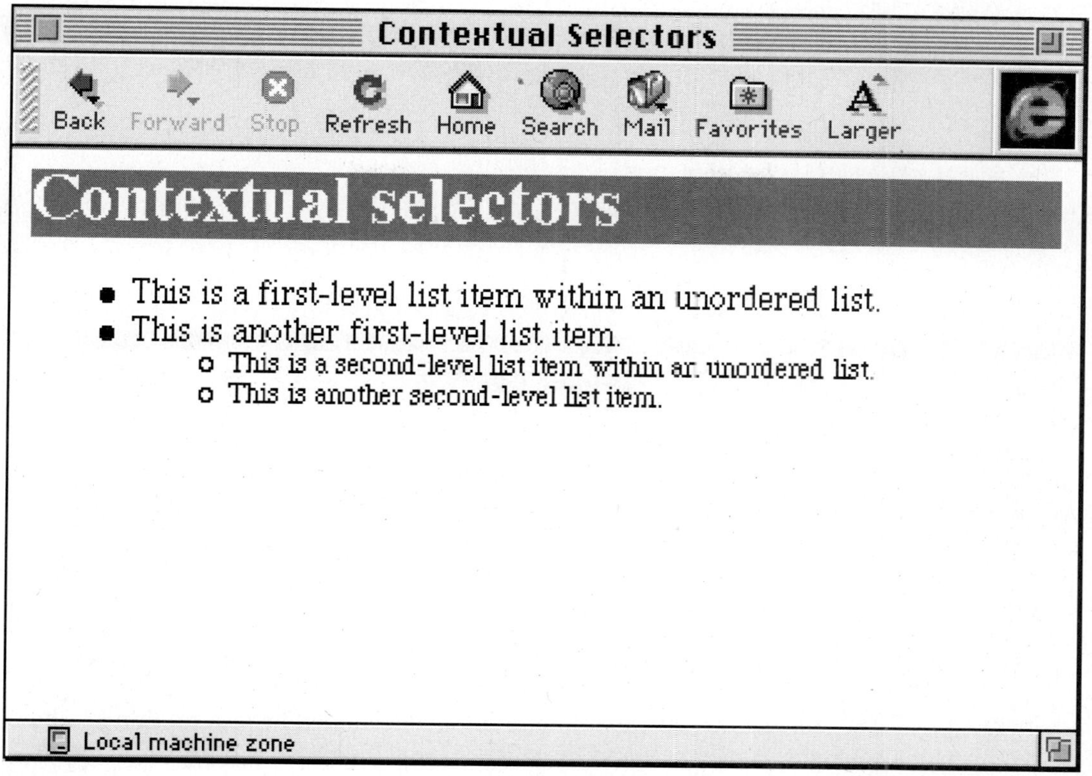

Figure 6.25

Importing styles

We have seen that style rules can appear in external style sheets, internal styles (using the `STYLE` tag), and inline (using the `STYLE` attribute for an HTML tag). There is one more way in which style sheets can be incorporated into a document. In the `STYLE` tag, CSS allows the insertion of an `@import` statement in place of a rule. This statement references a file by giving its URL. This file contains rules that are then inserted into the current document at the point of the `@import` statement. For example, consider Figure 6.26. This example will produce the same results as we saw in Figure 6.23 from the file shown in Figure 6.22. Instead of the `LINK` tag, however, we have used the `@import` feature. Notice that the `@import` statement is terminated by a semi-colon. In addition, notice that we have more than one `@import` statement. Any number are allowed but their positioning is important. The rules in later ones generally override the rules in the preceding ones if there is a conflict. We will examine this issue of conflicting rules shortly. If a particular URL doesn't exist, then no error will occur. Instead, the browser will simply use the rules that it has without that file. The full file can be found in `IQTravel_6i.html`.

File segment from: IQTravel_6i.html

```
<STYLE>
   <!--
   @import url(IQTstyle.css);
   @import url(IQTspecial.css);
   P {text-align: right}
   -->
</STYLE>
```

Figure 6.26

Cascading order

We've seen a number of mechanisms for associating style rules with a particular Web document. Often rules will conflict. One rule may make the font-size for `H1` headers 150 percent of the default font size. Another may make the font-size 200 percent. Which does the browser use?

Determining which rule applies in a particular situation can be somewhat complicated but the algorithm is explicitly laid out in the CSS specifications (see: `http://www.w3.org/TR/REC-CSS1`). The rule priority or cascading order is determined by several things. The browser assigns a weight to each rule and the rule with the highest weight wins. Here's a set of guidelines that will help sort out most cases.

The default style sheet for the browser will have less weight than styles that originate with the author of the Web document. Styles that appear in the `HEAD` portion of the document (either through the `LINK` tag or the use of an `@import` statement in a `STYLE` tag or rules placed in the content of a `STYLE` tag) will have less weight than inline rules. In the event that the weight of two conflicting rules is the same, the later one in the document wins.

Rules in imported style sheets are considered before any rules in the `STYLE` tag itself (which means the ones in the `STYLE` tag contents will win if they have the same weight as the imported ones). To make this easy to remember, it is wise to place all the `@import` statements before any local style rules. The following diagram demonstrates this graphically.

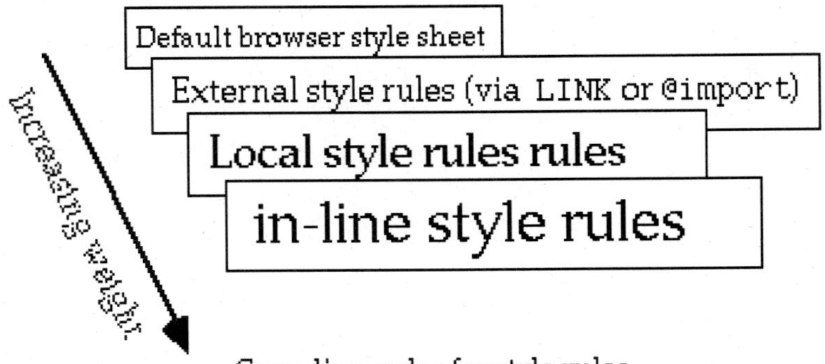

Cascading order for style rules

Style sheets in the browser wars

Cascading style sheets are part of the browser wars. Each of the major browser makers (principally Netscape and Microsoft) has been adding features to make their browser more attractive than their competitor's. These features are then submitted to the*World Wide Web Consortium* (W3C), the group having taken the role of standards body for HTML and related topics. The W3C eventually works out a standard that everyone is supposed to follow. Meanwhile some features work in one version of the browser but not others. Everyone is afraid to wait until nearly all of the bugs have been located. Besides, where else can you get millions of free testers than the Web! Consequently both Netscape and Microsoft have only partial support for all the features of CSS.

There are two Web sites that have a table showing which properties are "safe":

`http://style.webreview.com/safegrid.html`

and another table showing which properties are "unsafe":

`http://webreview.com/wr/pub/guides/style/unsafegrid.html`

Check these sites if you have trouble with CSS. You may also want to check the Web-Archipelago.com site to get links to many other CSS related pages that can help you.

Section review questions

True or false

1. CSS allows us to set up style rules that can apply to many HTML documents at once.

2. The style rules in an external style sheet must not conflict with the internal style rules of a document.

3. The style rules in an external style sheet must be contained in a `STYLE` tag.

4. Comments can be placed in an external style sheet by putting the two characters `/*` before the comment and the two characters `*/` after the comment.

5. The `LINK` tag that accesses an external style sheet can appear anywhere in the HTML document that utilizes that style sheet.

6. You can have either external style sheets that you access with a `LINK` tag or internal style rules using the `STYLE` tag but not both.

7. The way the browser determines the difference between a contextual selector and a group of selectors that have the same style rule is by context within the style sheet.

8. Any number of `@import` statements are allowed in the contents of a `STYLE` tag.

9. The order of the `@import` statements will not affect how a document will be rendered.

10. More specific style rules should appear first in the order of the `@import` statements; the most general style rules should appear last.

11. The default style sheet used by the browser carries the least weight in deciding among conflicting style rules.

12. The style rule

```
EM { font-size: large }
```

appears in a `STYLE` tag at the beginning of a particular HTML document. The tag

```
<EM STYLE="font-size: x-large"> wow </EM>
```

appears later in the document. The browser will render the word *wow* in the large font size.

13. The cascading order refers to the choice made by the browser to determine which rule to apply in the event that more than one rule has a selector that references a particular element.

Multiple choice

14. An external style sheet
    (a) must reside in the same directory as that of the HTML document that references it.
    (b) can reside in the same directory or a subdirectory of the one containing the HTML document that references it.
    (c) can be referenced anywhere on the Web provided its full URL is used in the `HREF` attribute of the `LINK` tag.
    (d) none of the above.

15. The rules in external style sheets
    (a) will always override any conflicting local style rules within the document.
    (b) will always be overridden by any conflicting local style rules within the document.
    (c) must not conflict with any local style rules within the document.
    (d) none of the above.

16. An external style sheet
    (a) can only contain style rules for blocks.
    (b) can contain any style rule except ones relating to margins.
    (c) can contain any style rule that does not conflict with an internal style rule.
    (d) none of the above.

17. A contextual selector
    (a) specifies how an element that appears within another element should be rendered.
    (b) is two or more selectors to which the declarations apply equally.
    (c) is specifically used to tell the browser how to render list items.
    (d) none of the above.

18. The style rule

    ```
    OL UL LI { font-size: x-small }
    ```

    (a) will apply to list items that are contained in either an ordered list or an unordered list.
    (b) will only apply to list items that appear in an unordered list within an ordered list.
    (c) will render all list items within an ordered list with an extra small font size.
    (d) none of the above.

6.5 Positioning Text for Interesting Effects

CSS allows positioning of elements directly. Recall that we were able to achieve positioning of elements using the `TABLE` tag (see the end of Section 4.4). That mechanism, however, is really only effective for simple layouts. With CSS positioning, you can even overlap elements, which you cannot do with tables.

That's the good news. The bad news is that CSS positioning is only a working draft and may not always work the way it is supposed to. Here we'll examine a few of the features that positioning is supposed to provide and develop an example showing you how to use them.

For each element (for example a paragraph, a header, or the contents of an `EM` tag) think of that element being contained in a box. With positioning we can place that box anywhere on the browser window by specifying the location of the upper left-hand corner of the box. As an example, look at Figure 6.27. We have declared a style class called bigText. We use some of the font properties (`font-size`, `font-family`, `font-weight`) that have appeared before as well as the `color` property. The new properties are `position`, `top`, and `left`.

These are positioning properties. The value of `absolute` for the `position` property tells the browser that any information given about the positioning of the affected element is an absolute location in the browser window, not a position relative to the elements that came before. All our experience to this point has been with relative positioning. Items are placed by the browser in the order in which they occur in the HTML document. Room is made for each new element in the window with the possible modification that some elements may be aligned on the right or left or may be centered in the window. Now we can place things in an absolute position in the window. The location is determined by the other properties. The `top` property tells the browser how far from the top of the screen to place the box containing the element. In this case we have chosen the value of 25 pixels. The `left` property tells the browser how far from the left edge of the window to place the box. We chose 30 pixels.

Finally, note that we place the text that will be affected within a `DIV` tag. This isolates the effects of the style class to that block alone. The resulting rendering of `Demo_6c.html` is shown in Figure 6.28

File: `Demo_6c.html`

```
<HTML>
<!--File: Demo_6c.html-->
<!--Project: CSS-->
<HEAD>
<STYLE TYPE="text/css">
  <!--
  .bigText {position:absolute; top:25px;
            left:30px; font-size:300%;
            color:#cccc00; font-family:Times;
            font-weight:bolder}
  -->
</STYLE>
<TITLE>Positioning Text</TITLE>
</HEAD>
<BODY BGCOLOR="white">

<DIV CLASS="bigText">
  QUEST
</DIV>

</BODY>
</HTML>
```

Figure 6.27

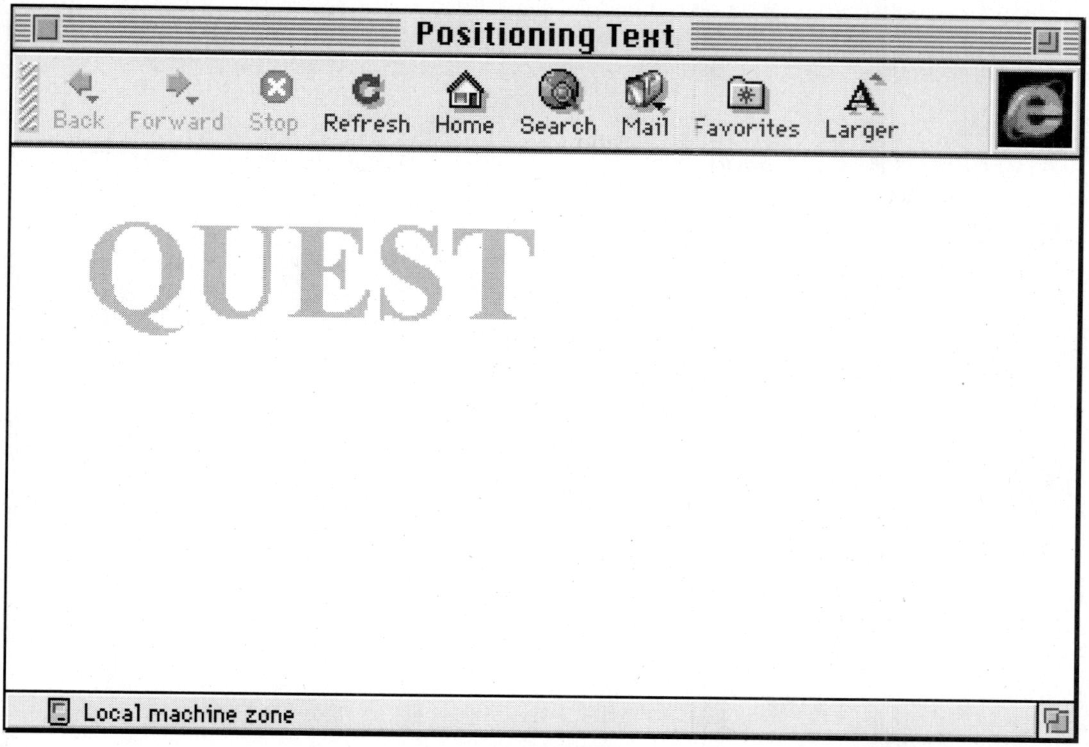

Figure 6.28

What happens if you place something in an absolute position that overlaps something that is already there? Well, that's where the fun starts. It's this ability that makes positioning such an effective way to get new effects that we haven't been able to do before now without building an image file and then placing the image on our Web document.

As an example, let's build on the previous example by adding additional elements. Figure 6.29 shows `Demo_6d.html` with two style classes which we've named "`loc1`" and "`loc2`." Each of these will allow us to place some large format text in a particular location in the browser window. Again we have used the `DIV` tag to localize the effect of the style class. Notice that even though the word ISLAND will be placed above and to the left of the word QUEST, we are not restricted to placing the block containing ISLAND before the block containing QUEST. The only impact of this order is that the browser will process the document in the order in which we placed the elements and the later one will be placed "on top" of the earlier one when they overlap.

By the way, we are utilizing the fact that the `background-color` property defaults to "`transparent`" which allows the earlier word to be seen behind the later word in the document. The file `Demo_6d.html` is shown in rendered form in Figure 6.30.

File: Demo_6d.html

```
<HTML>
<!--File: Demo_6d.html-->
<!--Project: CSS-->
<HEAD>
<STYLE TYPE="text/css">
  <!--
  .loc1 {position:absolute; top:25px;
         left:30px; font-size:300%;
         color:#cccc00; font-family:Times;
         font-weight:bolder}
  .loc2 {position:absolute; top:0px;
         left:0px; font-size:300%;
         color: blue; font-family:Times;
         font-weight:bolder}
  -->
</STYLE>
<TITLE>Positioning Text</TITLE>
</HEAD>
<BODY BGCOLOR="white">

<DIV CLASS="loc1">
  QUEST
</DIV>

<DIV CLASS="loc2">
  ISLAND
</DIV>

</BODY>
</HTML>
```

Figure 6.29

Figure 6.30

3D positioning

With overlapping elements, we have seen that the order in which they occur in the HTML document determines which elements appear in front of others. If we imagine each element being on a separate layer, then the layers corresponding to overlapping elements make up a stack. The bottom of the stack can be thought of as the most distant from us on the screen, the top of the stack is the element closest to us.

The `z-index` property takes an integer value. A value of 1 represents the bottom of the stack (things most distant). Higher values represent layers closer to us on the screen. The numbers do not have to be consecutive.

Figure 6.31 shows the file `IQTravel_j.html` in which we use the `z-index` property to display the Island Quest Travel name at the top of the document using what we have seen in the previous examples. As before, we use the `DIV` tag to isolate the effect of the style classes to particular blocks. Now, however, we must be careful to place all the material following the overlapping words into a separate block which we must position to avoid colliding with the block at the top of the screen. If we don't do that, the browser will start this material at the upper left corner of the display screen which will be right on top of the first block of words. In this case, we just used in-line styles in the last `DIV` block. The pixel values were determined by trial and error until the positioning was what we wanted.

File: `IQTravel_6j.html`

```
<HTML>
<!--File: IQTravel_6j.html-->
<!--Project: CSS-->
<HEAD>
<LINK REL="stylesheet" TYPE="text/css"
      HREF="IQTstyle.css">
<STYLE>
  <!--
  .level3  {position:absolute; top:0px;
            left:0px; z-index:3;
            font-size:300%; color: blue;
            font-family:Times; font-weight:bolder}
  .level2  {position:absolute; top:25px;
            left:30px; z-index:2;
            font-size:300%; color:#cccc00;
            font-family:Times; font-weight:bolder}
  .level1  {position:absolute; top:50px;
            left:60px; z-index:1;
            font-size:300%; color:#66ff99;
            font-family:Times; font-weight:bolder}
  -->
</STYLE>
<TITLE>Island Quest Travel</TITLE>
</HEAD>
<BODY BGCOLOR="white" TEXT="blue">
<DIV CLASS="level3">
  ISLAND
</DIV>
<DIV CLASS="level2">
   QUEST
</DIV>
<DIV CLASS="level1">
  TRAVEL
</DIV>
<DIV STYLE="position:absolute; top:100px">
  <H1>Island Quest Travel</H1>
  <P>
  <EM>Island Quest Travel</EM> can take you to exotic locations.

  <P>
  <HR>
  <P>
```

```
  <DIV STYLE="margin-left: 20%; background-color:#66ff99">
  <H2>Planning</H2>
  <P>
  We have dozens of locations that offer adventure and excite-
  ment.
  </DIV>

  <DIV STYLE="margin-left: 10%; background-color:#cccc00">
  <H2>Flight reservations</H2>
  <P>
  Just leave it to us. We'll get you there and back. We will
  handle reservations with the major airlines as well as the
  local pilots.
  </DIV>

  <DIV STYLE="background-color:#ccff00">
  <H2>Guide services</H2>
  <P>
  Islands often have jungles and we have the guides to take you
  to some of the temples from forgotten civilizations.
  </DIV>
</DIV>
</BODY>
</HTML>
```

Figure 6.31

The rendered version of `IQTravel_6j.html` is shown in Figure 6.32.

Figure 6.32

The following box shows the positioning properties for CSS. There a few particularly interesting ones that we have not covered (such as `clip` and `visibility`). `Clip`, for example, allows you to specify a rectangular region so that only that portion of the particular element that lies within the region will be shown. `Visibility` allows you to hide certain elements from being displayed while not giving up the region in the browser window where the element would appear. This can be used for setting up regions around which text will flow, for example. Check out some of the links from the Web-Archipelago.com site to find out more about these properties.

CSS Positioning properties

property	**values**
`position`	"`static`" or "`absolute`" or "`relative`"
`left`	"`auto`" or units such as pixels (px) or inches (in) or millimeters (mm) or a percentage of the window width (e.g. `10%`)
`top`	same values as `left` except that percentage applies to window height.
`width`	same values as `left` property.
`height`	same values as `top` property.
`clip`	"`auto`" or "`rect`(<top> <right> <bottom> <left>)" where <value> is in length units or percentage as in other properties.
`overflow`	"`visible`" or "`hidden`" or "`scroll`" or "`auto`"
`z-index`	"`auto`" or an integer value
`visibility`	"`inherit`" or "`visible`" or "`hidden`"

Section review questions

True or false

1. CSS positioning allows us to place an element in the exact position we want in the browser window.

2. If the `background-color` property of an element is not transparent, then it is possible that an overlapping element can hide part of the element being overlapped.

3. In the use of CSS absolute positioning, the order of the elements being positioned only affects how they overlap.

Multiple choice

4. The style class definition

```
.loc {position:absolute; top:20px; left:50px}
```

when combined with the DIV tag

```
<DIV CLASS="loc">
   imbedded elements
</DIV>
```

will cause the imbedded elements

(a) to be placed in a box whose upper left corner is 20 pixels below the previous element in the browser window and 50 pixels from the left edge of the browser window.

(b) to be placed in a box whose center is 20 pixels from the top and 50 pixels from the left edge of the browser window.

(c) to be placed in a box whose upper left corner is 20 pixels from the top and 50 pixels from the left edge of the browser window.

(d) none of the above.

5. If we position an element in an absolute position in the browser window using a DIV block, then subsequent sections of the HTML document

(a) will be placed in the browser window in a position following the position of the elements within the DIV block.

(b) will be placed in the same position as that of the DIV block.

(c) will be placed in the browser window without regard to the DIV block.

(d) none of the above.

Short excursion exercises

1. Modify `IQTravel_6a.html` so that H1 headers are 130 percent of the default font size and rendered in red and H2 headers are 120 percent of the default font size and rendered in green.

2. Change `IQTravel_6b.html` so that EM is rendered in aqua and 10 percent smaller than the default font size.

3. Modify the file `Demo_6a.html` (or create a new one) to examine the results of specifying only the font-size property of the Hn tags. For H1 through H6, use font sizes of xx-large, x-large, large, medium, small, and x-small. Create an appropriate header to display each font size.

4. Take the file you created in the previous exercise and set the font-family property to Arial. Try setting the value simply to sans-serif to see which font family the browser provides.

5. Starting with IQTravel_6c.html, add a style rule that will render the background color for paragraphs in aqua.

6. Modify the file IQTravel_6d.html so that the first line of each paragraph is rendered in light blue.

7. Modify the IQTravel_6d.html file and change the value of the background-repeat property to repeat. What is the result?

8. Place the blue stripe down the middle of each paragraph in IQTravel_6d.html.

9. Instead of using the background-color property in the style rule for H1, H2, create another style class called "redBack" and use the CLASS attribute for the H1 and H2 headers to get the same result.

10. Modify the tourInfo_6a.html file by picking a different color instead of the one used there for the alternating rows of the table. Use the colorTable.html file from the CD-ROM to locate the hex values for the color you want.

11. Modify the tourInfo_6a.html file to add another style class (call it "mint-color") similar to the yGreen-color style class. Set the background-color property for this new class to #ccff99. Now use the CLASS attribute for the TABLE tag to set the table background to the yellow-green color and use the new class to alternate the color on the rows.

12. Starting with the IQTravel_6f.html file, modify the in-line style rules so that the style blocks are larger at the top and smaller at the bottom (reverse the margin-left values). From a design point of view does this look better or worse than the earlier arrangement?

13. Modify the IQTravel_6f.html file so that the style blocks are indented from the right margin by the same amounts (instead of the left margin). What change should you also make to the H1, H2 style rule to accommodate this change in the design? Modify the H1 style rule so that the "staircase" effect extends to the H1 header.

14. Add a style class to the file IQTstyle.css to create a white background and blue text. Then remove the BGCOLOR and TEXT attributes from the BODY tag in IQTravel_6g.html and replace them with the appropriate CLASS attribute. The rendered file should look the same as the previous version.

15. Use contextual selectors to have any EM elements within a TABLE element rendered in small caps. Then modify the tourInfo_6b.html file to demonstrate that your style rule is working.

16. Create a file named `IQTspecial.css` and place the following style rule in that file:

```
H1, H2 {text-align: left;
        background-color:blue;
        color:white}
```

    Place the file in the same directory as a copy of `IQTravel_6i.html` and the file `IQTravel.css`. View `IQTravel_6i.html` in your browser and determine if the `H1` and `H2` headers have text that is aligned right or left. Now switch the order of the `@import` statements and repeat the experiment. Did your browser do the right thing?

17. Modify the value of the position parameters in the `Demo_6c.html` file to place the text near the right margin of the browser window. By "grabbing" the lower right corner of the browser window with the mouse, change the width of the browser window and see if the text stays near the right edge. (You probably don't want to use pixel values for some of the positioning properties; even under the best of circumstances, you will be unable to defeat the attempt to keep the text in the visible window).

18. Switch the order of the `DIV` blocks in `Demo_6d.html`. Does the order matter?

19. Start with the file `IQTravel_6j.html` and adjust the value of the top property in the in-line `STYLE` rule for the `DIV` tag that surrounds the bulk of the document. Set the value so that the `H1` header will partially overlap the word TRAVEL. Then add a `z-index` property value to the `DIV` tag to make the `H1` header be rendered on top of the larger type.

Longer voyage exercises

20. Define a style rule for the `STRONG` tag so that using the `yellowBox.gif` file, you create what appears to be yellow-highlighted text such as a student would use to highlight elements in a text book. Modify one of the files in this chapter to use this tag. Experiment to make sure everything works when the `STRONG` text spills from one line to the next.

21. Repeat the same exercise as the previous one but use the background-color property instead to accomplish the result. Why would you pick one of these methods over the other?

22. Although this may still be a buggy feature, how would you place the blue stripe in `IQTravel_6d.html` so that it ran top to bottom of each paragraph about three-fourths of the way from left to right? Use the background-repeat together with the background-position properties to see if you can get the right half of the background of each paragraph to be rendered with a light blue background.

23. Create another style class in `IQTravel_6e.html` that will allow you to place a yellow stripe down the left edge of an element. Use the `yellowBar.gif` file provided with the CD-ROM. Then modify the `IQTravel_6e.html` file so that paragraphs alternate between a blue stripe and a yellow stripe along the left edge. That is, the first paragraph has a blue stripe, the second has a yellow stripe, and so on.

24. This produces an interesting effect. Start with IQTravel_6e.html and set the BGCOLOR attribute of the BODY tag to blue (the TEXT attribute already has this value). Now alter the style rule for paragraphs so that the background color is white. Although the colors in this make it look too much like a Fourth of July banner, try playing with the colors to make this a more subtle effect.

25. Create a style class in IQTravel_6e.html that will place white text on a blue background (call it "whiteOnBlue") and a second style class that will place blue text on a white background ("blueOnWhite"). Now, starting with the paragraph after the horizontal rule, use one style class for the first paragraph and the other style class for the next paragraph, and repeat.

26. Redo the previous exercise using the CLASS attribute in the BODY tag and using inheritance to eliminate the use of the CLASS attribute in half of the paragraphs.

27. Using style classes and inheritance, create a checkerboard color pattern for all the cells in the table in tourInfo_6b.html. Try to minimize the number of times you have to use the CLASS attribute. Experiment with the colors from the colorTable.html file on the CD-ROM.

28. Create a new external style sheet file by starting with IQTravel.css and adding three new style class definitions to that file. These will correspond to the three paragraphs that were indented and colored in IQTravel_6g.html. Then replace the inline style rules used with the DIV tag in that file with appropriate CLASS attributes.

29. As an extension of your notebook project that you began in the exercises of Chapter 3, put together a sequence of Demo_x.html files (x = a, b, ...). Each of these files will exhibit the results of various style rules. A suggestion is to have Demo_a.html demonstrate the font properties, Demo_b.html demonstrate the color and background properties, Demo_c.html demonstrate text properties such as text-align and text-indent. Each demonstration page should show the same block of elements repeated with different style rules applying to each so that you can record the differences that will result from changes in the style rules.

    For each file, display the style sheet rules on your notebook page with a link to the appropriate Demo_x.html file.

30. Extend the notebook project to cover positioning. Use the same idea as the previous exercise using another Demo_x.html file to display the result of various choices for the positioning properties.

31. Starting with Demo_6c.html, use style rules to obtain the effect shown in Figure 6.33.

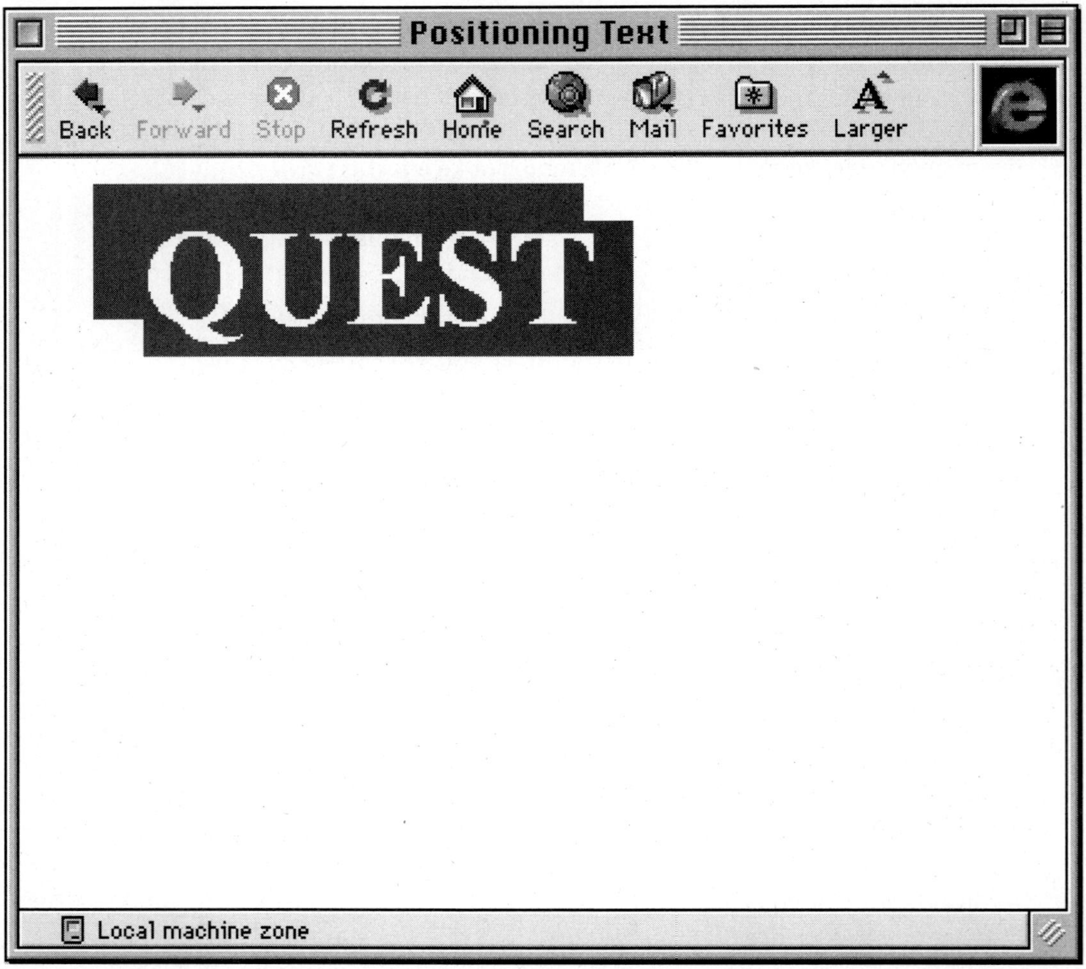

Figure 6.33

32. If you have some knowledge of (or are just interest in) what SGML is, see if you can locate any other languages besides HTML that use SGML for their definition. The Web is a good place to start. See if you can find out what a DTD is and how it relates to HTML.

Appendix A: HTML Syntax

Each HTML document is of the form

```
<!DOCTYPE HTML PUBLIC "-//W3C//DTD HTML 3.2 Final//EN">
<HTML>
<HEAD>
<TITLE>The title of the document </TITLE>
... other head elements
</HEAD>
<BODY>
... document body
</BODY>
</HTML>
```

The first line identifies the version of HTML used in the document. This line is used by validators that parse an HTML and report any syntax errors that may be present in the document.

Notes relating to this appendix:

1. An attribute displayed in boldface type means that the attribute is required.
2. There may be significant differences in how a tag is used depending on the particular attributes that are chosen. In these cases, each distinct tag-attribute type is given its own entry.
3. In a small number of instances, rarely-used tags or tag-attributes are omitted.

Attributes:
Notes:

1. Virtually all tags support the `STYLE` or `CLASS` attribute in support of cascading style sheets. These attributes are not listed separately. See Chapter 6 for their use.

Tag: `A` `(HREF` attribute`)` Hyperlink

Attributes:

`HREF`="URL"

The URL of the document to which the "clickable" element will link.

`TARGET`=*name*

The name is a string identifying a sub-window (see Appendix B on Frameset documents) whose content is to be replaced by the document named in the `HREF` attribute.

The value of *name* can also be one of the following:
`_blank` (to tell the browser to place the new document in a separate window),
`_self` (to tell the browser to replace the contents of the sub-window

containing the hyperlink),
`_parent` (to tell the browser to replace the contents of the parent window—the one that was subdivided to produce the window containing the hyperlink), or
`_top` (to tell the browser to replace the contents of the full browser window).

Purpose:

Identify a hyperlink element and the location to which the element is linked.

Notes:

1. The end tag is required.
2. The content of the tag becomes the "clickable" element in the viewed document.
3. The URL must be quoted.
4. The named URL will appear after the link with the start of the document at the top of the browser window.
5. The URL can be a "mailto" value of the form
   `mailto:`*`e-mail-address`*
   where *e-mail-address* is a typical e-mail address (e.g. `avila@demo.sjsu.edu`). In this instance, if the user clicks on the clickable element, the browser will open a window in which the user can compose and send an e-mail message to the named party.
6. `A` tags may not be nested.

Example:

```
Visit our <A HREF="http://sparky.sjsu.edu/">Web site</A>
or <A HREF="mailto:avila@demo.sjsu.edu">send us a message</
A>.
```

Tag: A (NAME attribute) Anchor for a hyperlink

Attributes:

NAME="anchorName"

AnchorName is a string which uniquely identifies this particular named anchor within the document.

Purpose:

Provides a mechanism to link to locations other than the beginning of a Web document. This tag identifies the target of a hyperlink.

Notes:

1. The end tag is required.
2. The content of the tag may not be empty.
3. `A` tags may not be nested.
4. The named anchor identifies a location to which hyperlinks can attach. For example assume `NAME`="label1" is the attribute for a particular `A` tag within the document whose URL is `http://demo.sjsu.edu/myDoc.html`. Then the corresponding hyperlink **within** the `myDoc.html` document would appear as:
   `<A HREF="#label1">linked text</A>`
   and in **another** document would appear as
   `<A HREF="http://demo.sjsu.edu/myDoc.html#label1">`

```
        linked text</A>
```

Example:

```
<A NAME="label4">Section 4</A>
```

Tag: ADDRESS Address and author information

Attributes:

none

Purpose:

Specifies information about the document such as authorship and address.

Notes:

1. The end tag is required.
2. Content is restricted to paragraphs and plain text elements.

Example:

```
<ADDRESS>
Programmer: J. H. Avila<BR>
Last modified: 2/8/98<BR>
e-mail: avila@sparky.sjsu.edu
</ADDRESS>
```

Tag: APPLET Java applet

Attributes:

CODEBASE="URL"

The URL is the base URL for the applet, i.e. the directory in which to look for the Java applet class file. If this attribute is not used, the URL for the document containing the APPLET tag is used instead.

CODE="classFile"

This is the name of the Java class file containing the Java applet. This name is relative to the base URL; it cannot be an absolute name (showing the full path).

ALT="alternateText"

The alternateText string will be displayed instead of the Java applet if the browser is not capable of running Java applets.

NAME="appletName"

The appletName string identifies this particular applet in the event that more than one may appear in a Web document. This is used by some applets to communicate with others in the same document.

WIDTH="pixels"

HEIGHT="pixels"

The values of WIDTH and HEIGHT make up a sub-window in which the applet will be viewed within the Web document. This does not include any other windows that the applet itself may produce.

ALIGN="top|middle|bottom|left|right"

These values apply to the sub-window allocated to the applet and behave in the same manner as the corresponding attribute for the IMG tag.

HSPACE="pixels"
VSPACE="pixels"

These values allow the given number of pixels between the edge of the applet sub-window and the surrounding elements in the Web document.

Purpose:

Provides a means to execute a Java applet which usually displays within the browser window for the Web document containing the tag.

Notes:

1. The end tag is required.
2. Parameters to the applet program can be passed using a PARAM tag within the contents of the APPLET tag.
3. Non-PARAM elements within the APPLET tag contents will be displayed if the browser is not able to display Java applets. Since this method allows text markup tags to be utilized, it is recommended over the use of the ALT attribute.

Example:

```
<APPLET CODE="ZoomText.class" WIDTH=400 HEIGHT=100>
  <PARAM NAME="text" VALUE="Island Quest Travel">
  <PARAM NAME="backGroundColor" VALUE="black">
  <PARAM NAME="fontSize" VALUE="36">
  <PARAM NAME="fontName" VALUE="Helvetica">
  <PARAM NAME="fontBGcolor" VALUE="cyan">
  <PARAM NAME="fontFGcolor" VALUE="red">
   This applet is viewable only with a Java-capable
   browser.
</APPLET>
```

Tag: AREA Client-side image map clickable region

Attributes:

SHAPE="rect|circle|poly|default"

Determines the shape type to use for the region identified by the AREA tag.

COORDS="v1, v2, ..., vn"

Depends on the type of shape.

For rect: "x1, y1, x2, y2" where x1, y1 are the coordinates of the upper-left corner of a rectangular region and x2, y2 are the coordinates of the lower-right corner.

For circle: "x1, y1, r" where x1, y1 are the coordinates of the center of the circle and r is the radius (in pixels).

For poly: "x1, y1, x2, y2, ..., xn, yn" where the x and y are the coordinates of a succession of points surrounding the clickable region formed by connecting x1, y1 to x2, y2, to ..., to xn, yn to x1, y1.

HREF="URL"

URL is the location of the document to be linked to if the user clicks in the region identified by this AREA tag.

NOHREF

If this attribute is present (it takes no values), then the region identified by this AREA tag will **not** respond to mouse clicks.

ALT="textString"

This required attribute provides a means of allowing text-only browsers to present the hyperlinks to the user as a text menu. It may also be used by some graphical browsers to display the textString in the status line as the mouse or other pointing device is moved over the clickable region.

Purpose:

Identify a region within an image that is sensitive to mouse clicks and the location of the document to which the sensitive region is linked.

Notes:

1. There is no end tag.
2. If the SHAPE attribute is omitted, a rectangular region is assumed.
3. Coordinates are relative to the upper-left corner of the image (x increases to the right, y increases downward).
4. If the % character follows one of the list items in a COORDS attribute, then the item is interpreted to mean a percentage of the full width or height as appropriate.
5. If two or more regions identified in AREA tags overlap, the region defined first in the MAP tag contents takes precedence over later regions. This means the AREA elements with NOHREF should generally be placed before ones with the HREF attribute.

Example:

```
<MAP NAME="townMap">
   <AREA SHAPE="rect" HREF="BrentsRestaurant.html"
         ALT="Brent's Restaurant"
         COORDS="109, 60, 136, 82">
   <AREA SHAPE="rect" HREF="cowboyMuseum.html"
         ALT="Cowboy Museum"
         COORDS="302, 82, 328, 108">
   <AREA SHAPE="circle" HREF="westCircle.html"
         ALT="West Circle"
         COORDS="109, 150, 16">
   <AREA SHAPE="poly" HREF="LucTheater.html"
         ALT="Luc Theater"
         COORDS="205, 133, 205, 166, 257, 173,
                 257, 146">
</MAP>
```

Tag: B   Bold font

Attributes:

none

Purpose:

1. Render the enclosed text using a bold text style.
2. The end tag is required.

Notes:

none

Example:

```
<B>This text will be rendered in bold style</B>
```

Tag: BASE Starting location for relative URLs

Attributes:

HREF="URL"

the base URL for dereferencing relative URLs

Purpose:

Provide a base URL from which relative URLs will be determined.

Notes:

1. Must appear in the document's HEAD.
2. HREF attribute must be present

Example:

```
<BASE HREF="http://sparky.sjsu.edu/">
```

Then later the URL in a tag such as

```
<IMG SRC="graphics/watermark.gif">
```

will be dereferenced as

```
http://sparky.sjsu.edu/graphics/watermark.gif
```

Tag: BASEFONT Default font size

Attributes:

SIZE="value"

The value can be an integer from 1 to 7.

Purpose:

Set the default font size for the text within the document.

Notes:

1. There is no end tag.
2. The size applies only to normal text and text appearing within the content of the PRE tag but not to headings unless these are modified with the use of a FONT tag using a signed value for the SIZE attribute.

Example:

```
<BASEFONT SIZE="3">
```

Tag: BIG Larger font

Attributes:

none

Purpose:

1. Render the enclosed text one font-size larger.
2. The end tag is required.

Notes:

none

Example:

```
<BIG>This text will be displayed one size larger than the
text surrounding it.
</BIG>
```

Tag: BLOCKQUOTE Extended quotations

Attributes:

none

Purpose:

To render a large quotation from another work.

Notes:

1. The contents of a BLOCKQUOTE are usually rendered with indented margins and possibly in italics.
2. Don't use BLOCKQUOTE just to get indented text. Not all browsers will render BLOCKQUOTEs in the same way.

Example:

```
<BLOCKQUOTE>
"Well," said George, "we'll have a big vegetable patch and a
rabbit hutch and chickens. And when it rains in the winter,
we'll just say the hell with goin' to work..."
<BR> from "Of Mice and Men" by John Steinbeck.
</BLOCKQUOTE>
```

Tag: BODY Document body

Attributes:

BACKGROUND="URL"

A background image used to tile the window displaying the document.

BGCOLOR="color"

The background color of the document.

TEXT="color"

The color of the text in the document.

LINK="color"

The original color of text hyperlink elements.

VLINK="color"

The color of text hyperlink elements after they have been visited.

ALINK="color"

The color of text hyperlink elements while the mouse button is down over the element.

Colors are given in the RGB color space as hexadecimal numbers (e.g. BGCOLOR="#C0FFC0"), or as one of 16 widely understood color names. These colors were originally picked as being the standard 16 colors supported with the Windows VGA palette.

Color names and RGB values:

Black = "#000000"	Green = "#008000"
Silver = "#C0C0C0"	Lime = "#00FF00"
Gray = "#808080"	Olive = "#808000"
White = "#FFFFFF"	Yellow = "#FFFF00"
Maroon = "#800000"	Navy = "#000080"
Red = "#FF0000"	Blue = "#0000FF"
Purple = "#800080"	Teal = "#008080"
Fuchsia = "#FF00FF"	Aqua = "#00FFFF"

Purpose:

The `BODY` tag announces the start of the body of the document and establishes basic document-wide color attributes.

Notes:

A matching `/BODY` tag is placed at the end of the document's body.

Example:

```
<BODY BGCOLOR="white" TEXT="blue" LINK="aqua"
      VLINK="navy" ALINK="red">
... body of the document
</BODY>
```

Tag: `BR` Forced line break

Attributes:

`CLEAR="left|right|all"`

Purpose:

Force the browser to issue a line break so that subsequent elements begin on a new line.

Notes:

1. There is no end tag.
2. `CLEAR="left"` will force subsequent elements to appear **after** any floating images that are aligned on the left margin (such as would happen if text were flowing around the right of such an image just prior to the `BR` tag). `CLEAR="right"` does the same thing for images that are currently aligned on the right margin and `CLEAR="all"` does the same for images aligned either on the left or the right margins.

Example:

```
<BR CLEAR="all">
```

Tag: `CAPTION` Place a caption above or below a table

Attributes:

`ALIGN="top|bottom"`

This controls the position of the caption either above or below a table.

Purpose:

Provides a mechanism to create and place a short descriptive title for a table.

Notes:

1. Markup tags are allowed in the `CAPTION` text.
2. The `CAPTION` tag must appear within the contents of the `TABLE` tag.
3. The end tag is required.

Example:

```
<TABLE BORDER="2">
   <CAPTION>Rainfall by Month</CAPTION>
   <TR>
      <TH>Month
      <TH>Rainfall
   </TR>
   <TR>
      <TD>January
      <TD>13.5
   </TR>
   ...
</TABLE>
```

Tag: `CENTER` Centering a block of elements

Attributes:

none

Purpose:

To center all elements within the contents of this tag.

Notes:

1. The `CENTER` tag will terminate a paragraph as determined by a `P` tag.
2. Equivalent to the use of the `DIV` tag with `ALIGN='center"`.
3. The end tag `/CENTER` is required.

Example:

```
<CENTER><IMG SRC="graphics/island_horizon.gif"></CENTER>
```

Tag: `CITE` Short Citations

Attributes:

none

Purpose:

Render the enclosed text to reflect that the text is a reference to another work.

Notes:

1. This is a logical tag describing *what* the enclosed text is, not how to display it. The browser determines how to render the text.
2. The text is usually rendered in italics.
3. Use this to identify titles of other documents but not for longer references.
4. Use the `BLOCKQUOTE` tag for longer quotes from referenced work.

Example:

```
For more information see <CITE>HTML for Web Programmers</
CITE>.
```

Tag: CODE   Code segment from a program

Attributes:

none

Purpose:

Render the enclosed text to reflect that the text is part of a program. This usually means a constant-width font.

Notes:

1. This is a logical tag describing *what* the enclosed text is, not how to display it. The browser determines how to render the text.
2. The text is usually rendered in a constant-width font.
3. This is designed for code segments that appear within a paragraph. Newline characters are ignored. If you want longer segments, use the `PRE` tag.

Example:

```
Use <CODE>public class</CODE> to indicate that objects from
your class should be available to all other classes.
```

Tag: DFN   Definition

Attributes:

none

Purpose:

Render the enclosed text to indicate the definition of a new term.

Notes:

1. This is a logical tag describing *what* the enclosed text is, not how to display it. The browser determines how to render the text.
2. The text is usually rendered in italics.
3. This is usually used the first time one introduces a term in a document.

Example:

```
The <DFN>World Wide Web</DFN> is the collection of all com-
puters connected to the internet that can view or deliver
HTML documents.
```

Tag: DIV   Identify a division in a document

Attributes:

`ALIGN="left|center|right"`

Purpose:

Establish a default alignment for all enclosed block elements (e.g. `P`, `Hn`).

Notes:

1. Alignment attribute values for elements within a DIV block override the ALIGN attribute value of the DIV tag.
2. The use of the CENTER tag to create a center alignment is more widely used (and suggested) than the DIV tag with ALIGN="center".
3. The presence of the DIV tag will terminate a paragraph as identified by a P tag.
4. The end tag /DIV is required.
5. An important mechanism to isolate style rule scope.

Example:

```
<DIV ALIGN="right">
Text to be right-aligned...
</DIV>

<DIV CLASS="bigText">
   ISLAND
</DIV>
```

Tag: DL Definition List

Attributes:

none

Purpose:

Displays a list of definitions. Each item consists of a term and its corresponding definition.

Notes:

1. Items within a definition list are identified by the DT (to indicate the term) and DD (to indicate its definition) tags.
2. The end tag is required.

Example:

```
<DL>
   <DT>The first term to be defined.
      <DD>The definition of the first term.
   <DT>The second term to be defined.
      <DD>The definition of the second term.
</DL>
```

Tag: EM Emphasized text

Attributes:

none

Purpose:

Render the enclosed text to indicate emphasis.

Notes:

1. This is a logical tag describing *what* the enclosed text is, not how to display it. The browser determines how to render the text.
2. The text is usually rendered in an italic font.

Example:

```
<EM>This is an important point</EM>
```

Tag: FONT Font appearance

Attributes:

`SIZE="size"`

Sets or modifies the size of the font used to display the text in the contents of the tag.

`COLOR="color"`

Sets the color of the text within the contents of the tag.

Purpose:

Set or modify the appearance of the text within the contents of the tag.

Notes:

1. The end tag is required.
2. The value for the `SIZE` attribute is determined by the browser and is not directly mapped to point sizes. The value may be from 1 to 7.
3. If the `SIZE` value is signed (+ or -) then the size is relative to the value of the base font size as set using the `BASEFONT` tag. Thus `SIZE="+2"` will render the text enclosed in the `FONT` tag content two sizes larger than the base font; `SIZE="-1"` will render the text one size smaller than the base font.
4. The value of the `COLOR` attribute can be one of 16 color names recognized for the `BGCOLOR` attribute of the `BODY` tag (see the `BODY` tag) or can be a six-digit hexadecimal value preceded by the # character in the form `COLOR="#RRGGBB"`. The first two hex digits represent the red component, the next two represent the green component and the last two represent the blue component.

Example:

```
<FONT SIZE="+1" COLOR="red">
   Be careful when you modify the file.
</FONT>
```

Tag: FORM User-fillable form

Attributes:

`ACTION="URL"`

URL refers to an executable file (on a server) that will process the data from the form.

`METHOD="get|post"`

"Get" means that the form data will be delivered to the form processing program by means of an environment variable.

"Post" means that the form data will be delivered to the form processing program using the standard input stream.

Purpose:

To provide a mechanism to record user input in a Web document so that it can be transmitted to a server program for processing.

Notes:

1. The end tag is required.
2. The content of a FORM tag will contain all form (data gathering) elements.
3. Form elements or fields are created using other tags:
see INPUT, TEXTAREA, SELECT.

Example:

```
<FORM ACTION="http://sparky.sjsu.edu/cgi-bin/Echo"
      METHOD="post">
   Your name:
   <INPUT TYPE="text" NAME="name" SIZE="30">
</FORM>
```

Tag: Hn (where *n* = 1, 2, 3, 4, 5, or 6) Section headers

Attributes:

ALIGN="left|right|center"

Determines the horizontal placement of the text header (left is the default).

Purpose:

To display text headers (such as the titles of chapters or sections). H1 is the most important header, H6 is the least important.

Notes:

The end tag is required.

Example:

```
<H1>Chapter 1: Basic HTML tags</H1>
```

Tag: HR Horizontal rule

Attributes:

ALIGN="left|center|right"

Determines the placement of the horizontal line in the browser window. Default is center.

NOSHADE

No assigned value. If this attribute is present, the line is rendered in a solid color instead of the traditional two-color 'groove."

SIZE="pixels"

The number of pixels used for the height of the line.

WIDTH="length"

The length of the line in pixels (e.g. WIDTH="300") or the percentage of the total browser window width (e.g. WIDTH="80%"). Default is 100%.

Purpose:

Place a horizontal line in the Web document to separate one section from the next.

Notes:

The end tag is forbidden (the tag does not represent any contained elements).

Example:

```
<HR WIDTH="50%">
```

Tag: `I` Italic font

Attributes:

none

Purpose:

1. Render the enclosed text using an italic text style.
2. The end tag is required.

Notes:

none

Example:

```
<I>This text will be rendered in italics style</I>
```

Tag: `IMG` Imbedded image

Attributes:

`SRC`="URL"

URL is the location of the image file.

`ALT`="alternateText"

The alternateText string is placed in the document instead of the image if the browser does not support graphical elements (such as one that provides speech for sight-impared persons).

`ALIGN="top|middle|bottom|left|right"`

"Top" aligns the top of the image with the top of the current text line.

"Middle" aligns the middle of the image with the baseline of the current text line.

"Bottom" (default) aligns the bottom of the image with the baseline of the current text line.

"Left" places the image against the current left margin, temporarily changing this margin so that subsequent text is flowed along the image's right-hand side. Results may depend on other previous left-aligned images or text.

"Right" places the image against the current right margin, temporarily changing this margin so that subsequent text is flowed along the image's left-hand side. Results may depend on other previous right-aligned images or text.

`HEIGHT`="pixels"

The height of the image in pixels.

`WIDTH`="pixels"

The width of the image in pixels.

`BORDER`="pixels"

Used when an image element is a hyperlink. Then the value of pixels is the width of the border around the element. If the value is 0 then the border will not be displayed.

`HSPACE`="pixels"

The number of pixels to be placed horizontally between the image and surrounding elements.

`VSPACE`="pixels"

The number of pixels to be placed vertically between the image and surrounding elements.

`USEMAP="label"`

Used for client-side image maps. The label is associated with the `NAME` attribute of a `MAP` tag within the current document. The `MAP` tag is used to identify clickable regions in the image.

`ISMAP`

If this attribute is present, then the `IMG` tag must be contained within an `A` tag whose `HREF` attribute identifies the URL of a file on the server that identifies clickable regions within the image.

Purpose:

Place an image in a Web document.

Notes:

1. Currently, most browsers only support files in GIF or JPEG format.
2. The value of the `ALT` attribute cannot contain any markup tags.
3. The use of the `WIDTH` and `HEIGHT` attributes allows the browser to reserve space in the window to place the image before it actually arrives. This may allow the user to begin viewing text information more quickly.
4. Netscape allows the `WIDTH` and `HEIGHT` values to be incorrect and then modifies the image to fit the values given. This can produce poor image quality. Other browsers may not support this "feature".

Examples:

A simple image

```
        <IMG SRC="graphics/smallWhiteBall.gif">Planning ser-
vices:
```

A "clickable" image using a client-side image map

```
        <IMG SRC="graphics/townMap.gif" USEMAP="#townMap">
```

A "clickable" image using a server-side image map

```
        <A HREF="graphics/townMap.map">
                <IMG SRC="graphics/townMap.gif" ISMAP>
        </A>
```

Tag: `INPUT` (Type = checkbox) User-checkable form field

Attributes:

`TYPE="checkbox"`

`NAME="fieldName"`

A unique name associated with the particular field so that the association can be made later between the field and whether or not it was checked.

`CHECKED`

If this attribute is present, the checkbox will be initially displayed as checked.

Purpose:

Allows the user to check a box to represent a simple choice (e.g. yes/no).

Notes:

1. There is no end tag.
2. This tag must be contained within the contents of a `FORM` tag.
3. If the user selects the checkbox, then the value associated with the field name will be "on". If the user does not select the checkbox, then no data will be transmitted for this field (as if the field didn't exist).

Example:

```
Yes I want to receive more information:
   <INPUT TYPE="checkbox" NAME="choice">
```

Tag: `INPUT` (Type = file) Form field to contain a file name

Attributes:

`TYPE="file"`

`NAME`="fieldName"

A unique name associated with the particular field so that the association can be made later between the field and the data associated with it.

`SIZE`="number"

The allowable number of characters to be displayed in the input box shown on the screen.

`MAXLENGTH`="number"

Maximum number of characters to accept for this field.

Purpose:

Allows the user to supply a file name either in a one-line input box or by clicking on a related button to browse the local file system for the file whose name will be transmitted.

Notes:

1. There is no end tag.
2. This tag must be contained within the contents of a `FORM` tag.
3. Only the file name is transmitted, not the file.
4. There is an `ACCEPT` attribute (which we have not shown) that restricts the types of files that can be selected (e.g. `ACCEPT="image/*"`). See the site: `http://www.w3.org/` for more detailed information.

Example:

```
Please identify the file:
<INPUT TYPE="file" NAME="dataFile" SIZE="30">
```

Tag: `INPUT` (Type = hidden) Hidden form field

Attributes:

`TYPE="hidden"`

`NAME`="fieldName"

A unique name associated with the particular field so that the association can be made later between the field and the data associated with it.

`VALUE`="textString"

The textString will be sent to the server bound to the value of the `NAME` attribute.

Purpose:

Allows the writer of the HTML document to embed information that will always be transmitted with this form but will not be displayed on the browser window.

Notes:

1. There is no end tag.
2. This tag must be contained within the contents of a FORM tag.
3. This tag can be used to carry identifying information over from one form to another if the second is generated "on the fly" by the program processing the data from the first form.

Example:

```
<INPUT TYPE="hidden" NAME="userDateID"
       VALUE="u2365-d980214">
```

Tag: INPUT (Type = image) Graphical submit button

Attributes:

TYPE="image"

SRC="URL"

Identifies the graphical image to be used as a submit button to send form data to the server.

ALIGN="top|middle|bottom|left|right"

Provide alignment options for the layout of the image.

NAME="fieldName"

A unique name associated with the particular field so that the association can be made later between the field and the data associated with it.

Purpose:

Provides a graphical button that the user can click to send the form data to the server.

Notes:

1. There is no end tag.
2. This tag must be contained within the contents of a FORM tag.
3. The name attribute is not required but is recommended.
4. The x and y coordinates of the mouse click relative to the upper left corner of the image are transmitted using fieldName.x&fieldName.y.

Example:

```
Click on the button to send in your request
<INPUT TYPE="image" SRC="icons/sendButton.gif"
       NAME="sendButton">
```

Tag: INPUT (Type = password) User-fillable form field

Attributes:

TYPE="password"

NAME="fieldName"

A unique name associated with the particular field so that the association can be made later between the field and the data associated with it.

`SIZE`="number"

The number of characters to allow to be displayed in the input box shown on the screen.

`MAXLENGTH`="number"

Maximum number of characters to accept for this field.

Purpose:

Allows the user to enter text in a one-line input box. The typed characters are not displayed in the box, but instead a character such as * is shown for each character typed.

Notes:

1. There is no end tag.
2. This tag must be contained within the contents of a `FORM` tag.
3. There is no encryption of the data as transmitted to the server for processing.

Example:

```
Your password:
   <INPUT TYPE="password" NAME="pass" SIZE="8">
```

Tag: `INPUT` (Type = radio) User-checkable form field

Attributes:

`TYPE="radio"`

`NAME`="fieldName"

A unique name associated with the particular field so that the association can be made later between the field and whether or not it was checked.

`VALUE`="data value"

The data value is the text that will be attached to the field name when the data is transmitted to the server.

`CHECKED`

If this attribute is present, then this radio button will be the selected one.

Purpose:

Allows the user to choose precisely one of a number of choices.

Notes:

1. There is no end tag.
2. This tag must be contained within the contents of a `FORM` tag.
3. Each instance of an `INPUT` tag with `TYPE="radio"` produces a separate radio button choice.
4. Exactly one of the radio buttons must have the attribute `CHECKED`.
5. Radio buttons occur in families. Each button in the same family must have the same `NAME` attribute value.

Example:

```
I would prefer to travel during:
<BR>
   <INPUT TYPE="radio" NAME="season"
          VALUE="spring">Spring
   <INPUT TYPE="radio" NAME="season"
```

```
        VALUE="summer" CHECKED>Summer
<INPUT TYPE="radio" NAME="season"
        VALUE="fall">Fall
<INPUT TYPE="radio" NAME="season"
        VALUE="winter">Winter
```

Tag: `INPUT` (Type = reset) Clear all form fields

Attributes:

`TYPE="reset"`

`VALUE=`"textString"

The textString will be displayed as a label on the button.

Purpose:

Allows the user to clear all data from a form with one mouse click.

Notes:

1. There is no end tag.
2. This tag must be contained within the contents of a `FORM` tag.
3. No data from a reset button will be transmitted to the server.

Example:

```
<INPUT TYPE="reset" NAME="Clear form">
```

Tag: `INPUT` (Type = submit) Submit form data to server

Attributes:

`TYPE="submit"`

`NAME=`"fieldName"

A unique name associated with the particular field so that the association can be made later between the field and the data associated with it.

`VALUE=`"string"

The string will be displayed as a label on the button that is produced by this tag.

Purpose:

Provides a button that the user can click to send the form data to the server.

Notes:

1. There is no end tag.
2. This tag must be contained within the contents of a `FORM` tag.
3. The name attribute is not required.
4. There can be more than one submit button. If so, the `NAME` attribute should be used and the value associated with the name will be the text string given for the value attribute.

Example:

```
<INPUT TYPE="submit" VALUE="Send my request">
```

Tag: `INPUT` (Type = text) User-fillable form field

Attributes:

`TYPE="text"`

`NAME="fieldName"`

A unique name associated with the particular field so that the association can be made later between the field and the data associated with it.

`SIZE="number"`

The allowable number of characters to be displayed in the input box shown on the screen.

`VALUE="text string"`

If this attribute is used, the text string will appear as a default string in the input box.

`MAXLENGTH="number"`

Maximum number of characters to accept for this field.

Purpose:

Allows the user to enter text in a one-line input box.

Notes:

1. There is no end tag.
2. This tag must be contained within the contents of a `FORM` tag.

Example:

```
Your name:
   <INPUT TYPE="text" NAME="name" SIZE="30">
```

Tag: `KBD` Sample keyboard input to a program

Attributes:

none

Purpose:

Render the enclosed text to reflect that the text is input to a program as a user would enter it from the keyboard. This usually means a constant-width font.

Notes:

1. This is a logical tag describing *what* the enclosed text is, not how to display it. The browser determines how to render the text.
2. The text is usually rendered in a constant-width font.
3. This is designed for small segments that appear within a paragraph. Newline characters are ignored; if you want longer segments, use the `PRE` tag.

Example:

```
Users are required to type <KBD>java TextFileUpdate </KBD> to
execute the program.
```

Tag: `LI` List item

Attributes:

Within `UL` tag:

`TYPE="disc|square|circle"`

"disc" will place a filled circle at the start of the item.
"square" will place a small square at the start of the item.
"circle" will place an open circle at the start of the item.

Within `OL` tag:
`TYPE="1|a|A|i|I"`
"`1`" for Arabic numbers (1, 2, 3, ...).
"`a`" for lower case letters (a, b, c, ...).
"`A`" for upper case letters (A, B, C, ...).
"`i`" for lowercase Roman numbers (i, ii, iii, ...).
"`I`" for uppercase Roman numbers (I, II, III, ...).

Purpose:

Identify list items within ordered or unordered lists.

Notes:

1. Not all browsers support attributes for the `LI` tag.

Example:

```
We offer the following tours:<BR>
<UL>
   <LI>Guided luxury tours—everything is provided
   <LI>Supported tours—we provide the guides
   <LI>Self-guided tours—we get you there and back
</UL>
```

Tag: LINK   Link to support documents

Attributes:

`REL="stylesheet"`
identifies the other document as a cascading style sheet.

`TYPE="text/css"`
identifies the type of file as text containing `css` style rules.
(other values are possible to support things like JavaScript).

HREF=url
locates the file containing the cascading style rules.

Purpose:

Identify a file containing cascading style rules so that the rules can be applied by the browser to the document containing the `LINK` tag.

Notes:

1. Not all browsers support cascading style rules.

Example:

```
<LINK REL="stylesheet" TYPE="text/css"
      HREF="IQTstyle.css">
```

Tag: `MAP` Client-side image map

Attributes:

`NAME`="nameString"

The nameString must match the value in the `USEMAP` attribute of the `IMG` tag associated with this `MAP` tag.

Purpose:

Provides information that allows the browser to associate regions in an image with hyperlinks.

Notes:

1. The end tag is required.
2. The contents of the `MAP` tag must contain one or more `AREA` tags, one for each "clickable" region of the image.

Example:

```
<MAP NAME="townMap">
   <AREA SHAPE="rect" HREF="BrentsRestaurant.html"
         ALT="Brent's Restaurant"
         COORDS="109, 60, 136, 82">
   <AREA SHAPE="rect" HREF="cowboyMuseum.html"
         ALT="Cowboy Museum"
         COORDS="302, 82, 328, 108">
   <AREA SHAPE="circle" HREF="westCircle.html"
         ALT="West Circle"
         COORDS="109, 150, 16">
   <AREA SHAPE="poly" HREF="LucTheater.html"
         ALT="Luc Theater"
         COORDS="205, 133, 205, 166, 257, 173,
                 257, 146">
</MAP>
```

Tag: `META` Store meta-information about the document

Attributes:

`NAME ="keywords|description"`

`CONTENT`="*text* "

Purpose:

If the value of `NAME` is "keywords", then the value of `CONTENT` is a list of keywords that may be used by search engines for this document.
If value of `NAME` is "description", then the value of `CONTENT` is a short description of this document that may be used by search engines for this document.

Notes:

1. Must appear in the document's head.
2. `NAME` and `CONTENT` attributes must be present.

Example:

```
<META NAME="description" CONTENT="Travel to exotic island
locations with Island Quest Travel">
```

Tag: `OL` Ordered (numbered) List

Attributes:

`TYPE="1|a|A|i|I"`

use "1" for Arabic numbers 1, 2, 3, ...
use "a" for lower case alpha characters a, b, c, ...
use "A"for use upper case alpha characters A, B, C, ...
use "i" for lower case roman characters i, ii, iii, ...
use "I" for upper case roman characters I, II, III, ...

`START="number"`

The number is the starting sequence value for the list items.

Purpose:

Display a list of items and number each item.

Notes:

1. Leaving out the `START` attribute will result in starting with the number 1.
2. Lists can be nested.
3. List items are identified with the `LI` tag.
4. The end tag is required.

Example:

```
<OL TYPE="a">
   <LI>This is the first item.
   <LI>This is the second item.
</OL>
```

Tag: `OPTION` Menu Option

Attributes:

`VALUE="textString"`

TextString is the value that will be associated with the name of the `SELECT` field containing this `OPTION` tag.

`SELECTED`

If this attribute is present, then this option will be displayed when the browser displays the pop-up menu.

Purpose:

Provide one of the menu items in a pop-up menu as created with the `SELECT` tag.

Notes:

1. The end tag is recommended.
2. The content of the `OPTION` tag is the string that will be displayed to the user as one of the choices in the pop-up menu.
3. Since the textString associated with the `VALUE` attribute will be attached to the name of the `SELECT` field in which the `OPTION` appears, it should uniquely identify which of the options were chosen by the user.

Example:

```
<SELECT NAME="islands">
   <OPTION VALUE="cayman">Grand Cayman</OPTION>
   <OPTION VALUE="fiji">Fiji</OPTION>
```

```
    <OPTION VALUE="molokai">Molokai</OPTION>
    <OPTION VALUE="aruba" SELECTED>Aruba</OPTION>
    <OPTION VALUE="lucia">St.Lucia</OPTION>
</SELECT>
```

Tag: P Paragraph

Attributes:

`ALIGN="left|center|right"`

Purpose:

Identifies a paragraph in a document. The alignment attribute determines how the entire paragraph is rendered: flush left, centered, or flush right.

Notes:

The end tag is optional. The parser will determine the end of a paragraph from the presence of other tags.

Example:

```
<P>
This is the start of a new paragraph...
<P>
This is the start of another paragraph...
```

Tag: PARAM Parameter tag for Java applets

Attributes:

NAME="parameterName"

This name is used by a Java applet to obtain run-time values from the HTML document.

VALUE="parameterValue"

The parameterValue must be appropriate for the Java applet and will be associated with the NAME value.

Purpose:

Provide a means to supply parameters from an HTML document to a Java applet.

Notes:

1. The PARAM tag must appear within the contents of an APPLET tag.
2. PARAM tags must appear at the beginning of the contents of an APPLET tag.
3. Any number of PARAM tags may be present.
4. The NAME value must correspond to the one expected in the Java applet program.

Example:

```
<APPLET CODE="ZoomText.class" WIDTH=400 HEIGHT=100>
  <PARAM NAME="text" VALUE="Island Quest Travel">
  <PARAM NAME="backGroundColor" VALUE="black">
  <PARAM NAME="fontSize" VALUE="36">
  <PARAM NAME="fontName" VALUE="Helvetica">
  <PARAM NAME="fontBGcolor" VALUE="cyan">
  <PARAM NAME="fontFGcolor" VALUE="red">
   This applet is viewable only with a Java-capable browser.
</APPLET>
```

Tag: PRE Pre-formatted text

Attributes:

WIDTH="number"

Provides advice to the browser to indicate the maximum number of characters to appear on a line. This can be used to select an appropriate font size or indentation.

Purpose:

Render text in a fixed-width font preserving spacing associated with white space characters such as the blank space and newline characters.

Note:

Tab characters should be avoided. If present, they should (but may not) be rendered to reflect a tab setting every 8 characters.

Example:

```
<PRE>
/* This is a short C++ program */
int main(int argc, char *argv[])
{  cout << "Hello, world.";
   return 0;
}
</PRE>
```

Tag: SAMP Sample output from a program

Attributes:

none

Purpose:

Render the enclosed text to reflect that the text is output from a program. This usually means a constant-width font.

Notes:

1. This is a logical tag describing *what* the enclosed text is, not how to display it. The browser determines how to render the text.
2. The text is usually rendered in a constant-width font.
3. This is designed for output segments that appear within a paragraph. Newline characters are ignored; if you want longer segments, use the PRE tag

Example:

```
Users of this program will see <SAMP>access denied</SAMP> if
they attempt to access a local file.
```

Tag: SELECT Selection menu

Attributes:

NAME="fieldName"

FieldName will be the name associated with the data from this form field when it is transmitted to the server.

SIZE="number"

The number of menu items that are visible at one time.

`MULTIPLE`

If this attribute is present, then the user can select more than one item.

Purpose:

Provide the ability to select one or more items from a pop-up menu.

Notes:

1. Must appear in the content of a `FORM` tag.
2. The items in the pop-up menu are supplied by `OPTION` tags within the content of the `SELECT` tag.
3. The `SELECT` tag must appear within the content of a `FORM` tag.
4. If `MULTIPLE` is used, then one should set `SIZE` to a value greater than 1 so that the user can see more than one item at once.
5. How to select more than one item is platform-dependent.

Example:

```
<SELECT NAME="islands">
   <OPTION VALUE="cayman">Grand Cayman</OPTION>
   <OPTION VALUE="fiji">Fiji</OPTION>
   <OPTION VALUE="molokai">Molokai</OPTION>
   <OPTION VALUE="aruba" SELECTED>Aruba</OPTION>
   <OPTION VALUE="lucia">St.Lucia</OPTION>
</SELECT>
```

Tag: `SMALL` Smaller font

Attributes:

none

Purpose:

1. Render the enclosed text using one font-size smaller.
2. The end tag is required.

Notes:

none

Example:

```
<SMALL>This text will be displayed one size smaller than the
text surrounding it.
</SMALL>
```

Tag: `STRIKE` Strike-through font

Attributes:

none

Purpose:

1. Render the enclosed text using a strike-through appearance.
2. The end tag is required.

Notes:

none

Example:

```
<STRIKE>This text will be displayed with a line through the
middle of the text
</STRIKE>
```

Tag: STRONG — Strongly emphasized text

Attributes:

none

Purpose:

Render the enclosed text to indicate a strong emphasis.

Notes:

1. This is a logical tag describing *what* the enclosed text is, not how to display it. The browser determines how to render the text.
2. The text is usually rendered in a bold font.
3. If you must have bold type, use the `B` tag.

Example:

```
<STRONG>This is an very important point</STRONG>
```

Tag: STYLE — Style markup

Attributes:

`TYPE="text/css"`

(other values are possible to incorporate other types of style rules)

Purpose:

Provide style rules to the document containing the `STYLE` tag.

Notes:

1. Cascading style sheets are not supported by all browsers.
2. For browsers that do not support the `STYLE` tag, you can enclose the contents in quotes to "hide" the contents from these browsers.

Example:

```
<STYLE TYPE="text/css">
   <!--
   H1 {font-size:150%}
   H2 {font-size:125%}
   -->
</STYLE>
```

Tag: SUB — Subscript

Attributes:

none

Purpose:

1. Render the enclosed text as a subscript which will place it slightly lower on the line than the surrounding text.

2. The end tag is required.

Notes:

- none

Example:

```
The first variable is denoted by A<SUB>1</SUB>.
```

Tag: `SUP` Superscript

Attributes:

none

Purpose:

1. Render the enclosed text as a superscript which will place it slightly higher on the line than the surrounding text.
2. The end tag is required.

Notes:

none

Example:

```
The square of a variable x is denoted by x<SUP>2</SUP>.
```

Tag: `TABLE` Table rendering (rows and columns)

Attributes:

`ALIGN="left|center|right"`

This controls the horizontal position of the entire table in the browser window. Default is left.

`WIDTH`="length"

Length is the width of the table. It can be in pixels (e.g. `WIDTH="400"`) or a percentage of the total browser window width (e.g. `WIDTH="100%"`). If this attribute is missing, the width is determined from the table contents.

`BORDER`="size"

Size is the number of pixels for the outer border around the table. If `size="0"`, then the border will be suppressed.

`CELLSPACING`="pixels"

Each cell has its own border as rendered by the browser. The value of pixels represents the number of pixels between adjacent cell borders and also between an edge cell and the table border.

`CELLPADDING`="pixels"

This specifies the number of pixels between the contents of a cell and the border of the cell.

Purpose:

Provides a mechanism to place document content in a two-dimensional array of rows and columns. This can be used for presenting data that is commonly viewed in tabular form or for precise layout of document elements.

Notes:

1. The contents of rows and columns are determined using the `TR`, `TH`, `TD` tags.
2. A caption can be attached to a table using the `CAPTION` tag within the contents of

the TABLE tag.
3. The end tag is required.
4. Using pixel values for the WIDTH attribute is not recommended since it forces the browser to render the table with a particular value. This may require the user to resize the window to be able to view the table.

Example:

```
<TABLE BORDER="2">
   <CAPTION>Rainfall by Month</CAPTION>
   <TR>
      <TH>Month
      <TH>Rainfall
   </TR>
   <TR>
      <TD>January
      <TD>13.5
   </TR>
   ...
</TABLE>
```

Tag: TD Table Data cell

Attributes:

NOWRAP
: If this attribute is present (it takes no value), then automatic word wrap will be disabled within this cell.

ROWSPAN="number"
: Number is an integer representing the number of rows that this cell will cover.

COLSPAN="number"
: Number is an integer representing the number of columns that this cell will cover.

ALIGN="left|center|right"
: Determines the horizontal alignment of the contents of the cell.

VALIGN="top|middle|bottom"
: Determines the vertical alignment of the contents of the cell.

WIDTH="number"
: Suggests the width (in pixels) for the cell. This may be overridden if it conflicts with the width of other cells in the same column.

HEIGHT="number"
: Suggests the height (in pixels) for the cell. This may be overridden if it conflicts with the height of other cells in the same row.

Purpose:

Used for table cells.

Notes:

1. Appears within the contents of the TR tag.
2. The end tag is not required but is recommended to avoid errors either by the

programmer or the browser in complicated situations.
3. Table cells can contain essentially all HTML element types including tables.
4. An empty cell is rendered differently than a cell with just whitespace inside. To obtain the same appearance as a non-empty cell, place the metacharacter `" "` within the cell.
5. If you place an image in a table cell, use the `WIDTH` and `HEIGHT` attributes, otherwise the browser will have to determine these values from the size of the image. This will force a potentially long wait to render the table until all images have been downloaded.

Example:

```
<TD ROWSPAN="2" WIDTH="30" HEIGHT="60">
   <IMG SRC="graphics/logo.gif">
</TD>
<TD>Aruba</TD>
<TD>January 12</TD>
```

Tag: `TEXTAREA` Multi-line data entry form field

Attributes:

NAME="fieldName"
FieldName will be the name associated with the data from this form field when it is transmitted to the server.

ROWS="number"
This is the number of rows of characters that the data box will accommodate.

COLS="number"
This is the number of characters per row that the data box will accommodate.

Purpose:

Provide a multi-line box into which the user can supply data.

Notes:

1. Must appear in the content of a `FORM` tag.
2. The end tag is required.
3. The content of the `TEXTAREA` tag (which can only be text) is used to display default content in the field when it is first displayed.
4. Text entered by the user is usually not auto-wrapped at the right edge of the box.

Example:

```
<TEXTAREA NAME="feedback" ROWS="5" COLS="40">
   Your comments here...
</TEXTAREA>
```

Tag: `TH` Table cell Header

Attributes:

`NOWRAP`
If this attribute is present (it takes no value), then automatic word wrap

will be disabled within this cell.

`ROWSPAN`="number"

Number is an integer representing the number of rows that this cell will cover.

`COLSPAN`="number"

Number is an integer representing the number of columns that this cell will cover.

`ALIGN="left|center|right"`

Determines the horizontal alignment of the contents of the cell.

`VALIGN="top|middle|bottom"`

Determines the vertical alignment of the contents of the cell.

`WIDTH`="number"

Suggests the width (in pixels) for the cell. This may be overridden if it conflicts with the width of other cells in the same column.

`HEIGHT`="number"

Suggests the height (in pixels) for the cell. This may be overridden if it conflicts with the height of other cells in the same row.

Purpose:

Used generally for cells that are "header cells" at the top of a column. These cells usually contain labels for the corresponding column.

Notes:

1. Appears within the contents of the `TR` tag.
2. The end tag is not required but is recommended to avoid errors either by the programmer or the browser in complicated situations.
3. Table cells can contain essentially all HTML element types including tables.
4. An empty cell is rendered differently than a cell with just whitespace inside. To obtain the same appearance as a non-empty cell, place the metacharacter `" "` within the cell.
5. If you place an image in a table cell, use the `WIDTH` and `HEIGHT` attributes, otherwise the browser will have to determine these values from the size of the image. This could mean a long wait to render the table while all images are being downloaded.

Example:

```
<TH>Island locations</TH>
<TH>Excursion start dates</TH>
```

Tag: `TITLE` Document Title

Attributes: none

Purpose:

To supply the title of the document as it will appear in the title bar of the browser window.

Notes:

1. Every HTML 3.2 document must have exactly one `TITLE` element in the document's `HEAD`.
2. Closing tag required.

Restrictions:

Other tags are not allowed within the tag content.

Example:

```
<TITLE>Island Quest Travel</TITLE>
```

Tag: TR Table Row

Attributes:

`ALIGN="left|center|right"`

Determines the horizontal alignment of the entire row of cells.

`VALIGN="top|middle|bottom|baseline"`

Determines the vertical alignment of the entire row of cells. If the value is baseline then the first line of text in each cell of the row should share the same baseline.

Purpose:

To identify a row of a table.

Notes:

1. Appears within the content of a `TABLE` tag.
2. The end tag is optional but recommended for readability and to avoid errors by the browser in complicated use of tables (such as nested tables).

Example:

```
<TR>
   <TH>Month
   <TH>Rainfall
</TR>
```

Tag: TT Teletype font

Attributes:

none

Purpose:

Render the enclosed text in a fixed-width font

Notes:

1. Enclosed text is not treated like preformatted text. Whitespace is collapsed and newlines are ignored.
2. The end tag is required.

Example:

```
<TT>This text is displayed in a fixed-width font</TT>
```

Tag: U Underlined font

Attributes:

none

Purpose:

1. Render the enclosed text using an underlined text style.
2. The end tag is required.

Notes:

Since many browsers display hyperlinks in underlined style, it is recommended that this style not be used since it may confuse readers.

Example:

```
<U>This text will be displayed in underlined style</U>
```

Tag: UL Unordered List

Attributes:

`TYPE="disk|square|circle"`

This determines the character displayed to mark each list item. The disk (usually the default) is a filled circle. The displayed character will be different for nested lists.

Purpose:

Display an unordered list of items (i.e. the list items are not numbered).

Notes:

1. The end tag is required.
2. Individual list items are identified with the `LI` tag.
3. Lists can be nested.

Example:

```
<UL>
   <LI>First item in the list.
   <LI>Second item in the list.
</UL>
```

Appendix B: Frameset Documents

Frameset documents announce to the browser that the browser window is to be partitioned into frames or sub-windows. They also determine the arrangement of these frames and the initial content of each frame. A frameset document is similar to an ordinary HTML (BODY) document and is of the general form

```
<HTML>
<HEAD>
<TITLE>The title of the document </TITLE>
</HEAD>
<FRAMESET attributes >
... FRAME tags
</FRAMESET>
</HTML>
```

Tag: FRAMESET Frame document layout

Attributes:

COLS="w1, w2, ..."

The presence of this attribute signals that the browser window or sub-window is to be partitioned into vertical columns. Each of w1, w2, ... is an indicator of the column width to be assigned to each column. These may be the number of pixels (e.g. 40) the percentage of the available width (e.g. 50%) or an asterisk (*). In the case of an asterisk, each column partition with an asterisk is given an equal amount of width after the columns assigned pixel values or percentages for widths have been taken care of.

ROWS="h1, h2, ..."

The presence of this attribute signals that the browser window or sub-window is to be partitioned into horizontal rows. Each of h1, h2, ... is an indicator of the row height to be assigned to each row. These may be the number of pixels (e.g. 40) the percentage of the available height (e.g. 50%) or an asterisk (*). In the case of an asterisk, each row partition with an asterisk is given an equal amount of height after the rows assigned pixel values or percentages for heights have been taken care of.

Purpose:

Provides a mechanism to subdivide the browser window into sub-windows.

Notes:

1. The end tag is required.
2. A frameset document may be responsible for the subdivision of the original browser window or it may be responsible for the subdivision of a sub-window identified in a parent frameset document.

Example:

```
<HTML>
<HEAD>
   <TITLE>Island Quest Frameset document</TITLE>
</HEAD>
```

```
<FRAMESET ROWS="80, *">
   <FRAME SRC="IQTravel_head.html"
          SCROLLING="no"
          MARGINHEIGHT="0" MARGINWIDTH="0">
   <FRAME SRC="IQTravel_home.html" NAME="content">
</FRAMESET>
</HTML>
```

Tag: `FRAME` Initializes the content of a sub-window

Attributes:

`SRC`="URL"

URL refers to an HTML body document (a conventional HTML document) or to another frameset document. In the latter case, this will result in a subdivision of the sub-window to which this `FRAME` tag applies.

`NAME`="*frame_name*"

The given frame name must be a unique string. It will identify the particular sub-sub-window in an `A` tag as the sub-window whose contents are to be replaced by the document referenced in a hyperlink.

`NORESIZE`

If this attribute is present, then the user may not re-size the sub-windows by using the mouse to drag the bar between sub-windows.

`SCROLLING`="*value*"

value is either `yes`, `no` or `auto` to indicate if the sub-window **must** have a vertical scroll bar (`yes`) or **must not** have a vertical scroll bar (`no`), or if the vertical scroll bar will be present if needed (`auto`).

`MARGINHEIGHT`="*value*"

value is the number of pixels to be allocated to the vertical space between the content of the sub-window and the edge of the sub-window itself.

`MARGINWIDTH`="*value*"

value is the number of pixels to be allocated to the horizontal space between the content of the sub-window and the edge of the sub-window itself.

Purpose:

Identifies the initial content of a sub-window. May also give the sub-window a name which will allow hyperlinks to target this sub-window as the location in which the referenced document will appear.

Notes:

1. There is no end tag.
2. The document appearing in the `SRC` attribute can be a frameset document. In that case, the sub-window identified by this `FRAME` tag is to be further subdivided.

Example:

```
<FRAMESET ROWS="80, *">
   <FRAME SRC="IQTravel_head.html"
          SCROLLING="no"
          MARGINHEIGHT="0" MARGINWIDTH="0">
   <FRAME SRC="lowerFrameset.html">
</FRAMESET>
```

Index

@import statement 193
Andreessen, Marc 3
animated GIF 44
Apache 13
applets 4, 136
    requirements 141
    restrictions 141
    sources 142
attributes 33
background color 43
background image tiling 47
background images 47
background, textured 47
Berners-Lee, Tim 2
Black, Roger 54
browser
    options menu 26
    resizing the window 26
browser wars 4, 195
browsers for persons with handicaps 87
Bush, Vannevar 3, 12
button links 70
byte code 137
cascading style sheets 158
CERN 2
character tags 29
checkbox 113, 225
citation tag 30
clickable image 83
clickable text
    attributes 66
    default colors 766
code
    color 33
color
    code 33
color choices 68
color names 33
color table 69
colors, safe 69
compression 44
    lossy 44
contextual selectors 191
copyright 43
copyright law 19
CSS 158
    3D positioning 201
    element positioning 197
    positioning
        properties 205
    postioning
        z-index 201
    support 159
CSS specifications 194
default style sheet 158
definition list 40, 221
design 117
dithering 68
DNS 72
document rendering 158
document root (directory) 39
domain name 40
domain name servers 73
e-mail 74
emphasize tag 29
error message 72
explicit anchor 76
external elements 51, 52
    copyright information 51
    modification date 51
    programmer 51
form processing 103
forms 102
frames 145

- body documents 145
- frameset documents 145
- hyperlinks 149
- multiple frames 150
- warnings 151

get method 103
GIF 43
GIF89A 43
Gopher 12
graphical elements
- downloading 39, 42

hardware 8
Hello, WWW World 16
hierarchical organization of Web documents 66
horizontal rule 24
hot text 63
HTML 2, 16
- indentation 35

HTML validators 142
http 4539
httpd 90, 93
hyperlink
- explicitly-anchored 76
- implicitly-anchored 62

hyperlinks 3, 62
- in frames 149

hypertext 12, 62
HyperText Markup Language 16
hypertext transfer protocol 39
image
- clickable 83
- coordinate system 85
- downloading 48
- hot-spot 83, 85
- sizes 48

image formats 43
image map
- client-side 83
- differences 93
- server-side 83, 89
  - CERN format 93
  - map file 90
    - NCSA format 90
    - overlapped regions 92
    - relative URL 92

imagemap 93
implicit anchor 62
Internet Explorer 4
Internet Protocol 72
IP address 72
Island Quest Travel 21
Java 4, 136
- virtual processor 137

Java applet parameters 139
Java-capable browsers 137
JavaScript 4
JPEG 44
keywords 53
layout 117
layout, using tables 125
link failure 72
links 62
lists 35
- LI 35, 230
- OL 35, 232
- UL 35, 243

logical tags 158
mailto 75
MapWiz applet 87
meta information 53
metacharacters 30
- &amp 52
- &copy 52
- &gt 30
- &lt 30

Microsoft 4

modem 48
Mosaic 3
multitasking 8
NCSA 3, 90
Nelson, Ted 12
Netscape Corporation 3
operating systems 8
Origami applet 140
PageMill 13
Pellow, Nicola 3
physical tags 158
PNG 44
pop-up menus 112
positioning 197
post method 103
preferences menu 66
radio buttons 115
relative path name 40
rendering 158
RGB color code 33
root directory 40
sampler test page 60
search engines 53
security 138
selector 160
server 9
SGML 158
software development 136
style
    block 182
    declaration 160
    definition 160
        in-line 181
    property 160
        background-color 169, 172
        background-image 172
        background-position 172
        background-repeat 172
        class 174
        CLASS attribute 175, 178
        color 164, 172
        color and background 169
        conflict resolution 177
        font-family 167
        font-size 160, 167
        font-style 167
        font-variant 167
        font-weight 167
        inheritance 178
        margin-left 183
        positioning properties 197
        text-align 183
style rules 160
    selector 160
    selectors
        contextual 191
style sheet 161
style sheets
    @import statement 193
    cascading order 194
    external 188
    LINK and STYLE together 190, 231, 237
sublists 36
Sun Microsystems 4
tables 119
    caption 119
    cells 120
    rows 120
tag 18
tag contents 18
tags
    A 63, 211
        e-mail 74, 212
        HREF 63, 74, 211
        NAME 76, 78, 212
        TARGET 149, 151, 211

with Hn tags 78
ADDRESS 51, 213
APPLET 139, 213
CODE 139, 213
AREA 84, 214
COORDS 84, 214
HREF 84, 214
SHAPE 84, 214
attributes 33
value 33
BODY 18, 217
ALINK 67, 217
BACKGROUND 47, 217
BGCOLOR 43, 68, 217
LINK 67, 217
TEXT 43, 67, 217
VLINK 67, 217
BR 24, 218
CAPTION 119, 218
CENTER 44, 87, 219
CITE 29, 219
Comment 22
DD 40, 221
DIV 182, 220
DL 40, 221
DT 40, 221
EM 29, 34, 221
FONT 32, 222
COLOR 33, 222
SIZE 33, 222
FORM 103, 222
ACTION 103, 222
METHOD 103, 222
get 103, 222
post 103, 222
formatting 18
FRAME 148, 246
FRAMESET 146, 245
HEAD 18
Hn 29, 223
HR 24, 223
HTML 18
I 30, 223
IMG 39, 44, 70, 224
BORDER 71, 224
ISMAP 89, 225
SRC 39, 224
USEMAP 84, 224
INPUT 105, 225
NAME 105, 225
SIZE 107, 226
TYPE 105, 225
TYPE="checkbox" 113, 225
TYPE="hidden" 108, 226
TYPE="password" 108, 227
TYPE="radio" 115, 228
TYPE="reset" 108, 229
TYPE="submit" 108, 229
TYPE="text" 107, 229
LINK 188, 231
logical 29, 34, 158
MAP 84, 231
META 53, 232
CONTENT 54, 232
NAME 54, 232
OL 35, 232
OPTION 112, 233
SELECTED 112, 233
P 24, 233
PARAM 139, 234
physical 29, 32, 158
PRE 34, 234
metacharacters 34
WIDTH 34, 234
SELECT 112, 235
STRONG 34, 237

STYLE 161
SUB 34, 237
SUP 34, 238
TABLE 119, 238
BORDER 119, 238
TD 120, 239
TD, TH
COLSPAN, ROWSPAN 123, 239, 240
TEXTAREA 109, 240
TH 120, 240
TITLE 18, 241
TR 120, 242
UL 35, 243
TYPE 36, 243
textured background 47
transparent background 43
Universal Resource Locator 39
Unix 8
URL 39
validators 142
W3C 8, 142, 195
watermark background 47
Web design 54
five do's 54
Web developer 6
Web document
development cycle 18
Web site 5
white space 24
Windows NT 8
World Wide Web 2
World Wide Web Consortium 8, 142, 195
WWW 2
Xanadu 12
z-index 201